MANY THINGS IN PARABLES

Extravagant Stories of New Community

MANY THINGS IN PARABLES

Frederick Houk Borsch

FORTRESS PRESS   PHILADELPHIA

Biblical quotations, unless otherwise noted, are from the Revised Standard Version of the Bible, copyright 1946, 1952, © 1971, 1973 by the Division of Christian Education of the National Council of the Churches of Christ in the U.S.A., and are used by permission. In some cases the quotations have been slightly altered by the author. Translations of sayings from the *Gospel of Thomas* are by T. O. Lambdin and are taken from *Nag Hammadi Library*, ed. J. M. Robinson (San Francisco: Harper & Row, 1977).

COPYRIGHT © 1988 BY FORTRESS PRESS

Library of Congress Cataloging-in-Publication Data

Borsch, Frederick Houk.
  Many things in parables.

  Bibliography: p.
  1. Jesus Christ—Parables. I. Title.
BT375.2.B58 1987   226'.806   86-46410
ISBN 0-8006-2042-9

2986E87   Printed in the United States of America 1-2042

To
Rebecca and Rebecca
Margaret and Margaret
Emily, Mary, Robert
Curtis and Jacob
—all godchildren

CONTENTS

PREFACE

If multiplicity of interpretations is the measure, many of the Gospels' parables have been and are extraordinarily successful. A number of these stories are found in more than one version in the Gospels, and almost all of the stories have been given a variety of emphases and readings through the Christian centuries. Although this openness to different hearings is unsettling for some people, it was evidently characteristic of the parables from their early tellings and may have been part of their original purpose. This study is concerned not only with the reasons that Jesus is said to have taught in parables, nor just with the uses of the parables by the early Christian communities, but also with the hearings that may be given to these stories in a variety of settings and circumstances today. The capacity of the parables to help shape the interpretation of contemporary life and to encourage the telling of new stories is an additional interest of these researches and reflections.

The book is in several ways a companion volume to my study of the healing stories in the Gospels (*Power in Weakness: New Hearing for Gospel Stories of Healing and Discipleship*), which also sought to bring historical, literary, psychological, and theological insights to bear on significant biblical narratives. Both studies reflect the concern in stories of and about Jesus to engender a new sense of community in conjunction with the advent of the kingdom of God. Many of the parables and stories of healing convey through their extravagant terms a passion for the inclusion of those whom others have been willing to set outside the sphere of God's care.

These observations have been developed and honed over a number of years in teaching undergraduates and graduate students at several universities and seminaries. Versions of the chapters have been presented at conferences and institutes for clergy and for laity in many parts of the United States, in Great Britain and Panama, and in Jerusalem and the West Bank. Special thanks are due to responsive audiences at Ursinus College and the Protestant Episcopal Theological Seminary in Virginia, and to the sponsors of the Brennan Lectures in the Episcopal Diocese of Kentucky and the Cheney Lectures at the Berkeley Divinity School of Yale Divinity School.

The questions and responses of many friends and participants have helped me to think more closely about the stories and to develop my understanding.

I am particularly grateful to Gary Commins, John Koenig, Mary Boys, Sue Anne Steffey Morrow, and Dan Via for reading through the entire manuscript and giving me their criticisms and suggestions. John Hollar and Barry Blose of Fortress Press offered numerous improvements. Susan Buck carefully prepared the manuscript and gave me good advice. Barbara Borsch, as always, helped me in too many ways to count. The final responsibility of what now appears in print can, of course, only be mine, but I do want these many good people to know how much their listening and responding has helped me discover with them "many things in parables" (Mark 4:2; Matt. 13:3).

Princeton University
February 1987

PROLOGUE

TELLING IT SLANT

Frequently in the Gospels people come to Jesus with questions or Jesus provokes their concern:

How often shall my brother sin against me and I forgive him? (Matt. 18:21)

What shall I do to inherit eternal life? (Luke 10:25)

Why do you eat and drink with tax collectors and sinners? (Luke 5:30)

With what can we compare the kingdom of God, or what parable shall we use for it? (Mark 4:30)

Jesus is heard responding with stories. In part he seems regularly to answer in this way in order to point to living experience as the arena in which life's meanings are to be discovered. The Gospels' stories more than imply that the only way one can realize what the coming kingdom of God is like is to participate in the particular experience of it. This emphasis does not mean that abstractions and more general observations and analyses have no value. They, too, can help in efforts to interpret life, but Jesus' most frequent response was evidently to press his disciples and those who wished to question him back toward primary experience—to the particular and everyday character of life. These stories can then be heard to allude to more universal themes and understandings, but not until they are heard in all their singularity.

So do the Gospels' stories tell of vineyards and pastures, of dinner parties, of servants and masters, brothers, fathers and sons, times of sowing and reaping. They are not religious in some special way, dealing with only certain aspects of life. Rather, human destiny is "at stake in . . . ordinary creaturely existence—domestic, economic, social. The world is real. Time is real." Each individual "is a toiler and an 'acter' and a chooser."[1]

INVITED TO PLAY

The everyday, lifelike character of these stories allows each hearer, whether friend, opponent, or observer, to enter in. More than this, the stories seem in many ways designed to lure hearers to become participants. They are invited to play the parts—in some sense to become the characters and to see and hear and feel what is happening from their perspectives. And "play" is the right word. In order to share in the experience of the story one steps a little outside oneself and dresses up in the clothes of another. For a

1

few minutes hearers are meant to let go of certain critical faculties in order to play in the story.

Often the shape of the story will tend to direct one toward its major figure and the role one is primarily meant to play. But often, too, the story may invite participation in several roles—sometimes as actors, sometimes as observers of others from within the story's frame. By playing different parts hearers are enabled to gain several vantages and finally a more complex perspective and insight.

The parable of the Good Samaritan is such a story. The lawyer (who has asked, "Who is my neighbor?"; see chap. 7), together with the parable's other hearers, is drawn into the circumstances of a robbed and injured traveler. The hearers experience despair as the victim is avoided by two of his own countrymen who, one would certainly think, ought to have stopped to help. Instead it is a despised Samaritan who offers compassion and care. What happens by way of such a story can be compared with looking through a window and then in a mirror (or, in a complex story, in a series of mirrors) and then through a window again, now with a new perspective upon life.[2] The lawyer and the other hearers, having in the story seen themselves helped by one who had every reason to contend that he was not their neighbor, find their ideas about goodness and responsibility radically challenged. They may well see themselves and their concerns differently when next confronted with an opportunity to be of help to another.

The parable has the virtue of allowing the lawyer first to invest himself and learn for himself and then make the transference to circumstances in his own life. The good novel or play or story allows its audience this measure of play and freedom. "Tell all the truth but tell it slant, / Success in circuit lies," wrote Emily Dickinson.[3] While most artists might not go so far as Wallace Stevens, who said, "The poem must resist the intelligence / Almost successfully . . . ,"[4] they recognize the importance of requiring exploration, self-investment, and discovery on the part of their audience. The good poem, story, or play hides as well as discloses. Indeed, it hides in order that an insight might not just be given but be discovered.

BEYOND APPEARANCES

There may at times be even an element of artifice or entrapment in an interesting work of art. In his painting *The Ambassadors*, Hans Holbein the Younger presented two well-to-do and established young men. About them are many of the artifacts of the Renaissance: a globe, a lute, what look like a telescope and other scientific instruments, a book. At their feet is a long whitish object with no identifiable shape. Only when one stands at an angle to the picture—when the object is seen "slant"—is it recognized to be a human skull. Suddenly the up-and-coming young men, and even the renaissance of human endeavor, are viewed in a more complex, mortal perspective.

That rather typical conceit of the time may seem like only a trick, but it is part of the craft and intrigue of a good painting and a good story to suggest relationships and possibilities that might not be perceived if one observed only more obvious appearances. All art forms use measures of intensification in order to cause certain aspects to stand out. The spatial surface or the time scheme may be altered so that objects, persons, or events can be seen in significant relationships that otherwise might go unnoticed. Many people are today most familiar with this possibility through film, where a close-up may for a moment cause the audience to forget all else that is happening in order to focus on the reaction of a single character. Then the movie may suddenly switch from the face of one character to the face of a loved one in another city. Or through a flashback the audience may be given a glimpse of a childhood act that years later is having its consequences.

"Art does not reproduce the visible but makes visible," held Paul Klee.[5] Some artists are more vigorous than others in their use of several vantages at once, distortion, juxtaposition of the unlikely, exaggeration or other means of intensification, in order to insist that their audience see or hear more than appearances and gain insights that might otherwise go unobserved. But the best painters and tellers of stories are also adept at leaving spaces and ambiguities that the imaginative intelligence is courted into puzzling and wondering over and for which it is invited to make analogues from its own life. The audience is brought well into the experience of the work of art. There it is asked to discover at least as much as it is told. Good artistry never leaves its audience in a passive role.

The audience is also invited to wonder about more than can be told because the life the artist is seeking to represent is so often problematic and mysterious. Not everything can be clearly stated, because not everything is understood or known. The faithful story also conveys that awareness, at the same time trying to intimate more than can otherwise be said. Such stories do not so much comprehend an insight as try to penetrate more deeply into what is experienced—or even seems just about to be experienced—but cannot be clearly articulated. The hearer is invited to probe in that direction.

What is exciting but sometimes maddening about having participated in such a story is that it cannot be shared in more direct ways. I attend a performance of King Lear and, still overwhelmed by it all, try to tell my friends what I have learned. "True love," I say to them, "will not advertise itself for its own advantage and may tragically be recognized too late." Their unanimated faces show that they have not yet grasped my revelation. I try to explain to them about Lear and Cordelia and her two sisters, but they cannot seem to share what I have experienced. Finally I can only urge them to experience the play.

The good play or story expresses what often can be said in no other way. The insight or insights cannot be separated from the story because the total experience of the story offers a way of talking about what otherwise cannot fully be brought to expression. The narrative is not just an illustration for the understanding to which it points; it is itself a way of telling about the existence of that insight.

It is not surprising that, for these reasons, much of the Bible is in narrative form. Story was found to be the best way—at times the only way—to reflect upon and interpret the mystery of God's presence and absence in the everyday reality of human affairs. Sometimes that was done by presenting two versions of a story—one in which we hear of human adventures and foibles without any mention of God, another in which God is at least just offstage if not directly involved in the action. So did the biblical authors seek to involve their hearers in the mysterious tension and interplay of human freedom and God's plan, of chance and providence. Through human character and dialogue, through those seeking God's will and failing to find it, and others denying it yet being led by it, through repeated basic plot themes and the counterpoint of subplots, the audience is induced by means of narrative to explore the significance of life lived before God.

PUTTING THIS BY THAT

Many of Jesus' stories are called parables because explicitly or implicitly they make a form of comparison, suggesting that this can somehow represent that or is like that. The Greek word *para-bolē* is itself made up of two smaller words that together mean "tossed near," "put beside," and so "compared." The number of such comparisons that are preserved in the Gospels suggests that Jesus very frequently taught and proclaimed his message in these terms.

Some of the parables are quite brief: "Every scribe who has been trained for the kingdom of heaven is like a householder who brings out of his treasure what is new and what is old" (Matt. 13:52). "You are the light of the world" (Matt. 5:14). Often, however, parables are somewhat longer stories in which the comparison is developed or extended in some way. The different developments are sometimes put into four general categories: illustrative stories, similitudes, allegories, and what we may call the open parable, in that the narrative gives fewer clues to its significance and is more open to interpretation. It should quickly be said, however, that the study of parables is an art and not a precise science. Despite a sense of often being able to distinguish an open parable from its cousins, we are rarely capable of doing so on strictly formal grounds or with absolute agreement. The forms of parable bear a number of resemblances, and some cousins look and act more like their relatives than others. The context in which they are found influences how one understands them. Distinctions are frequently made more on the basis of inner character than outward features.

It is important to recognize the similarities from the outset, because in the history of the interpretation of parables there has been a tendency to try to understand most parables in terms of categorization. For many hundreds of years that predominant way of interpretation was allegorical. In the late nineteenth century Adolf Jülicher did a great service for the study of parables by directing attention away from allegorical interpretation to the central impression or thrust that he believed lay within them. There was then a tendency, however, to turn this insight into a new orthodoxy and so heavily to concentrate on the central thrust as to overlook or underemphasize other aspects and intricacies of the story. Many of the parables, even if the interpreter said otherwise, seemed to become illustrative stories.

HISTORICAL VERSUS LITERARY

More recent discussion of the parables has stressed what has been called their polyvalence—their openness to be heard in different ways. Not only may a story be heard differently in different contexts but interpreters are found to bring varying expectations to its hearing. The multiplicity of interpretations which has grown up in and around many of the parables attributed to Jesus can be understood as a sign of their success as parables, but this hearing of the parables in different ways obviously raises a number of critical questions about standards for interpretation. Earlier in this century most approaches stressed historical considerations and asked what the parable meant to the evangelists and to Jesus. Interpreters tried to understand the parable as it passed through its early history. The tendency was to attempt to fix its meaning at various stages and often to see the one attributed to Jesus as the correct one. Sociological questions came also to be asked regarding the composition of the community in which a parable was heard and how that influenced its telling and hearing.

These issues continue to be of great importance for the understanding of parables. The starting point is, of course, with the Gospels. The first individuals that can be seen seeking to apply the parables to their own life situations are the evangelists. Clearly they believed that they were being guided to use the stories to tell the message of and about Jesus in the context of the questions of their time and often trying circumstances.

Since the evangelists' presentations provide the primary texts, it is important to hear the parables in their specific settings in the Gospels, recognizing not only how a parable will have been fitted into the concerns and outlook of the particular Gospel but also how the parable's telling may have been influenced by the Gospel.[6] Sometimes one may conclude that a particular parable is a composition of the evangelist, but through careful listening to the Gospels it is also often possible to hear behind their versions something of the voices of the generation or two of Christians who used the parables before the Gospels were written. In some cases one can then try to understand the place the parables may have had in Jesus' preaching and teaching.

A number of recent studies of the parables have, however, tended to be more concerned with the parables as literature, asking how a parable can be listened to apart from historical considerations. How may it be heard as a story that might be told at any time and in a variety of contexts? In one sense the church has long used the parables and other portions of the Gospels in this way, especially in liturgical settings and for preaching, where the story was read or retold apart from its context in a particular Gospel. Now, however, the story might even be considered apart from its relationship to the story of Jesus' ministry, and more purely literary questions were raised about the form of the story and the interrelationship of its different aspects. Strategies were sometimes applied that examined the basic structures of the stories, looking for ways to compare the fundamental components and inner workings of narratives from different eras and cultures. It was often possible to make certain anthropological and psychological observations on the basis of these analyses. Still more complex are questions of epistemology: How do human beings think and come to know and see life through their stories? Yet more recently some studies have concentrated on the tensions within stories and their discrepancies, which allow for still more openness of interpretation and even a sense of the enigmatic and perhaps meaningless character of all story and life.[7]

Other discussions of the parables have emphasized the more purely psychological aspects. The parable of the prodigal son, for instance, can be "internalized" and experienced as the interrelationship between the id (prodigal), superego (elder brother), and ego (father), or, in other terms, between the willful child, censorious parental figure, and the mature and reconciling adult.

All these more literary approaches have their values and can add to the richness of the interpretation of parables. They also have their critics, particularly among those who are concerned with the more historical issues and most especially among those who ground much of their theology in historical considerations. What, they are more prone to ask, was the author's (the evangelist's and/or Jesus') primary purpose when telling the story? Explicit or implicit in their question is the understanding that this is what the story meant and means, other interpretations being at best subsidiary.

This historical concern and emphasis upon authorial intention has important value, but it also has its share of problems. Whether one likes it or not, ancient history does not easily yield to efforts to understand its minds. Interpreters must also deal with the fact that they are inevitably asking questions about the intentions of people of long ago from the context of their own interests and attitudes.[8] Moreover, then as now, distinctions can and often should be made between how a story may have been intended and how it was heard. Then as now, in other words, there are differences between teller and audience. The matter becomes more intricate when one reckons with the possibility that the teller of the story could have had more than one purpose in mind when sharing it. Or the teller may have used it on several different occasions, varying the purpose somewhat with the audience and occasion. In some instances the storyteller's strategy may have been yet more complex. The intention may have been to provoke hearers to make their own interpretation and to draw their own conclusions on this basis.

Finally in this regard interpreters more concerned with literary issues are right to recognize that authors are subject to societal and psychological forces, and basic patterns and functions of stories along with people's expectations of them, of which authors are often unaware. Yet these may have had much to say about how the story was shaped and thus the ways in which it was heard and can be heard. There is, in other words, a more universal, aesthetic dimension to stories which is important for a full hearing of them.[9] Although it is very helpful, for example, to know the historical circumstances behind the story of Macbeth and Shakespeare's writing and staging of the play, it is also valuable to hear the story as a tale that transcends its connections with Scottish history and early seventeenth-century English theater.

HISTORICAL AND LITERARY

Actually this understanding helps make a useful bridge between the more literary and more historical approaches. By learning things about how a particular story might be said to function and act in any time or setting, contemporary hearers may be able to draw closer to the earlier audiences and may come to believe that they can share ways of appreciating the story with them. Alternatively, the appreciation of how the story functions as a story can certainly be deepened by studying how it was heard in particular times and contexts. As most scholars have now come to recognize, "the parables of Jesus seem treated best when they are viewed within the twin coordinates of history and literature and when these two focuses come together as hermeneutics."[10]

This collaboration also helps deal with the concern that the variety of approaches to a story could result in such a breadth of interpretation that a given parable could seem to mean anything depending on how one wanted to hear it. Are there no canons of interpretation that dictate that a particular interpretation is in some way inappropriate or ill fitting? Was it, for example, in any sense in keeping with the parable for certain theologians of the Middle Ages to interpret the story of the weeds being permitted to grow up along with the wheat but then at harvest being burned (Matt. 13:24–30) as a justification for the burning of witches?

In fact, it can now be seen that there are a number of considerations that may sometimes be in tension but at other times work together to instruct with regard to ways in which a story was once heard and ways in which it might appropriately be heard. One will examine the stories' early contexts and ask about their relation to the character and purposes of other stories told by the same author. Most critics, even among those who use more literary approaches, would probably grant a form of primacy to basic historical considerations.[11] One can also compare and contrast similar stories of the period. A close reading will often discover signals within a story (e.g., rhetorical devices such as the patterning and repetition of words and phrases). These along with basic structures and functions of similar stories from other eras and cultures can guide interpretation.

The result will not necessarily be some one best interpretation, but certain understandings may be largely ruled out. What may emerge is a kind of direction, and paths in that direction, along which interpretation can most usefully proceed. Those paths, however, need not be narrow. The width of the possibilities that are opened up can allow audiences to explore along the ways and to see details and aspects of the landscape that will enrich their appreciation and understanding.

This more multifaceted approach to parables will sometimes mean that a parable should not be heard only as an open parable, similitude, allegory, or illustrative story. Some parables may be heard differently in different contexts, and there can be mixed types. Several of the parables are found in as many as four versions in the Gospels. The inner workings and significances of the Gospel stories are more interesting and intriguing than simple classifications allow.

TYPES OF PARABLES: EXEMPLARY
AND SIMILITUDE

Some of the similarities and sharings between these cousins being recognized, it is, however, still useful to set out the broad distinctions. Obviously those who formed and passed along the early Christian narratives did not ask formal questions about what kind of stories they were using; nevertheless, they were adept at different storytelling strategies. Hearers many centuries later can be helped in their listening by becoming more alert to the ways of storytelling. When a parable is seen to be working in a largely allegorical manner or more as an open parable or illustrative story, the recognition of its essential function will certainly aid in its interpretation.

The illustrative or exemplary story may be the easiest of the types of story for the general reader to identify. These stories are usually available to general understanding, and hearers often do not require any specialized knowledge to realize their import. The stories of the poor widow who contributes everything she has (Mark 12:41–44; Luke 21:1–4), of the rich fool who stores up treasure without reckoning with his mortality (Luke 12:16–21), of the proud Pharisee and the humble tax collector (Luke 18:9–14), and of the Good Samaritan (Luke 10:25–37) are among the parables regularly put into this category. At least on their usual hearing they offer a moral point that can readily be expanded to other similar circumstances and developed for teaching or preaching purposes. They function by the principle of wider application, and hearers are explicitly or implicitly advised to "go and do likewise" or cautioned not to do likewise. The stories can be said to be "satisfying," in that listeners usually feel they have got the point and been properly edified.

For this reason there is often a tendency to interpret or hear many a story as an exemplary story although it may, in fact, have other dimensions to it.

The similitude is also recognized fairly readily and at least its general meaning is understood without much difficulty. In this kind of parable a simile is extended into a short narrative. In a simile one learns that one thing is "like" another, and there is the obvious suggestion that one can learn something from the comparison. In the Gospels Jesus instructs the disciples to "be wise as serpents and innocent as doves" (Matt. 10:16) and tells the scribes and Pharisees that they "are like whitewashed tombs." The latter simile is elaborated upon and the points of comparison made clear. Tombs "outwardly appear beautiful, but within they are full of dead men's bones and all uncleanness. So you also outwardly appear righteous to men, but within you are full of hypocrisy and iniquity" (Matt. 23:27–28).

"The kingdom of heaven is like leaven which a woman took and hid in three measures of meal, till it was all leavened" (Matt. 13:33; Luke 13:20–21) is an example of a simile extended into a very brief and simple narrative. Usually a similitude is drawn from such "a typical, familiar, recurring, everyday scene" that "gets its force from its appeal to what is universally acknowledged."[12] Other examples of parables usually regarded as somewhat longer, more complex similitudes are the stories of the woman and lost coin (Luke 15:8–10), the seed that grows by itself (Mark 4:26–29), and the mustard seed (Mark 4:30–32; Matt. 13:31–32; Luke 13:18–19).

Again, this form of storytelling is basically satisfying. The mind may be teased a bit, especially when the point or points of comparison are not made explicit, but hearers usually feel themselves edified.

ALLEGORY

The allegory is a more complex form of storytelling, although in many cases allegories are deliberately made to look more difficult to understand than they really are. "Allegory" literally means to speak so as to imply other than what is said. Once, however, one understands the other frame of reference or story that is being referred to, interpretation often becomes relatively simple. But to begin with, the allegory—unlike the similitude—does not tell what is being referred to. In this manner allegory is based more in a metaphorical activity in which one thing is directly substituted for another, with the overall context often providing the only clues as to what is being referenced.

Allegories are a relatively popular form in the Jewish Scriptures. The story that Nathan told David about the rich man who took the poor man's lambs (2 Sam. 12:1–4) is a kind of allegory, as is Hosea's description of his relationship with his whore wife, and Isaiah's parable of the vineyard (5:1–7). Ezekiel's best-known allegories tell of sheep and their true and false shepherds (chap. 34) and of the valley full of dry bones (37:1–14). Other of Ezekiel's visions and those of Daniel are more fully historical allegories that use a series of images (sometimes more descriptions than narratives) to allude to contemporary events or to what from the seer's view is soon to happen in history (though it may have already taken place in real time). The correspondence of the allegory to events that are or will be taking place offers a sense of a divine plan and even predestination in history. A number of these allegories (especially in periods when there is little sense of direction within human history) become rather surrealistic. The hearer or reader quickly realizes that it is a theology rather than a concern with realistic narrative that is in charge of the allegory. The Book of Revelation is the chief Christian example of an allegorical style that is also found in a number of Jewish writings of the intertestamental period.

A more sober form of allegory was important to theological argument and to the effort to make ancient Scripture speak directly to contemporary concerns. Philo of Alexandria, who lived at the beginning of the Christian era, was ingenious in his ability to discover by means of allegory the tenets of Greek philosophy in the Jewish Scriptures. In a more rabbinic manner Paul spoke, for example, of a building's foundation he had laid and those who built upon it with gold, silver, precious stones, wood, hay, and stubble (1 Cor. 3:10–15), and of Hagar and Sarah as corresponding to the two covenants, to freedom and slavery, and to the heavenly and earthly Jerusalem (Gal. 4:21–31).

Perhaps the most obvious example in the Gospels of a story using allegory is the one often called the parable of the wicked tenants (Mark 12:1–9; see Matt. 21:33–41; Luke 20:9–16). Sometimes in later generations the knowledge necessary for "translating" such a story is lost, but in this case one realizes that the early audiences would have had no trouble recognizing that the story as told was a kind of code in which the features and characters covertly referred to other events and actors. Even to modern hearers at all familiar with early Christian teaching the allegory is transparent. The vineyard's tenants are the Jewish people of the time, and it is God who plants and arranges the vineyard. God sent servants, the prophets, who were shamefully treated. Finally God's own Son, Jesus, was sent, whom they killed. The predicted destruction foretells the Roman despoliation of Jerusalem and the Jewish nation. The vineyard, the true Israel, has now been passed on to the largely gentile Christians.

Yet how does one know for sure when allegorical references are intended? To begin with, it is important to realize that allegory is not so much a particular form of story as it is a way of telling and hearing a story. There is a sense in which every story that sets forth or implies a form of comparison is allegorical.[13] It is one story referring to or hinting at another meaning. But the mode of storytelling or hearing which understands a number of features in one story to stand one after another for aspects of another story or set of circumstances is sufficiently distinctive so as to deserve its own classification. If there are more than a few of these kinds of correspondence in a story, hearers are probably right to recognize it as allegory.

Allegorical narratives have in the past been used for a variety of purposes. At times they may convey a politically dangerous message that has been "encoded" in such a way that only an inner circle will understand it. Often, however, they are more transparent and are employed as a means to attract hearers or readers to understandings they might otherwise have missed or given little heed to and so to make them more interesting and memorable.

Another way in which allegory is pleasurable is that it enables hearers to engage in the satisfying task of realizing for themselves what the various aspects of the story are referring to, and so also allows them to feel on the "inside" of things and a little superior. Others who do not know what is being signified remain "outsiders" to the implied story. These usefully didactic and pleasurable aspects of allegory have helped make it a favorite approach to teaching and interpretation over the years.

Problems can, however, arise when interpreters begin to look for allegorical significations that were not originally intended. Their allegorical interpretations may then be interesting and perhaps have other values while yet ignoring or otherwise missing other purposes and characteristics of the stories. The parable of the sower with its interpretation (Mark 4:3–9, 13–20; Matt. 13:3–9, 18–23; Luke 8:5–8, 11–15) may be a case in point.[14] It is even possible that this parable may have been somewhat rewritten to suit later interpretation, as could also be the case with the story of the wicked tenants.[15]

There is, of course, nothing wrong with such interpretations. In the past, allegorical readings were often used to adapt parables and other biblical materials to contemporary circumstances, and one can still learn from them. But because in New Testament times—and for many centuries since—allegorical interpretation has been so popular in Christian teaching and preaching, one wants at least to be aware of the possibilities that significations are being added that were not at first intended.[16]

At present there is considerable scholarly debate about whether a number of the Gospel parables were first devised as allegories of salvation history or whether they had a rather different purpose to start with and were later, under the pressure of Christian apologetical needs, retold and/or interpreted along these lines.[17] In the course of these discussions I shall argue that there is a marked tendency by the evangelists to add detail of an allegorizing character or otherwise to interpret the parables in a manner useful for fitting the narratives into their views of God's plan in history. This tendency is perhaps most identifiable when two or more evangelists produce different allegorical understandings of the same parable, as is the case, for instance, with Matthew's and Luke's presentations of the story of the great dinner party. But even when a parable may be discerned to have had an allegorical salvation-history or theology focus from the beginning, this concern need not exhaust its meaning, and a number of the parables may be seen to have other purposes. The matter is made more complicated because quite a few of the parables not readily susceptible to full allegorical interpretation may still have several allegorical features or at least features that are easily so interpreted. Interpreters can, of course, disagree among themselves whether, for instance, the king or householder in some parables should be seen as a figure for God in the earliest tellings of the particular parables. Given their intimate knowledge of the Jewish Scriptures, many in the first audiences of the Gospel parables probably could not have heard of a vineyard without thinking of Israel or of a harvest without imagining a time of judgment. Some interpreters today might prefer to understand these as only allusions rather than full allegorical features, but the distinction is at the least very fine.

OPEN PARABLES

That being said, however, there are a number of parables in the Gospels which, though using certain allegorical features, seem to resist any fitting full allegorical interpretation. They may seem to be full of metaphorical motion and to allude to some other story or perception about life but not in the definitive manner of a developed allegory.

These parables are in some ways like similitudes and in fact may begin with "The kingdom of God is like . . . ," although at least in some cases this phrase may be a later addition. In a number of instances, however, how or with what the story corresponds is not all that clear (partly because the kingdom itself is lacking in precise definition). Thus even in several of "The kingdom of God is like . . ." parables one seems to be dealing more with metaphorical activity than simile. At least it is not easy to keep to hard and fast distinctions.

Nor do these parables easily yield the kind of message that can often be drawn from illustrative stories. At times the hearers may feel they are bordering on this possibility, but there may also seem to be an excess or "surplus of meaning" that flows over the borders of any summing-up and even makes such seem trivial in the light of a rehearing of the parable.[18] More than this, there are found in many of the Gospel parables odd features or even a kind of strangeness to the whole story which seems designed to thwart at least any simple use as an illustrative story. They appear to be told more to provoke questions than to answer them. They seem to begin to talk about one thing, and then it is as though someone changed the subject. It is difficult for hearers to remain passive: they must wonder why this story is being told.

Perhaps the most distinguishing characteristic of what we will call the open parable is that it is unsatisfying—at least at first, and maybe in some sense always. The open parable is regularly interrogative and even argumentative—implicitly beginning and ending with, What do you think? Indeed, many of the stories are dotted with questions. Instead of leading to an insight one might try to put into other words, the parable tends to leave one reaching, even groping. It often surprises rather than confirms. At first, and maybe in the end, it may seem paradoxical as it suggests that what seems to

be self-contradictory is yet in some way true. Or it may even have the character of a riddle as it implies certain of the contradictions of life without
resolving them. Listeners might hear, for instance, of the necessity of human endeavor and responsibility and also of the gift of grace. Paul can exhort
Christians "to work out your own salvation with fear and trembling; for God
is at work in you, both to will and to work for his good pleasure" (Phil.
2:12–13). An open parable might tell that mystery. It would ask its hearers
to puzzle and leave them wondering—not just in order to involve them in
the issue but because the matter is puzzling and must be lived through to be
in some sense understood.

While usually beginning quite normally, and inviting hearers into commonplace circumstances, the open parable tends to become "unstable."[19]
Having created the expectation that one is about to hear an allegorical or illustrative story, the open parable soon takes twists and turns. It generates
dissonance as it starts stopping to make sense. Hearers are pulled up short
and made to listen and look more carefully. The surface of reality begins to
crack as the parable tells of other than is expected or perhaps even could be
expected. One thought one knew where one was—was reasonably sure of
what is possible and what is right and wrong. As fissures appear in that certainty, the parable may seem to have become not only odd but even threatening. Such parables are capable not just of giving hearers new perspectives
but of altering their situation. They can be (it would seem they were intended to be) in this sense *events* in people's lives. One can never look on a
member of another ethnic group or, indeed, see oneself when in need in
quite the same way after having shared the experience of the injured man
helped by the despised Samaritan.

REORIENTATION BY DISORIENTATION

An analogy might be made with what happens to one's understanding of
the world of natural laws as one begins to learn about subatomic physics,
quantum mechanics, the indeterminacy principle, and general and special
relativity. Contemporary students of physics have had to learn that appearances can deceive, and that in order to see with fresh eyes they need new
models—new metaphors for thinking and speaking of relativity and quantum mechanics.[20] Their world has had to undergo paradigm shifts for them
to be able even to imagine what is happening.[21] With the right paradigm or
metaphor, however, they are able to redefine reality.

A number of the Gospel parables seem also to be trying to shift perception. The Gospels speak of people having eyes and not seeing and ears and
not hearing, and then of new sight and new hearing. At times a kind of
riddling goes on as striking reversals are said to take place in the way people
think things were meant to be. What happens has been called "reorientation by disorientation."[22] First, hearers have their ways of seeing the moral
and spiritual order challenged and disrupted. They are made to see their

blindness in order that there can be the possibility of new vision. Or, as is more appropriate to the hearing of parables, they are made to hear dissonance in order that they can discover a new way of hearing. Things have first to be seen and heard to make no sense, so that another sense can be apprehended.

In the terms of Jesus' essential proclamation this reorientation is *metanoia*. The Greek word is usually translated "repentance," but in its basic meaning *metanoia* calls for a changed mind and heart. It is a turning-about —a *conversion* to a new way of thinking and hoping. "Repent, the kingdom of heaven is at hand" (Matt. 4:17). One can be sorry for past and present wrongs because the approaching kingdom of God has brought a new way of hoping and seeing the future and present.

A number of Gospel parables are set forward as occasions of this *metanoia*. They are not merely its illustrations. The advent of the kingdom—its new possibilities and ways of viewing the community of God's people—these are experienced in the hearing of the parable. It is, therefore, not only what is said that is important but how it is said. The way in which the parable works is essential to the experience. Hearers start off with a sense of knowing how things are or can be. As the parable takes its twists and turns they lose that surety. They are trapped into thought. They find themselves challenged and upset. They may even experience the story as calamity—as a disaster for their sense of self-worth and place in the moral order of things. Then, however, they are invited to search for new possibilities, new ways of hearing and seeing. While such effort on their part seems to be necessary, the new vision may also come with the shock of revelation and be appreciated as an insight that has been graciously given to them.

This experience of having, losing, and finding, or having, losing, and then being given a new opportunity for choosing, parallels the great central theme of the Bible: of a people repeatedly being given, losing, and finding their relationship with God and one another; of losing the place in the garden, in the promised land, as the first or privileged child, at the banquet or in the kingdom—of losing sight and hearing or life itself—but then finding or being surprised by the hope of grace or even grace in its fullness. The parable can never be discarded or simply summed up because the experience of its hearing is a kind of directional signal pointing toward this mystery it is trying to tell about. Only by following the *way* of the parable—by retelling and rehearing it—does one find that sense of direction.

EXTRAVAGANT STORIES

This kind of parabolic story begins to reveal its character by the instability noted earlier. That instability is often created by some manner of exaggeration or extravagance.[23] The sums of money mentioned seem very large or the punishment or reward out of keeping with what has happened. The suddenness of the reversals that take place appears hyperbolic and odd, even comic. This extravagance and hyperbole are offering other clues as well. They help hearers to realize that in the context of the ordinary the extraordinary is being talked about.[24] By a kind of alchemy the common and the surprising are suddenly juxtaposed. In the midst of the everyday details of human life there is the unexpected. Actions and events may go well beyond rational behavior intimating to hearers that they are involved in boundary situations—living on that frontier where Jesus proclaimed the inbreaking of the kingdom of God. By looking and listening beneath the surfaces of human life one discovers that ordinary decisions and actions are often fraught with all manner of unexpected consequences. Suddenly hearers are encountered by ultimate questions regarding reconciliation, forgiveness, acceptance, judgment, suffering, guilt, death, and new hope. All the open parables of the Gospels are eschatological in this sense—whether they explicitly speak of the end time of history or not. They indicate that *now* is the time for decisions of the greatest importance. Amid all the restrictions and limitations of mortal life that which is "without limit" is making its presence felt—making outrageous demands and offering incomprehensible grace and new ways of belonging.

The parable's "extravagance" presses the audience to recognize that the story cannot work well as a simple instructional or illustrative tale. Hearers are forced to search more deeply as they begin to realize that the story may be talking about more than on its surface it purports to be talking about. Such parables have an integrity and onceness about them that make difficult any easy application to other circumstances or areas of life, but one grows in the feeling that the story might be nudging its hearers to imagine some other stories or life situations, while one is not sure what they could be. There are only inklings and intimations.

This way of gesturing and hinting is a metaphorical activity of the highest order. The open parable seems to focus the force of several metaphors or in a sense to become itself a metaphor, motioning hearers toward what they must in many ways discover for themselves. The brevity of the story is an important factor, since it leaves space for allusion and imagination to interact and be at play. The other life stories that may come to mind need not parallel the details of the parable but rise to memory and imagination because of this more profound experience of the parable's movement.

GESTURING BEYOND

In the Gospels Jesus is presented as using a number of metaphors and metaphorical stories to talk about what is so difficult to talk about that at least some do not believe in its existence: God's presence and activity in the world. That presence is a kingdom, a dinner party, a wedding feast, and a treasure. Something is to be known about it from seeds and sudden growth, sowing, harvesting, a court of judgment, the returning of a master, finding what was lost, and new relationships between father and sons and masters and servants. Evidently no one or two metaphors are sufficient, because of the mystery of God's nearness. The excess of meaning and dissonance established by the variety of these ways of presenting God's activity are also an effective means of reminding that it is not to be simply or literally identified with any of them. God's ruling justice and love can be described as a place, but it is not a place; it is present, but it is yet to come. It is, although it is not, a kingdom, a judgment scene, and so forth.

Open parables are a way of pointing toward what is very hard to find words for. Because they are stories they can seek to accomplish even more than the usual function of metaphor and offer through the story something of the experience of God's nearness and what it is like to live on the threshold of the kingdom of God and its new community. Tension, however, remains because the metaphorical activity of the parable refuses to abandon its "is not" character and so to point beyond itself to what it can only approximate. One can never be sure that the father or judge or vineyard owner is or is not God, whether God or God's ruling has really shown up in the usually very secular parable, or whether the story is only gesturing toward the divine mystery—or maybe, somehow, both. Or perhaps it may even indicate that sometimes the possibility of God can only be recognized through an awareness of God's apparent absence. Through their paradoxical and often deliberately ambiguous character[25] open parables continue to incorporate aspects of life's enigmatic nature, though the final purpose of parables is not to delineate the enigmatic but to suggest the otherwise unspeakable and to bring human beings "before us in their moral mystery and in a perspective of divine severity and love."[26]

1

THE RESILIENT RASCAL

The Unjust Steward

There was a rich man who had a steward, and charges were brought to him that this man was wasting his goods. And he called him and said to him, "What is this that I hear about you? Turn in the account of your stewardship, for you can no longer be steward." And the steward said to himself, "What shall I do, since my master is taking the stewardship away from me? I am not strong enough to dig, and I am ashamed to beg. I have decided what to do, so that people may receive me into their houses when I am put out of the stewardship." So, summoning his master's debtors one by one, he said to the first, "How much do you owe my master?" He said, "A hundred measures of oil." And he said to him, " Take your bill, and sit down quickly and write fifty." Then he said to another, "And how much do you owe?" He said, "A hundred measures of wheat." He said to him, "Take your bill and write eighty." The master commended the dishonest steward for his astuteness; for the sons of this world are wiser in their own generation than the sons of light. And I tell you, make friends for yourselves by means of unrighteous mammon, so that when it fails they may receive you into the eternal habitations.

Luke 16:1–9

So successfully does this parable resist any satisfying allegorical cross-referencing or easy use as an exemplary story that it is regularly avoided by preachers. Its apparent commendation of what seems to be at best shady behavior has placed it on the banned list of Sunday-school texts. What is this, one asks? Is the Bible recommending cheating as a way of dealing with a difficult situation? Is, for instance, a Latin American dictator to be admired for stashing money in a secret Swiss bank account just before his regime is overthrown? Is one to congratulate a Pentagon worker for illegally saving defense contractors money so that he can later get a good job with one of them?

The first person that can be seen having difficulty with the interpretation of this story is the evangelist Luke. In succeeding verses (16:8b–13) he has, while evidently struggling with the meaning of the story, offered "notes for three separate sermons on the parable as text."[1] Frequently in his Gospel Luke is concerned with questions having to do with wealth and the use of money and this world's goods.[2] One recalls, for example, the parable of the rich man who stored up many goods only to find that that very night his soul was required of him (12:16–20) and the story of the conversion of the rich tax

17

collector Zacchaeus (19:1–10). The concern is especially evident throughout this section, and this parable, usually called the story of the unjust steward, is bracketed by the parables of the prodigal son and the rich man and Lazarus which begin similarly ("There was a [rich] man . . .") and tell of individuals who squandered, wasted, or made merry with the goods of this world. It has been suggested that Luke wrote his Gospel for a Christian community in which some members were people of means and questions about the right use of riches were very important.

The first sermon (vv. 8b–9) exhorts disciples to be at least as wise and shrewd as worldly people in dealing with "unrighteous mammon." There is probably a suggestion that by aiding and making friends of those less well-off now one will be helped in the future life. The second sermon (vv. 10–12) is also concerned with stewardship. One must learn to be faithful now with "unrighteous mammon" so that in the future one can be entrusted with true riches. The final sermon (v. 13) makes clear how dangerous money is if one is to try to live faithfully toward God.

One can sum up the three sermons by realizing that mammon may be used wisely but that its dangers and temptations are great. All of this may certainly be said to be good Christian advice, but it does not seem naturally to proceed from a story about a man who we are told was unjust. One can, at the least, think of better stories on which to hang such sermons.

Because this concern with the right use of riches is known to be a special interest of Luke's and because vv. 8b–13 do not readily flow from the parable, one also wants to hear the story apart from its Lukan interpretation. The next problem encountered, however, is the belief of several critics that the words "The master commended the dishonest steward for his astuteness" (v. 8a) are also part of the interpretation (added either by Luke or by a previous teller of the story) and do not belong to an earlier version of the parable. There would then be a story that concluded with the steward's behavior without a commendation of his astuteness or a mention of his unrighteousness and that would be interpreted as best it could be.[3] It does not make sense, these critics maintain, for the master or lord (*kyrios*) of the steward to commend him for his actions. If it is held alternatively that the *kyrios* is meant to be Jesus, then hearers would at least have to recognize that they are already outside the parable proper and into its interpretation by Jesus.

So many centuries distant from the first hearings of the parable one cannot, of course, be conclusive about a possible earlier form. It can be pointed out, however, that the very telling of the story (even without v. 8a) calls attention to the steward's evidently odd behavior. What is perhaps most unexpected, after all, is not that the steward is commended but that such a story is told at all. Yet, though a number of parables are open-ended, it does seem unlikely that the story terminated without some further development, and the commendation does provide that *twist* of surprise characteristic of other parables.[4]

It is, of course, also possible that the original ending of the parable has somehow been lost.[5] In a number of Jesus' stories the narrative concludes with the first actor talking in direct speech. Perhaps that is what has been lost and replaced with this version of the master's response to his steward's actions. Yet if a different ending did drop off, one could at best guess what it might have been, and no one has yet come up with another ending that would seem to make the tale worth making a point of and remembering. What is more likely is that the direct speech of the master was summed up in v. 8a. But that would leave the same essential story and evidently surprising ending.

Who then is the *kyrios* who commends the steward? It is conceivable that Luke intended a measure of ambiguity in this regard. Regularly *kyrios* in his Gospel is Jesus, but the internal consistency of the story (the steward's master is *kyrios* in vv. 3 and 5) certainly suggests that it is the parable's "rich man" that says a good word for the apparently unjust behavior.[6]

But maybe the steward's actions in response to the news that he was about to be fired were not all that wrongful. This has been the solution to the puzzle of the parable that has been provided by a number of commentators seeking to make sense of the story. Perhaps the originally required interest payments were usurious and the master commended the steward for having forgiven them, either because he now realized this was right or because it would put him in a good light with others. Or these were bad debts that the master was glad to receive as much on as could be collected. Or the interest on the debts was, in fact, the steward's normal profit, which he now overlooked in order to close the books on his master's accounts and also to earn favor with the debtors.[7]

Certainly none of these ways of understanding what the steward did are impossible, and maybe we today lack a comprehension of the customs that would make this story less odd to our ears. Yet, because the parable provides so little that would help one understand the steward's behavior as reasonable, and because several other parables that might reach back to early tradition seem unreasonable, these solutions may make too easily understandable that which may have been meant to be surprising, if not outrageous. The stern and apparently somewhat capricious master and the not always responsible steward, servant, or servants are rather frequent actors in the Gospel's parables. What would, of course, have seemed predictable (but made the story less memorable) is the denunciation by the rich man of his rascally steward. What is unexpected is that he evidently finds something commendable about his behavior.

This commendation has, in turn, led to questions about the rich man's morality. Possibly this is a cautionary tale about two "birds of a feather," neither one of whom is meant to be admired by the parable's audience. What the master comes to find that he values in the steward is that he is a bit of a shyster like himself—or, at least, a hard-nosed person who can finally get things done the way he would do them. He was cleverer than he took him for. What the audience might be meant to learn is how one should not behave!

This understanding of the story would permit it to be heard as morally acceptable and might make better sense of several of the comments that follow in Luke's Gospel. Yet hearing the story only in negative terms does not finally seem to fit well with Luke's overall context or with any readily imaginable setting in Jesus' teaching or that of the early churches.

One of the more interesting readings of the moral circumstances of the story leaves the steward as a clever rogue[8] but the master as still honorable if somewhat duped. The steward, who had been a kind of estate agent, when he finds out he is fired, calls in those who are renting land from his master. As no one yet knows he has been dismissed, the renters assume he is still acting for the master when he gives them a hurried opportunity to alter their bills by changing them in their own hand. He then presents the fait accompli to the master who has the choice of trying to undo what has happened or accepting the thanks and praise he is now receiving from the renters for his generosity. Being himself smart enough to see that what is best for the steward is also now best for him, he turns to the steward and says, "You are a wise fellow."[9]

This interpretation may read too much into the narrative, and several important questions remain, but a story along these lines does remind of tales from the Old Testament about escapes and cunning tricks, in which coping and conniving were paramount and standard morality took a back seat (Abraham saying Sarah was his sister, Jacob stealing Esau's birthright, David's letting others take the blame for his actions, and so forth). Most recent commentators, however, have tended to accept the parable's scandalous character and then to set it in the context of Jesus' proclamation of the approach of God's reign. They, too, note the sudden urgency of the steward's predicament, together with his hurried request to the first of the debtors that he should "quickly" sit down and write the revised amount of the bill and the abrupt "and you" to the second man. The nearness of the kingdom begins to force decisions other than those individuals might normally make and to call for what would otherwise appear extravagant ("Make friends quickly with your accuser, while you are going with him to court. . . ," Matt. 5:25). Seen in this perspective one now recognizes that the amounts under discussion seem to be unusually large. It has been estimated that the hundred measures of olive oil (= thousand gallons) and the hundred measures of wheat (= thousand bushels) would have each been worth the equivalent of at least five hundred days' wages for an average worker. The amounts to be written off, especially the fifty percent, also seem at least very sizable.[10] In the midst of the ordinary the extraordinary is happening.

Early in the parable it is said that the steward was "wasting" the rich man's goods (the root meaning of the Greek word *diaskorpizō* suggests that he was "scattering" them about as the prodigal son did with his inheritance). He still seems to be doing that, but now we are told that his behavior is also unjust, wrongful. Presumably earlier he was just a bad manager, but now he has compounded his behavior by in effect cheating his master in order that the debtors would later look with favor on him. What then could be commendable (or if we disregard v. 8a, noteworthy) about the steward's attempt to deal with his problem?

The master says that he was *phronimos*, meaning "wise, prudent, astute," perhaps even "shrewd." This word occurs in other Gospel passages strongly flavored by a concern with the nearness of judgment and the end of time. The young maidens who take flasks of oil with their lamps are said to be wise, and elsewhere Jesus asks who is the faithful and wise servant whom the master will set over his household after he returns suddenly (see Matt. 25:2–9; 24:45; Luke 14:42; also Matt. 7:24). According to a number of interpreters what is at least noteworthy and perhaps even earns the praise of his master is the steward's capacity to face up to the reality of his crisis—to see the facts of his predicament. He did not just mope and try to pretend that this really could not be happening to him. He did not say, "Maybe it will somehow turn out all right tomorrow." He was honest with himself, too, in that he realized he would be ashamed to beg from others and that he did not have the stamina to be a digger. But he had to do something, and he did it! There is something commendable in that.

One can imagine such a story being told with a little laugh, for the joke would be on anyone who missed what the story was getting at. One commentator draws out the same point and then makes the shift to Jesus' allied concern with the required response to the advent of God's reign. This steward "did not let things take their course, he acted, unscrupulously no doubt, . . . but boldly, resolutely, and prudently, with the purpose of making a new life for himself. For you, too, the challenge of the hour demands prudence, everything is at stake! . . . Evasion is impossible."[11]

The theme of making a new life for oneself seems to fit with Jesus' proclamation about the kingdom. Its breaking into present-day sensibilities and mores is at least disruptive and in many ways a catastrophe for people's sense of who is up and who is down—who is included in the kingdom and who not. One's sense of place (maybe even of what is right and wrong) is threatened if not shattered. That is evidently what the invasion of the present age by the age to come brings about as the end time begins to become the new time now.

Yet calamity can also become opportunity if one seizes upon the time of decision as a chance for a new life. Crooked he may have been, but the unjust steward recognized the significance of his moment of crisis and acted. At least that is worth remembering about him. Would that those who heard Jesus' teaching could also face the facts of their circumstances in the light of the nearness of the divine purposes for life. The future of faith belongs to those who can accept and adapt to the genuinely new and use their experience and imagination in doing so.

It is perhaps sufficient to leave this strange and still challenging parable here—maybe, despite its oddness, to be heard as a kind of exemplary story about resoluteness and single-mindedness in the face of what can upend life. Nor should one forget to enjoy the story and the way it works on its audience. The four questions in the dialogue that help to hold the story structurally together[12] also serve to invite the audience's participation, especially the first two: "What is this that I hear about you?" "What shall I do? . . ."

Hearers may begin by sympathizing with the steward with whom the master deals so sternly. This, one says, is just the way rich landlords behave. But next, as the steward seems to have associated himself with the upper class by being unwilling to do manual labor, hearers begin to wonder about him. Then, however, it is hard to resist the way in which he evidently dupes his master in order to gain future benefits. Listeners get into the spirit of that deception and vicariously enjoy getting even with all tough bosses. Behind his back they laugh at the master. But suddenly they realize that they are not being ethical by enjoying what the steward has transacted. Something will have to be done.[13]

Then comes the surprise ending. The steward was supposed to be caught and condemned. One is instead left with questions, probably at least as much about the master as the steward. As the first character to be introduced in the story, the master could be regarded as its main character. What kind of a master is this? Was he right to have given credence to those charges that were brought to him?

Many hearers of the story have likely found themselves in administrative positions dealing with such accusations and perhaps with shifty if imaginatively bright subordinates who have dealt irresponsibly and then even unjustly with what was not their own. What is one to think of a master who reacts like this?

Or what is one to think of Jesus reportedly telling a story like this? Is the steward another of the outcast ("the sinners") with whom Jesus kept associating himself and to whom he said the kingdom was open? Why this one? Is this justice? Does the kingdom include stewards like this as well as masters who do not seem to get even? Again, who is this master?

Over the years as I have continued to listen to the parable, further thoughts have come to mind. I have seen others, and once or twice found myself, in predicaments not unlike that of the steward. What in some ways may be most interesting about such a figure is the pluck and the faith he shows. Even after disaster has struck, he finds it possible to carry on. In that fortitude there may well seem something worth at least a measure of commendation and forgiveness—a trait even likable, perhaps on occasion lovable.[14]

Where does he find this resource? Do I have it? The parable can be heard asking that question as one puts oneself in the steward's place. And, actually, it does not require much effort to be in his shoes; after all, there is something of the rogue and dodger in most people. Most people are at least a bit phony. They do not always tell the truth. They cheat a little here and there—on their income tax—or they drive too fast. They cut corners and fudge things a bit. They try to get the advantage over others, and sometimes ambition masters their souls.

Most of the time they get away with it, but it is also sadly true that, sooner or later, if it has not happened already, they will come a cropper and find their own tragedies. Maybe it will not be their fault or, in more complicated ways, it will and it will not. They will lose some of their friends or their home or job or reputation or all of the above. Maybe their marriage breaks up. Or perhaps one year they are just overwhelmed by what seems the meaninglessness of much of life. Depression spread-eagles their spirits. They do not have what it takes anymore.

What then will they do? How will they respond? Will they be able to find hope? to try again?

What may seem most surprising about the rascally steward is that he does pick up and try again. One stands in at least some awe as he insists that this calamity of losing his job can be the basis of new opportunity—that there will be another chance—that in spite of losing, even through losing, there can be finding.

Now one may hear resonance with the story of a people who regularly sin and lose their place in the promised land—who are crushed and defeated, but who yet, even in exile, never give up believing that they are the Lord's people. And one day they do again find their way home.

Perhaps this is the story of all people: overstepping who they are, losing their place in the garden, yet believing that the one who created them will not totally abandon them. Still they can make at least a human life and even hope for more.

Then it becomes the story of the disciples who slept and lied when Jesus needed them, and who ran and watched from another hill while their Lord and all bright dreams about God's kingdom were brutally being put to death. What was it that later enabled them to tell his stories again? What mystery caused hope to be reborn in these disappointing disciples, enabling them to become the pioneers of new trust in God in the face of the world's cruelty?

And what is it that causes this to happen, not just once upon a time but again and again? One thinks of other rascally Christians: Frederick Buechner's Leo Bebb, ex–Bible salesman and convict, founder of the Church of Holy Love, who runs a theological correspondence school and diploma mill and is always in trouble with the IRS. Calamity is his constant companion. Yet he keeps dreaming up new schemes, and, amid all the chicanery and chaos, somehow manages to love life and people. In the end he may be a caricature for all the clergy—playing at being holy, pretending to know things about God while living off people's gullibility and need for someone to look up to—during which time grace passes through them almost in spite of themselves, beginning to make them commendable.

Then there is Graham Greene's whisky priest who has grown stout eating the peasants' food at their poor celebrations. Without much dedication he baptizes and regularly celebrates the sacrament of the mass, partly because this provides him with prestige and because these acts bring in fees and give him entree to the parties after the baptisms, weddings, and funerals. The sacrament of Christ's death is the means of his livelihood. As, however, the Mexican state becomes more and more opposed to the church, celebration of the mass becomes a dangerous act, punishable by death. But this undisciplined priest, who one drunken night impregnates one of his flock, still does not leave his home area and continues to offer the eucharistic sacrifice until it finally leads to his own—the death of an alcoholic priest who was able to turn wine into the blood of Christ until a firing squad splattered out his blood. The death of Christ becomes his death, and the people for whom he could not stop offering the sacrament now begin to see him as a martyr through whom they can have faith in life and in the hidden presence of God in an unbelieving world.[15]

Perhaps in recalling the story of an alcoholic, martyred priest too much has been read from this parable. This way of associating does at least indicate, however, the power of parable to make one think of other stories. And certainly such insights are not out of keeping with other parables and stories in the Gospels through which one discovers that grace can come to and through very unlikely people—tax collectors, the blind, prostitutes, Samaritans—and finally those deserting disciples. The fact that the steward in many ways did not really deserve to be commended may be a means of making the Gospel's point. Grace is surprise—as it was to the disciples. Grace comes anyway, even to the unredeemable—even to this steward.

Perhaps the greatest surprise, the greatest miracle, is that they do go on—Bebb, the whisky priest, Scarlett O'Hara, the disciples, the steward, we ourselves. Maybe that seems understandable when the sun is out, but in the darkness of so much wrong in the world thoughtful people struggle with what they call the problem of evil, and apparent meaninglessness. What the parable may leave one wondering about is the problem of good—not good over against evil but good even through evil, hope and grace enabling these characters to pick up again and cleverly carry on. That, after all, is a mystery too—that people will go on trusting that there is purpose and value in life. In spite of sin and roguery, just that people are survivors may be commendable, maybe even lovable, in the Creator's eyes.

2

THE JUST AND
THE UNJUST

The Pharisee and the Tax Collector

He also told this parable to some who trusted in themselves that they were righteous and despised others: "Two men went up into the temple to pray, one a Pharisee and the other a tax collector. The Pharisee stood by himself and prayed in this manner, 'God, I thank you that I am not like other men, extortioners, unjust, adulterers, or even like this tax collector. I fast twice a week, I give tithes of all that I get.' But the tax collector, standing far off, would not even lift up his eyes to heaven, but beat his breast, saying, 'God, be merciful to me a sinner!' I tell you, this man went down to his house justified rather than the other; for every one who exalts self will be humbled, but the one who humbles self will be exalted."

Luke 18:9–14

Here are two more characters. It is at least interesting to try for a few minutes to forget the framing verses of the story (vv. 9, 14) and to see and hear the Pharisee and the tax collector through the brief descriptions of them and their own words. With whom do hearers most easily identify?

Most contemporary listeners are so familiar with the story that they immediately bow their heads and beat their breasts. This must be an exemplary story about humility and repentance, and soon one can sing of "amazing grace, how sweet the sound, that saved a wretch like me . . ."

To be sure, most people are aware of the spiritual dangers of merely enjoying a sorrowing humility—wallowing in feelings of repentance and making this into a new claim to virtue. "I'm rather proud of how humble and repentant I am," would be one way of putting it. The last half of v. 14 (a repeated refrain in the Gospels which the evangelist may have added here) could be heard to suggest that the purpose of humbling oneself is to be exalted over others. "I am more repentant than thou," would then be the claim of the tax collector to the Pharisee.

The danger is nicely illustrated in the story of the senior minister who knelt at the altar rail one Good Friday and smote herself on the breast, saying, "Lord, I am not worthy." The assistant minister was so impressed by this act of piety that he too knelt, thumped his chest, and mumbled, "I am not worthy." Then from the back of the church they both heard the sexton beat his chest and add, "I am not worthy." The senior minister leaned over and whispered to the assistant, "Look who thinks he's not worthy now."

It is only a short step from that kind of penitence to a new self-righteous-ness. This parable, however, is clearly concerned with true penitence, hu-mility, and dependence on God's grace, and contrasts this attitude with the apparent smugness of the Pharisee. Verse 9 makes evident the opportunity to hear the story as a cautionary tale, warning against being like the Phari-see, and the first part of v. 14 presses home the moral. This is the traditional way of understanding the parable, and it certainly has its benefits.

Many modern hearers tend, of course, to miss the shock of the narrative's reversal by too quickly identifying the tax collector as the good guy and see-ing the Pharisee only as a stock figure of priggish self-righteousness. The story had more punch for the people of that earlier era who honored the Pharisees and knew what louts tax collectors could be. Tax collectors, it must be remembered, were acting as the agents of a foreign and occupying gov-ernment. Most of the tax collectors (who might better be thought of as toll collectors) entitled themselves to the right to collect levies on the transporta-tion of property by paying an advance fee. They then sought to make a profit on the transaction. The more money they could exact, the greater was their take. This offered scope for considerable bribery and extortion. The Gospels several times link tax collectors with sinners and prostitutes and, in so doing, reflect the general attitude of the times.[1] The tax collector Zacchaeus (who is encountered just a few verses later in Luke's Gospel: 19:1–10) was regarded as a sinner by the people of Jericho, and his own promise to make restitution indicates that he had been in the habit of defrauding people. On hearing a reference to a tax collector, in other words, the early audiences of this story would likely have thought of a well-to-do crook who worked hand in glove with the Romans and probably stepped all over people. To find a parallel in the eyes of the general populace today, one might imagine a weepy drug dealer standing at the back of a church.

The Pharisees, on the other hand, while often caricatured in the Gospels, were, in fact, regularly esteemed by the people. They were highly regarded not only for their studiousness and dedication but for their humility and charity. They lived sacrificially and were known for their care of the poor. Moreover, it was they who were working to keep alive and strengthen the traditions of Judaism in the face of the Roman occupation.

One can, of course, pick some faults with this particular Pharisee. His prayer, especially in comparison with that of the tax gatherer, sounds a bit long-winded. He appears to be self-centered and tends to concentrate on negative virtues. (Fasting, for instance, is meant to have its greatest signifi-cance in Judaism for its capacity to lead to compassion and care for others. See esp. Isa. 58:6–12.) Yet, by almost any standard and certainly in compari-son with most people then and now, he was a very religious and ethical per-son. This Pharisee seems sincere, and he does give thanks to God for his situation. In Jewish traditions that probably date back to this era, one can find prayers similar to his. Any reasonable person, after all, might thank God that he is not unjust and so forth. One can even hear a recognition of God's grace in his prayer.

Given the tenor of other parables that likely go back to the early tradition, it is not hard to imagine an earlier version of this one which ended with the prayers of the two men and then perhaps an implied or explicit question: Who is it that is acceptable with God? Once one adopts a fair and more realistic view of both the Pharisee and the tax collector such a question becomes more challenging. At least there is again more shock and surprise in the reversal of the story as it evidently suggests that the tax collector is not unacceptable.

What then is the trouble with the Pharisee? He is, in fact, found in other of Jesus' parables, or at least he is very reminiscent of the elder brother who has great difficulty dealing with his father's welcoming response to the return of his wastrel younger brother. One thinks of the all-day laborers who were upset because those who worked for only an hour received the same wage that they had agreed to. There can be heard again those who grumbled when Jesus chose to stay at Zacchaeus's house: "He has gone to be the guest of a man who is a sinner." What is evidently hard for the decent, hard-working folk of the world to deal with is the possibility that God cares for the prodigals and sinners. This, of course, was a problem not just for Jewish leaders but for everyone who was and is trying to be ethical. The Pharisees, in fact, were better than most in understanding that the God of Israel could care for the sinner—especially the repentant sinner. But preaching and talking about God's acceptance are one thing; acting it out in practice is much harder.

Some years ago a young clergyman was asked to help in a painful pastoral situation. The teenage daughter of a couple in the parish had been dating a man in his early twenties, and she became pregnant. By the time the clergyman was called in, an illegal abortion had taken place and the parents wanted counseling for their daughter and the young man, with whom she was still keeping company. What the parents most wanted, of course, was for them to be persuaded to stop seeing each other and for the man to go to a far country.

In those years of the early 1960s young men of this type were sometimes called motorcycle boys or hot rodders. The man's leather jacket seemed to have a hundred zippers on it, and his splendid mane of black hair concluded in what was styled a ducktail. The girl's parents, under very trying circumstances, wanted to be fair, but, in addition to everything else, this young man came from a very different background.

Unfortunately for the inexperienced clergyman, he did not really understand his assignment. As he counseled the motorcycle boy and tried to give him a Christian understanding of sexuality and life and service, the young man seemed to be quite taken by this vision. It may have been a fine confi-

dence job, but he appeared to be sincere in his way. A baptism and consequent membership in the parish were arranged.

The other members of this congregation were good people, thoughtful,
decent. Nevertheless, there was quite a lot of second-guessing and criticism.
It proved very difficult for the young man to find a place in the congregation.
His being accepted as an equal seemed to call into question the basis for the
membership of others. Did not being a regular churchgoer mean something
in the community?

Had Jesus only preached about accepting tax gatherers and sinners, his
words would not have caused much concern and perhaps would even have
been generally approved. The trouble came when he did it and, moreover,
seemed to claim that in so doing he was enacting God's will. According to
Luke, Jesus does so in this parable by entering into it, as it were, and de-
claring the tax collector justified. He also, according to Luke, offers to be the
guest of Zacchaeus, and the charge that he gave acceptance to tax gatherers
and sinners by eating with them is repeated in the Gospels. It emerges as
one of the most historically certain aspects of his ministry.[2] The company he
kept rubbed off on him in the eyes of others. It was hard for a number of people to see him as holy, for by his association he tended to make himself equal
with the types he hung around with.

Many of those types would likely have felt themselves unequal and outside God's acceptability. (The Greek word *hilaskomai,* "be merciful," in the
tax collector's prayer alludes to atonement and so to the hope of becoming
reconciled with God and thus, too, in the community.)[3] The leprous and
lame and blind may well have been made to see their problems as a sign of
God's disfavor. Others were at least on the borderline of acceptability because of their professions. In this story the tax collector's self-valuation is sig-
naled by his posture, the profound beating of his breast, and the shortness of
his petition, as well as by his keeping his distance from the good people and
their place of prayer. Jesus seems to have insisted to such tax collectors and
others like them that the kingdom of God was open to them. The care of God
was reaching out and seeking to include them. The sovereign freedom of divine mercy was not limited by human ideas of their righteousness and the
unrighteousness of others. The nearness of God's just grace meant that a new
community of relationships was being shaped.

The Pharisee of the parable wants to define his goodness over against the
tax collector. The most probable translation of the Greek text (*statheis pros
heauton*) suggests that he "stood apart" to offer his thanksgiving.[4] If he knew
the words attributed to Rabbi Hillel, he had on this day forgotten them:
"Keep not aloof from the congregation and trust not in thyself until the day of
thy death, and judge not thy fellow until thou art come in to his place."[5] For
this Pharisee there would be no community even at prayer. He makes his
judgment clear when he mentions extortion, for tax collectors, whose rates
of interest could be usurious, were often viewed as extortioners.[6] The Phari-

see's goodness in his own eyes comes at the price of separating himself from the tax collector and also causing the collector to distance himself from a sense of place in the community of Israel and God's care. The Pharisee is indulging in a kind of self-fulfilling prophecy. Because the tax collector is a "bad" person he cannot fully participate in the worship and the common life of God's people, and therefore he is a bad person. He "opens up a devilish gulf between himself and the tax collector, when he seizes the good for himself and pushes the other man into evil."[7] What the Pharisee becomes is a type for other of the world's figures of power who in one way or another will to exclude and oppress others. The first thing people do when they want to deny others' rights or any responsibility for their needs is to maintain that they have no membership in the community.[8] In telling this story Jesus is seen "taking sides with human beings in a concrete situation where the existing politico-religious structure has dehumanized people."[9] In his anger over this dehumanization Jesus is elsewhere reported to have said to some of the religious leaders, "The tax collectors and the harlots go into the kingdom of God before you" (Matt. 21:31).

What the Pharisee does is very human, and the bad news of the parable is that its hearers are that righteous man. The shock of the parable is that it is goodness defined in this good man's way that, by setting the tax collectors outside the kingdom, in fact makes the good man the outsider to the true community of Israel.

Once hearers of the parable have recognized themselves in the Pharisee, however, they are free also to associate themselves with the tax collector and to realize in how many ways they are that person too—at least sometimes fraudulent in their dealings with others, deep at heart doubting whether God can find them acceptable, often unobservant at prayer, though suddenly moved by a wave of penitence. One can imagine that Jesus might once have told this story in answer to a question like, How can a tax collector find favor with God? His response by way of parable invites both the askers of the question and tax collectors into the possibility of a new community of relationship with God and reconciliation with one another.[10] "Even sin against the law does not constitute a barrier for the God who is approaching in grace."[11]

This is the opportunity of the nearness of God's kingdom. Every group has its righteous people and "extortioners, unjust, adulterers." Can they together hear of God's insistent graciousness? Moreover, since the righteous do-gooder and a kind of crook live in each individual, the story also makes available the possibility of an inner acceptance and reconciliation. The do-gooder is called to acknowledge and offer healing acceptance to the sinful side of self, and the sinner has also to recognize and deal with the self-righteous penchant for defining goodness by setting oneself up as superior to others and so setting them out of the community.

A difficult and demanding insight offered by the parable of the righteous man and the tax collector is that religious zeal, faithfulness, and ethical living can separate one from one's brothers and sisters and cause their oppression. So can such goodness also separate one from God. In his teaching elsewhere Jesus shows that there is no crime for which his hearers do not have the inner desire and for which they could not be said to deserve punishment. This includes a readiness so to deprecate the life of others as to abuse them with words and call them fools—which Jesus suggests may in its way be even worse than killing them.[12] Since no one is able to be free from such attitudes, it is clear in this sense how the very desire to see oneself as good in relation to others makes one a sinner too. The message of hope is that the opportunity of acceptance with God does not depend on one's goodness and moral power. "The impossibility of fulfilling the intensified norms here becomes a pointer towards the grace of God."[13] Grace is needed by all and can come to all.

3

EQUAL PAY

The Laborers in the Vineyard

For the kingdom of heaven is like a householder who went out early in the morning to hire laborers for his vineyard. After agreeing with the laborers for a denarius a day, he sent them into his vineyard. And going out about the third hour he saw others standing idle in the market place; and to them he said, "You go into the vineyard too, and whatever is right I will give you." So they went. Going out again about the sixth hour and the ninth hour, he did the same. And about the eleventh hour he went out and found others standing; and he said to them, "Why do you stand here idle all day?" They said to him, "Because no one has hired us." He said to them, "You go into the vineyard too." And when evening came, the owner of the vineyard said to his steward, "Call the laborers and pay them their wages, beginning with the last, up to the first." And when those hired about the eleventh hour came, each of them received a denarius. Now when the first came, they thought they would receive more; but each of them also received a denarius. And on receiving it they grumbled at the householder, saying, "These last worked only one hour, and you have made them equal to us who have borne the burden of the day and the scorching heat." But he replied to one of them, "Friend, I am doing you no wrong; did you not agree with me for a denarius? Take what belongs to you and go; I choose to give to this last as I give to you. Am I not allowed to do what I choose with what belongs to me? Are you jealous because of my generosity?" So the last will be first, and the first last.

Matt. 20:1–16

Through the centuries this parable has been given interesting allegorical interpretations. One of the best-known and easiest to understand in terms of how and why it was conceived was devised by Irenaeus toward the end of the second century C.E. According to Irenaeus this Gospel story covertly referred to the stages of salvation history. Those who began work first were the people God called at the beginning of creation; then others were called and still others during the "intermediate period" (perhaps Irenaeus is here referring to the time of Jesus). Others were called after a long period of time, and finally God calls those at the end of time. The equal wage they all receive is the coin having stamped upon it the "royal image and superscription, the knowledge of the Son of God, which is immortality."[1]

Irenaeus's interpretation echoes a lovely image found in a Jewish book written about the year 100 C.E. There, in answer to a question about what will happen at the time of judgment to those who have come before as well as the ones who live at present and those who are yet to be, the angel answers, "I will compare the judgment to a circle: the latest will not be too late nor will the earliest be too early."[2] In a not dissimilar vein this parable has often been used in sermons to demonstrate that every person will be equally accepted into God's kingdom no matter at what stage in life the person is called—young, middle-aged, or old. Using this theme preachers have encouraged the elderly and even the dying to be baptized and to have faith in their full reception in the age to come.

An allegorical hearing for the story could certainly have been the first inclination of the earliest audiences of the parable. Isaiah 5:1–7 tells of a vineyard that is Israel and the owner of which is God. It is a familiar image from the Scriptures, as are also the time of harvest and the payment of wages, which represent the time of judgment. The Gospels' parable of the wicked husbandmen (Mark 12:1–12; Matt. 21:33–46; Luke 20:9–19) seems clearly to be an allegory told on the basis of such cross-references, and it has been maintained that (not all that differently from Irenaeus's interpretation) Matthew understood this story of workers all paid the same amount as an allegory of salvation history in which the divine favoring of Christians is to be viewed as not unjust to Jews.[3] One wonders how well this hearing squares with Matthew's usage of the saying about the first becoming last and the last first, which seems the evangelist's major interpretation of the parable, and his talk elsewhere of the rejection of at least some of the Jews and transference of their heritage. But it was certainly Matthew's penchant to read other parables in historical allegorical terms, and it may be true in this case as well.

Yet, despite this history of interpretation and the apparent inducements of its general imagery (encouraged when the householder is referred to as the lord [kyrios] of the vineyard, v. 8), other aspects of the detail and structure of the parable appear to resist allegorical explanation. In this awareness modern hearers may be appreciating what the earliest audiences would have recognized. It may well be that the parable deliberately created certain allegorical expectations and then defied them in order that hearers might be surprised and made to listen for something different in the story.

A similar surprise seems to be in store for those who are looking for a basic moral message. The evangelist Matthew appears to have been among the first to encounter this difficulty. He has placed the parable in the setting of instructions to the disciples about their eventual rewards but also the dangers of seeking places of privilege (as James and John do through their mother), leading to the admonition that "the one who would be great among you must be your servant" (20:26). That is an intriguing context, and Matthew may be saying something to the effect that the priority of disciples in their calling does not assure them of priority in rewards. But Matthew's use of the summary statement (found at other places in the Gospels) about the first being last and the last first (reversed in 20:16) to bracket the parable does not then seem to follow well from the story itself. The normal order in which one would expect the workers to be paid is reversed, but the story says that the workers called at different hours were made equal. That may involve a kind of reversal, but one imagines a more complex reordering than the refrain seems to indicate. Perhaps, as will be seen, when others are given more than they seem to have deserved, those who are only given their deserving feel that they have been treated unequally and so, in a way, have been put last. Equality can sometimes feel very unfair.

More recent efforts to draw a message from the economic circumstances and actions described in the narrative do not appear to fit well with the parable either. Sermons based on this parable have called for care for the unemployed and a more just and equitable distribution of income. People's needs, it is held, should be considered along with their abilities and hours of work. The poor have at least minimum rights.

It is possible that the parable may finally have something radical to say about economic arrangements in society, but that message is at least not obvious. The evident unworkability of the vineyard owner's pay scheme in the normal marketplace challenges one's efforts to apply such a practice more generally. Business leaders hear the parable and respond to the preacher, "Well, it's an interesting story, Pastor, but you can't expect us to operate our business that way. It would lead to chaos among the work force. The hardest workers wouldn't have it." Labor-union officers are even more adamant. "We're always glad to hear the Bible, Padre, but you can't expect people to give up the just deserts of overtime and seniority."

Told in the classroom, the story provokes interest until it is suggested that at the conclusion of the course the professor might give everyone the same grade. Some lazy students, of course, would rejoice, but those who had burned the midnight oil and were concerned about graduate school would be greatly upset. And when the faculty heard about such a system, they too would object. "A school can't be run that way."

What can be run that way? Again one realizes how a parable has lured its hearers in by the surface plausibility of its opening scenes but then gone in a surprising direction. One also begins to sense the artfulness of this narrative related in but a few quick scenes. The story might only have told of the hirings of the all-day laborers and then those who worked only one hour, since these are the groups to be compared, but the series of recruitments builds tension and allows hearers to ask questions: Why are various groups of these workers unemployed? What is the householder's tone of voice when he says to them, "Why do you stand here idle all day?"? Are they lazy? Is the answer of those hired at the eleventh hour ("Because no one has hired us") a lame excuse or the fact of the matter, or a bit of both? Perhaps in difficult economic circumstances the workers would have felt that it was an act of grace that they were hired at all.

Is the vineyard owner cross because there is not enough labor to go around? What kind of man is he? He sounds tough, ordering people about. Like other masters and owners in the Gospels' parables he seems rather arbitrary and unpredictable, as in his remark "Am I not allowed to do what I choose with what is mine?"

One remembers that this was a basically hierarchical society with a gulf between owners and workers—between the rich and the harsh life of the poor. Although the owner is said to agree with the laborers on a fair wage, it is hard to imagine that there would really have been much negotiating—that the workers had any rights or much leverage. It certainly sounds as if it was an employer's market with many more workers than jobs.

Still the audience is led to wonder about the master's motives. Is the harvest larger than he expected? Has the weather become threatening? Or does he have other reasons for employing people? Perhaps he does not like the idleness of these men. He knows that idleness can lead to trouble. Or perhaps he is genuinely concerned for their welfare and wants to see that there is enough work to go around.

In any case, as he keeps on hiring people through the day, the circumstances start to strain and a sense of instability develops. What is going to happen when the end of the workday comes, the time for payment—of reward, justice, and judgment? The feeling of oddness is heightened when the owner tells his steward to pay first those he has hired last.

As the instability and tension grow, words and phrases are repeated and begin to resound: "first," "last," "hour," "day," "denarius," "go"; "after agreeing" (v. 2) with "did you not agree with me?" (v. 13); "whatever is right [or "just," *dikaion*] I will give you" (v. 4) with "I am doing you no injustice [*adikō*]" (v. 13). What is the master's tone when he calls the spokesman for the grumbling all-day workers "friend"?[4] Some interpreters suggest that an earlier version of the parable ended with v. 13 and the owner's question "Did you not agree with me for a denarius?"[5] (so nicely leaving listeners to respond as they will to that rhetorical question), but the version through v. 15 also effectively closes with a series of provocative statements and questions.

As the parable progresses the audience is invited to hear it from the several perspectives, especially those of the all-day and one-hour workers and the master, although in the end it is clear that listeners are meant to react as best they can as the tired, agitated individuals who have labored the twelve hours. Their story begins at six in the morning. The marketplace where they gather is like a labor hall. A number of them probably came from miles around hoping for work and are glad for the opportunity. Likely they agree with the vineyard owner pretty quickly on a denarius for their work, a basic day's wage for poor farm laborers of the time. They go into the vineyard and begin their work—not unpleasant in the cool of the morning, but becoming uncomfortable and tiring as the sun mounts and the day wears on.

Three hours later, at nine o'clock, the owner returns to the marketplace and sees more men standing idle. Presumably these were workers who were not in the marketplace earlier. He sends them into his vineyard. They do not seem to have much negotiating right or power, and he tells them only that he will pay them what is right. Attentive hearers already begin to ask what is right.

Again at noon, and then at three o'clock, the householder does the same. What is happening with the harvest? What is this owner up to? Why are these men now standing about in the marketplace? How do the all-day workers feel about the fresh laborers coming into the vineyard?

Finally at five, with only an hour left in the working day, the owner hires a last group of workers. He asks them, "Why do you stand here idle all the day?" "Because no one has hired us," they respond. "You go into the vineyard too," he tells them. They have time only to pick several dozen grapes, perhaps eat a few. They hardly get dirty. The air is again cooler and they barely work up a sweat. Then the gong rings and it is six o'clock, the end of the working day.

Why the master tells the steward to pay the last hired first and the first hired last is unclear,[6] but for the purposes of the story it is in order to begin the surprise and to have the all-day workers present when those who have worked but an hour are given their wages. At first hearers are glad to be those one-hour laborers. Probably they and other observers had just a moment to try to figure out what they most likely were to be paid: what was one-twelfth of a denarius? But now they are given the whole basic wage.[7] They laugh with one another and perhaps smirk a little uncertainly at those standing behind them. No matter what the others are to receive, "isn't grace wonderful?" What a strangely generous master!

Then, however, hearers must go to the end of the line and share the bemusement of the all-day workers. What is this master's game? they ask. Why should these men who have no dirt under their fingernails, whose bodies are not aching and sticky with perspiration, be paid a whole denarius? Funny business! But then they also begin to rub their fingers together. Surely this means they will get something more. For them it is bonus time! But then they too are paid the single denarius.

What is this? every hearer must ask. It may be splendid from the perspective of those who received more than they expected and seem to have deserved, but it certainly would seem to be upsetting for those who were paid only what they had agreed to. Why? "Because," they grumble, "these last worked only one hour and you have made them equal to us who have borne the burden of the day and the scorching heat." But, the owner responds to one of them, "Friend, I am doing you no injustice. Didn't you agree with me for a denarius? Take what belongs to you and go; I choose to give to this last as I give to you. Am I not allowed to do what I choose with what belongs to me? Or are you jealous because of my generosity"? Literally, the owner asks, "Is your eye evil because I am good?" a question which is more concerned with the worker's attitude than the master's.

In one sense it might seem reasonable enough. If the owner wants to be this extravagant with his money, why should that be questioned? And, after all, the all-day laborers have what they agreed to. Why can they not leave it at that? Clearly it is very hard to do that. What one has deserved appears like less than that when others get the same without the deserving. Indeed, if one has really entered into the story with "ears that hear," one probably feels quite angry. This is not the way things are supposed to be. Perhaps for the first time one begins to realize that Jesus evidently did not just tell nice stories. It is often difficult for people today to understand how this nice man who traveled about in Palestine telling such nice stories got himself crucified. But, one recognizes, some of his stories could be very challenging. At the conclusion of this parable the audience are left trying to sort out emotions and to reflect on their reactions. Jesus is presented as radically questioning his hearers' readiness for the new ways of the kingdom.

As was indicated in the Prologue, a parable may well suggest a *direction* for interpretation, but there need not be one single message or teaching. As one interpreter, I will not try to tell readers what this parable should mean for them. That is for them and the community in which they participate to reflect upon. I will, however, present what the parable has come to mean to me, for it is in the telling of our own stories that the values of the gospel are best shared. For some years, especially as one who taught the New Testament, I struggled to find "the way" of this story and to imagine what kind of other stories the metaphorical movement within this story could be gesturing toward. This is what then happened to me.

When my wife first became pregnant, I found that I had an inordinate desire to have a son. I feel apologetic about that now. It seems rather sexist, and I realize how much fun it would be to have a daughter. But I had two sisters and no brothers as I was growing up. The sisters were and are very nice, and I love them dearly. Still it would also have been nice to have a brother, and the idea of having a son seemed sort of like having a very much younger brother. But when you want something that much, you figure it probably will not happen.

But it did! Benjamin was born, and all my parental heart went out to him with more love than I knew I had inside me. There was nothing I would not have done for him. I gave away all my parental love, unconditionally and irretrievably.

So much was this true that, when two years later my wife was pregnant again, I discovered that I had a very worrisome problem. When the second child was born and as it grew, how was I going to hide from it the fact that I could never love it as much as the first? There was no way which I could understand that this could be done. It would be very difficult to take back even a small part of what I had given so completely away. I must have thought that love was like a pie. The more people that came to share it, the smaller the slices had to be.

Then, as though to make matters worse, we had twins! But most readers will have guessed what then happened. It was like a miracle to me. Suddenly I loved Matthew and Stuart with the same love with which I loved Benjamin, without taking any love from him. This was a strange new arithmetic. The pie seemed to have become larger.

This parental loving was no special virtue of mine. This is what the loving of a parent is like—to love in this reckless and even-handed way. There was then and is now no point in asking me which of my sons I love the most. One of them may become a very illustrious man, another a junkie. If anything, I will probably try to bend my love toward the one who appears to need it the most. That is the way of love and seems to be what Jesus meant when he said that "those who are well have no need of a physician, but those who are sick; I came not to call the righteous, but sinners" (Mark 2:17).

By responding to the love that is offered by the parent, one child or another may, of course, make that love more effective and in returning that love share more fully in relationship. But that reciprocity is not a condition on the initial giving of the love by the parent. That love is there no matter what—no matter which child has been with the family the longest, no matter who is more industrious, no matter whether they are good or bad. Such love is a gift that does not work by normal human standards of deserving.

Sometimes it is hard for children to understand that although they can make such love more effective, they do not earn it. Moreover, it does not make any differences how hard they work or how well they behave; they cannot get more than their brothers and sisters. In this basic need of life they are all equal. At times that is so difficult to appreciate that in their insecurity children will think they want to see a brother or sister punished so that in their own not being punished they might somehow feel more loved ("Mother, you have to spank Billy"). This is an insecurity that unfortunately carries over into too much adult behavior. But while the love of the good parent remains complete for each child, it is also at heart completely equal.

Human parents are, of course, imperfect in their loving, but most people as children and/or parents gain some sense of what good parental love can be like—giving, sacrificing, unconditional, equal. These characteristics seem to have been among the reasons that Jesus frequently used the analogy and the metaphor of parent to speak of God. "Which one among you, if his child asks for a loaf, will instead give a stone? Or if the child asks for a fish, will give a serpent? If you then, who are evil, know how to give good gifts to your children, how much more will your Father in heaven give good things to those who ask him?" (Matt. 7:9–11; Luke 11:11–13).

The parent-God evidently wishes to relate to all the children with a radical equality. Most people probably tend to think of God's chief responsibility as rewarding the good and seeing that the bad people are punished or at least unrewarded. But in Jesus' surprising proclamation of the opening of the kingdom, rewarding and punishing seem to have much more to do with people's ways of responding than with the offering of God's love. God, Jesus maintains when calling disciples to be children of their parent-God by loving their enemies, "makes his sun rise on the evil and on the good and sends rain on the just and the unjust" (Matt. 5:45).

In such a family all are offered not only equality in their relationship with the parent but a new sense of equality with one another. Once individuals and groups of people realize that they have their place in this community and that they can neither lose nor earn more of their acceptance, they begin to be freed from the need to compete with one another for what they most need in life.

This equality does not, of course, mean that all human beings are the same in their skills and interests, and different people and activities require different equipment and resources in society.[8] Yet the sense of essential human equality being alluded to by the parable offers a radical way of thinking about and interpreting justice. What is most undercut is the tendency to see and use things not for their own value and out of real need but out of an insecurity that prompts constant comparison with others.[9] This often blinding insecurity, which demands not only enough for life but always more than enough, never sees an end to its need and is the source of much of the unending rivalry and greed in the world.

Clearly there were groups of early Christians who were trying to understand and live out the new sense of equality and sharing. Matthew has evidently used the parable to speak to those who, like the early disciples in the preceding story, have "left everything and followed you," and to James and John in the subsequent narrative, whose mother requests for them special places of honor in the kingdom. "You know," Jesus admonishes all the disciples, "that the rulers of the Gentiles lord it over them, and their great men exercise authority over them. It shall not be so among you." Instead, following the pattern of the Son of man, it is service and not being served that is now to be regarded as primary (20:20–27).[10] This corresponds, too, with Matthew's concern for the "little ones" of his community, the teaching that it is to children that the kingdom of heaven belongs (19:13–14), and the message of the Beatitudes that it is the meek, the mourners, and the poor in spirit who are blessed. This is indeed a reversal of what the world normally expects in terms of rewards; the last are becoming first, but the parable suggests that those who were formerly first need not become last and excluded —unless they choose to interpret the inclusion of others as their being passed over.

Yet maybe the offer of acceptance into the new community of the kingdom should not be interpreted this unconditionally. As some of the apostle Paul's critics objected when he proclaimed a similar message about God's grace, "Why not then do evil that good may come?" (Rom. 3:8). In other words, would not the moral order of the universe then be subverted? Could this be what Jesus meant? Then, as though in response to the question, we find another parable—this time one of the most familiar.

4

A MAN HAD TWO SONS

The Prodigal Son

And he said, "There was a man who had two sons; and the younger of them said to his father, 'Father, give me the share of property that falls to me.' And he divided his living between them. Not many days later, the younger son gathered all he had and took his journey into a far country, and there he squandered his property in loose living. And when he had spent everything, a great famine arose in that country, and he began to be in want. So he went and joined himself to one of the citizens of that country, who sent him into his fields to feed swine. And he would gladly have fed on the pods that the swine ate; and no one gave him anything. But when he came to himself he said, 'How many of my father's hired servants have bread enough and to spare, but I perish here with hunger! I will arise and go to my father, and I will say to him, "Father, I have sinned against heaven and before you; I am no longer worthy to be called your son; treat me as one of your hired servants."' And he arose and came to his father. But while he was yet at a distance, his father saw him and had compassion, and ran and embraced him and kissed him. And the son said to him, 'Father, I have sinned against heaven and before you; I am no longer worthy to be called your son.' But the father said to his servants, 'Bring quickly the best robe, and put it on him; and put a ring on his hand, and shoes on his feet; and bring the fatted calf and kill it, and let us eat and make merry; for this my son was dead, and is alive again; he was lost, and is found.' And they began to make merry.

"Now his elder son was in the field; and as he came and drew near to the house, he heard music and dancing. And he called one of the servants and asked what this meant. And he said to him, 'Your brother has come, and your father has killed the fatted calf, because he has received him safe and sound.' But he was angry and refused to go in. His father came out and entreated him, but he answered his father, 'Lo, these many years I have served you, and I never disobeyed your command; yet you never gave me a kid, that I might make merry with my friends. But when this son of yours came, who has devoured your living with harlots, you killed for him the fatted calf!' And he said to him, 'Son, you are always with me, and all that is mine is yours. It was fitting to make merry and be glad, for this your brother was dead, and is alive; he was lost, and is found.'"

Luke 15:11–32

The first surprise of this story is the younger brother's failure. Hearers familiar with folk tales about younger brothers who eventually dumbfound everyone by becoming heroes will keep waiting for that turn of events. The little dullard who goes off without anyone thinking him brave or wise (least of all his older brother or brothers) returns either rich or having conquered the monster or some other form of evil. Perhaps he ends up both bigger and smarter than the others. Or, if it is not by his own virtue that he succeeds, he is at least lucky. One imagines that in almost every culture mothers told such stories to little brothers who felt inferior to their bigger siblings and were perhaps abused by them—boys who feared that they would never grow up to be anything. Yet they would! But in this story one certainly cannot find much to admire in the younger son.

Of course, in a sense he does win out in the end, and the story recalls the repeated biblical plot of the younger brother who becomes God's chosen channel of grace. Jacob supplants Esau; Joseph saves his family,[1] and David becomes king of Israel. Yet finally in those stories hearers are able to see what God had, as it were, seen in these young men. But this younger son does not work hard and prosper like Jacob, show wisdom and resourcefulness like Joseph, or courage and love like David. He merits nothing, and the parable's first half is almost like a parody of the familiar biblical and folk narratives about the younger son coming home as a great success.[2]

The circumstances of his asking for his share of the inheritance and his leave-taking are sketched so briefly that the audience can only guess at the thoughts in the son's and the father's minds. Nor is enough known about the rules and customs of inheritance of that era to be sure whether what is described was in any sense a normal set of events. Probably what happened was unusual but still roughly in accordance with the understandings of the time. The oldest brother would inherit the fixed property and the land, on which the younger might well have had no real place after the father's death. The younger brother was entitled to a share of the rest of his father's property, and it is for this that the son asks in the parable. It may seem foolish for the father to give it to him, and hearers of the parable may already begin to ask what kind of father this is. Some readers of the story have also suggested that there must have been a serious breach in the relationship between this father and son.[3] Perhaps the son was angry with the father and/or the father was for some reason just as glad to see the son go. The story, however, does not even hint at that possibility, and in fact what is heard later suggests that it may have been very painful for the father to let his son leave. One, however, can imagine a father recognizing that the young man had to make such an effort if ever he was to grow up and have some control over his own life.

What would have been expected of the younger son was that he be careful with his inheritance. As long as his father was living, he had at least a moral obligation to preserve the legacy in order to protect his father against calamity in his old age. Indeed, hearers of the parable are probably meant to notice the shift in v. 12 when the son asks for his share of the goods or things, after which the father is said to divide his living (*bios*), his means of livelihood. It would have been a good part of the son's shame in squandering his property in loose living that he did not observe this filial responsibility. He had in effect disobeyed the Fifth Commandment, to "honor your father and your mother."

It would certainly have added to the disgrace of his circumstances that as a Jew he ended up in a pigsty tending unclean pigs ("Cursed be the man who keeps swine" was a Jewish saying)[4] and that he was in the employ of Gentiles in a land where there was little opportunity to keep the Jewish torah with respect to the Sabbath, proper foods, and so forth. What seems most to have depressed him about his circumstances, however, was his hunger. His condition sounds desperate. The carob pods the pigs were eating were edible for humans but barely palatable.

Many sermons have taken their theme from this point in the parable, stressing the young man's apparent repentance. Yet the story is so artfullly related that one cannot really be sure what is in his mind and heart as he "comes to himself." The switch to his own words (the whole story is full of direct speech) means that the audience hears his words, but the narrator steps back for a moment so that listeners may interpret the words for themselves. Having been invited to play the several roles in the story, they are also asked to think about what they might do and say if they were in the young man's shoes, and so also to begin to prepare for their response as the father.

The young man's confession may, of course, be heartfelt and sincere. On one hearing the lad sounds repentant enough—even abject. Yet the immediate cause of this conversion is his hunger, and the way he rehearses his little speech could create at least the suspicion that this is something of a ploy. Or maybe, in the way of human emotions, the young man's motives are more mixed and difficult to plumb. Even he may not be sure of all his heart as he heads home. One can imagine that it was all a kind of jumble and that mostly he was apprehensive and afraid.

One thing he does seem clear about are the terms on which he thinks he might become part of the household again. It does not look as though he has any hope of being received back as a son. He apparently cannot imagine his father's care, after what he has done, to be any greater for him than that he be treated as one of the servants. The unearned relationship of a son is lost, but perhaps he can at least earn room and board (a trace of work ethic here?) as one of the many hired hands. He leaves the far country and comes "to his father."

Flashes of recollection begin to light up in the theater of the listener's memories—perhaps of kindly fathers or harsh, even cruel, fathers, unpredictable fathers, or of no fathers and father substitutes. In the way of memory they may at the same time recall mothers—disappointed and angry mothers and teary, embracing ones. Because fathers, however, are often thought of in terms of discipline, the memory tape that begins to run may sound something like, "Just wait until your father gets home!"—or, in this case, ". . . until you get home!"

What will the father do? What should the father do? However he may feel, the father has certain responsibilities—in front of the servants, toward other fathers and sons, and if to no one else, certainly to the elder son. One can hardly pretend that nothing has happened.

The father is perhaps in his upper room—maybe looking out the window as he has half-consciously for many months. A long way off there is a figure. It looks like—but, no, it could not be. But as the figure draws nearer, it is! It is his son—his boy! He runs down the stairs, out the door, down the road, and throws his arms around his son come home. The young man is trying to get out his rehearsed speech: "Father, I have sinned against heaven and before you; I am no longer worthy to be called your son. . . ." But he is not able to finish, so busy is his father embracing and kissing him.[5] Nor is he allowed to humiliate himself by falling to his knees. If anyone, it is the father who has humbled himself by running out to offer this effusive greeting. The kiss is a sign of respect as well as affection and means that the son is being fully accepted by the father.

More than this! The father calls to the servants for a robe (a garment of honor), a ring (a sign of authority), and sandals (in a land where not everyone wore sandals, an indication of being a free person). There is to be a party. The calf that was being fattened up for an important occasion is quickly slaughtered and prepared. The contrasts between needing to swallow carob pods with swine (and harboring the meager hope of at least eating with the hired servants) and feasting with his father could not be more sharply drawn. Physically and also psychologically and spiritually the young man had been (as the father will soon describe it) in a life-and-death situation. In story time he has passed suddenly from famine and near-death to abundant new life.

The parent is portrayed as the father everyone might wish to have, but he appears almost too good to be true. His reception of his son seems not only loving and generous but extravagant—out of all proportion with what we have been told about the wastrel. Although he must have disapproved of his son's earlier behavior, he is not censorious and, in fact, replaces his son's prodigality with a more legitimate form of merrymaking, in the bosom of the family.[6] The young man is treated as though he were a great success, a returning hero. Evidently it is not the son's deserving but the father's emotions that are being acted out. As with the worried parent who has been waiting up all night for the teenager to come home, when the child is seen coming through the door anger and ideas about discipline are suddenly overwhelmed by relieved and happy love. This father apparently cannot help himself to respond in any other way.

Questions continue to arise. It may be nice to give in to one's emotions, but should not the father, even in fairness to the prodigal, also do what duty demands? What kind of example is being set? It would be a funny world were it run this way and failures treated as great achievers. Who would be able to tell the difference?

Probably for the moment, however, even listeners have their questions drowned out by all the feasting and merrymaking. Parties are wonderful! Grace is wonderful! Unmerited acceptance is a beautiful gift. Hearers cannot help laughing and joining in. The dishes are moved aside, and dancing begins.

But now the audience is made to leave the party and go out to be with the elder brother (having worked all day as he apparently does almost every day) as he comes in from the field and draws near the house. "What's all this music and dancing?" he asks of one of the servants, probably already piqued because no one told him there was going to be a party. The servant tells the elder brother the good news: "Your brother has come, and your father has killed the fatted calf, because he has received him safe and sound." Clearly, however, this does not seem like good news to the elder brother. Listeners are not sure whether he is angry because this poor excuse for a brother has returned or more particularly because of the reception his father has given him. Perhaps he is already realizing that, now that his brother has wasted his share of the inheritance, he will in effect be using part of his by living at home. This is what their father is already so generously giving him by this party. But whatever the wellspring of the anger, the elder brother is mad enough to stay out in the fields and not go in to the party.

Hearers of the parable will now *feel*, even if they do not otherwise observe, the balanced structure of the two halves of the parable, inviting notice of similarities and contrasts between the two sons and their relationships with their father. The younger son reveals something of his character in his self-dialogue, the elder in his dialogue with the servant. Both brothers are out in the fields or field when they do this. The younger *comes* to himself and then *comes* to his father, while the elder *comes* toward the house but, upon hearing that his brother has returned, refuses to *come* in, whereupon his father *comes* out to him. Indeed, in both parts the father goes out to his son, and one hears the son's words to the parent and his response. The nearly identical wording in vv. 24 and 32 (". . . was dead and is alive again; he was lost and is found") and the repetition of the expression "make merry," *euphrainō*, help link the halves and sharpen the comparison between the prodigal who has squandered and the elder who has served these many years and never disobeyed his father's command.

It does not take much imagination to feel sorry for a father with two sons like this—each selfish in his own way. Neither seems to have much regard for his father's feelings. One hears this disregard particularly in the tone of the elder brother's complaint and most especially in those bitter words "this son of yours" as he refuses either to address his parent as father or to recognize the younger sibling as his brother. He virtually reads himself out of the family. Perhaps being unable directly to express his anger toward his brother, he blames his father not only for the way he received the prodigal but for what happened in the first place—to which he adds the charge (maybe implied but never stated earlier in the story) that the wastrel has devoured his part of the living (which he notes was "your living") with harlots. Probably his protest also says more than he intended: "Lo, these many years I have served [i.e., "slaved for"] you." He has found little sense of joy or reward in his work as a *doulos*.

The father patiently responds to him using a term of endearment, "son" (*teknon*, "child"), and reminding him that it is "this your brother" who was lost and is found. Quietly the father points out that the elder's relationship with him as his son is unchanged. He has given him everything he can as his father. "You are always with me, and all that is mine is yours." In effect the father reminds him that what he has is his because of their father-son relationship, while it is just on this basis that he also wills to accept and restore the younger brother. This relationship goes beyond the meriting of the elder son's many years of work or the demeriting of the prodigal's sinning or what the law says about inheritance. "You are always with me, and all that is mine is yours."

The parable now stops with the question very much up in the air as to what the elder son will do. Will he stay out in the field until the party is over? Will he come in, grudgingly shake his brother's hand, but then go up to his room to play his lute? Or will he come in and join in the party?

It is perhaps easier to answer the question what he should do. In the interests of family harmony, out of deference to his father's feelings, and perhaps in recognition of the fact that his father need not care less for him because of his love for the younger son, the older son ought to go in and greet and accept his brother. Yet that is much easier said than done. After all, the older brother has a legitimate complaint. He feels he has had no special sign of his father's favor—not even a kid to make merry with his friends—whereas this wastrel gets the special fatted calf. Does one have to go off and do something stupid or immoral in order to get a special indication of acceptance? It is fine to say that "you are always with me and all that is mine is yours," but somehow it feels like less when the undeserving brother is treated with such great honor and happiness. It seems as if his father must prefer him.

The parable stops rather than concludes in a psychological and spiritual dilemma. One does not know what the older brother will do, yet it is recognized that his decision is crucial for his future. He who has everything can now choose to make himself last because, by refusing to accept his brother and his father's acceptance of his brother, he will no longer be able to know his father's love for himself. By refusing to join and rejoice in the party, he will set himself outside the family. What had been a life-and-death situation for the younger brother has now become one for him—complicated by the awareness that he now must in a sense die to the self-image of one who has earned a special relationship with his father, in order to live in the relationship that is always there for him. The parable stops at this decisive juncture in life's road. What does one really want? What does one truly need? There is potential for tragedy, but also new life.

A number of early Christian interpreters heard this parable as an allegory about the sinful but repentant Gentiles realizing God's love while the Jewish people remained unable to recognize the unconditional character of God's care for them and the fact that the Gentiles had now been accepted. Some scholars have suggested that Luke, too, may have had these thoughts in mind and that he could even have fashioned the story as an allegorical commentary on salvation history.[7] Yet, though the evangelist may have had such an interpretation in mind, it does not seem his primary reason for presenting the parable. He does not offer many of the little clues that would help hearers identify the figures as allegorical characters in this scheme. Moreover, the regular pattern in the New Testament is to speak first of the rejection by the Jews; here it would be a case of the Gentiles first being accepted. Also in the parable it is the father's care that is being accepted or rejected, not the Messiah. Nor is there any hint here of God's displeasure, since the father goes out to the elder brother and tenderly calls him "son." To the extent that the parable might be heard as an allegory of salvation history it is more subtle and nuanced than what is found elsewhere in the Gospels in this regard.

The parable does, however, contain a number of more obvious Lukan themes and interests: from dealing with this world's wealth and wasting and making merry with it (see 16:1, 19) to "having compassion" (cf. 15:20 with 10:33 and 7:13). This Gospel has seven important stories that tell of repentance and turning to God.[8] Luke also stresses the motif of the lost being found, not only in the two parables of the lost and found sheep and coin, which immediately precede the story of the prodigal, but elsewhere in his Gospel.[9]

Of chief importance for Luke's understanding of the parable is its context having to do with the lost and found, and most especially the introductory verses (15:1–2), which indicate that Jesus told the following parables as a defense against the charge that "he receives sinners and eats with them." One interpreter, maintaining that this context is Luke's creation, has argued that a parable like this was more the cause of the way Jesus lived, and thus this kind of accusation, than a response to it.[10] His life and ministry, in other words, were shaped by the stories he told, and the parables he told were, in part, the cause of opposition, not his defense. Yet, although one can agree that parables both reveal and affect the stance of their teller, it seems best to see the interplay between his stories and his actions as reciprocal. Clearly Jesus was remembered as one who received prodigal types and was critical of the unaccepting attitude of others. The doing and the telling were demonstrations and ways of saying the same thing, and it would make sense to use them each to explain or illustrate the other. While, then, the Lukan context

well fits the dramatizing purposes of the evangelist, it is not out of keeping
with circumstances that would have arisen in Jesus' ministry, and, although
Luke has evidently emphasized his motifs in the telling of the parable, its essential character and flavor (both in what is related and how it is told) are
congruent with other Gospel stories.

In whatever setting it is placed, the story invites participation in all its
roles, but hearers are finally to see themselves as the older brother—
the one who in the name of righteousness can become his brother's oppres-
sor. In him is glimpsed the shadow side of morality, that tendency (recalling
the same attitude in the vineyard's laborers, the Pharisee toward the tax collector, and Zacchaeus's detractors) to establish one's own goodness and ethical rightness at the expense of others.[11] One needs only to have met a few
of the world's ethical captains (ministers, politicians, prominent citizens, ed-
ucators, leaders of causes) to have seen that shadow side in operation. One
may also have seen and heard it in an "older" sister (such as Martha in Luke
10:34–42) or brother.

How does one, should one, can one, respond to that censorious attitude?
How should the father respond?

*Yet, darn it—those who work hard and do good deeds and make sacri-
fices have rights! What kind of world would it be if, when it came to their basic place in the scheme of things, they were treated the same as everyone else
(especially the good-for-nothings who always have to be helped rather than
being helpers), and even made to feel that some of the recognition and approval that they deserved was being taken away when it was demonstra-
tively bent toward the prodigals?*

What kind of world would it be? That appears to have been the question
Jesus was asking in at least several of his parables. Or, as seems to have been
even more the force of his insight and faith, what kind of world is it beginning to be as the kingdom of God disrupts and transforms the moral order?

5

THE DINNER PARTY

The Great Supper

A man once gave a great banquet, and invited many; and at the time for the banquet he sent his servant to say to those who had been invited, "Come; for all is now ready." But they all alike began to make excuses. The first said to him, "I have bought a field, and I must go out and see it; I pray you, have me excused." And another said, "I have bought five yoke of oxen, and I go to examine them; I pray you, have me excused." And another said, "I have married a wife, and therefore I cannot come." So the servant came and reported this to his master. Then the householder in anger said to his servant, "Go out quickly to the streets and lanes of the city, and bring in the poor and maimed and blind and lame." And the servant said, "Sir, what you commanded has been done, and still there is room." And the master said to the servant, "Go out to the highways and hedges, and compel people to come in, that my house may be filled. For I tell you, none of those who were invited shall taste my banquet."

Luke 14:16–24; see Matt. 22:1–10

A lot of partying and eating together is reported by the evangelists. The Gospels tell of wedding feasts, dinners, killing the fatted calf, Martha bustling about to serve everyone, the feeding of crowds, and quieter meals together—including the last supper of Jesus with his disciples. Jesus himself evidently ate with many different kinds of people and was, of course, accused of keeping indiscriminate company. The charge was "Behold, a glutton and a drunkard, a friend of tax collectors and sinners" (Luke 7:34; Matt. 11:19). Frequently Jesus is pictured at a meal or telling a story about one or he is involved with both at once. In chapter 14 alone Luke has assembled no less than four such stories.

One can understand why so many meals are told of. In that era even more than today eating together was a way of establishing community, offering hospitality, and building trust and friendship.[1] The actions of inviting to a meal and accepting the invitation were full of significance. People laid aside weapons and at least many animosities when they said, "Come eat with me," or, "Yes, I'll dine with you." Probably for most peoples a happy occasion of sharing food and company intimates a time of greater human community and peace. In the life and hopes of the people of Israel a fine meal easily had a symbolic import, alluding to a consummate age when God's peace and justice would be established.[2]

47

The version of this parable found in Matthew's Gospel has clearly taken up the symbolic understanding of the meal as the time of fulfillment for the kingdom of God and developed its potential as an allegorical narrative. To the banquet and its attendant circumstances "the kingdom of God may be compared." The man is a king, and the dinner is a marriage feast for his son. To any hearer of the time this would represent the consummation God effects for the Son, the Messiah. Those who do not come even though they are clearly twice called are representative of the Jewish people for whom this feast was originally intended. Those sent to invite them are the prophets who are shamefully treated and killed, and clearly there are now references to the similar allegorical story of the wicked husbandmen which immediately precedes in Matthew's Gospel (21:33–41, on which see pp. 10, 11, 148 n. 15). This apparently motiveless killing is one of the signs that a historical allegorical interest has superseded a concern with realism in the narrative. This development becomes even more evident when those first invited who "are not worthy" are destroyed and their city burned—an apparent reference to the destruction of Jerusalem in 70 C.E. Others then are invited to the marriage feast, and the wedding hall becomes full of guests "both bad and good." This last phrase is Matthew's way of recognizing that the now largely gentile church is a mixed community. In his parables of the wheat and weeds and of the net (13:24–30, 47–50) he also alludes to the presence of both the good and the bad in the church, along with the sorting-out that will take place at the end of the age (see chap. 9 and Matt. 5:45).

To this wedding-feast story Matthew then adds as a concluding scene a parable that stresses the need to be always ready for the coming of the kingdom that can happen at any time (22:11–14). It no doubt strikes the hearer as strange that one of the individuals who were invited to the marriage feast without any advance warning should now be cast into the outer darkness because he was not dressed for a wedding party. But this is the evangelist's way of emphasizing the importance of constant preparedness.[3]

It is almost surely Matthew, with perhaps some help from his sources, who has so interpreted and presented the story of the banquet. In one sense his rendition is a little inconsistent in that the messianic feast is usually seen as happening at the end of the age. By including the bad as well as the good, Matthew has evidently made reference to the ongoing life of the church, and one presumes a further sorting-out. But the evangelist's overall view of salvation history is made quite clear through the story, and it has had a powerful if not always healthy (because of its anti-Jewish use) influence upon subsequent Christian understanding.

Luke's version of the parable can be described as more secular, for it does not have many of the details that Matthew uses for his salvation-history allegory. This has led to speculation that there may once have been two separate if somewhat similar stories about a banquet which were used by the respective evangelists. When Matthew and Luke have a similar story or saying, many scholars ascribe it to a common written source that, they believe, both of them used. In this case, however, the differences are such as to suggest at least separate sources if not distinctive narratives. Luke's parable has, in fact, much more in common with yet another version of a dinner story which is found in the *Gospel of Thomas* (saying 64). This parallel creates still further possibilities. Thomas may have known Luke's version or both may derive from a common core narrative, and Mattew's parable can be understood to be related in various ways to Luke's rendition, and/or Thomas's, and/or the core story, or to none of them. The best solution to this question of possible sources seems to be that all three Gospels are presenting versions of a core story that Matthew narrates in the most distinctive and amended form. The differences are sufficient to indicate that he and Luke did not here share a common source but that the versions they inherited came to them through traditions that had branched apart earlier. Luke and Thomas, on the other hand, were independently making use of a story passed along that other branch, although the branch had most likely divided again before reaching them. Not to be ruled out, however, is the possibility that Thomas knew and used in his own distinctive way the parable from Luke's Gospel or that he knew Luke's version as well as a form from another source. Such is but a brief description of the possibilities and complications one must deal with when trying to understand the history and uses of what appears to be a common story now presented in three ancient documents.[4]

While it may be held that Luke's story of the dinner party stands considerably closer than Matthew's to the core story, it is still evident that Luke has made the parable very much a part of his Gospel with its particular concerns and emphases. Probably most important in this regard is the context—especially the immediately preceding little homily that urges hearers to invite the poor, maimed, lame, and blind to their dinners rather than friends, kinfolk, and rich neighbors capable of repaying the invitation. That this understanding of true charity as distinct from hospitality was known in Judaism of the time is indicated by a story that partly parallels the Gospels' banquet parable. In this story a rich tax collector who had not led a very pious life was nevertheless given a splendid funeral at the same time that a poor scholar died with little notice taken of his passing. Why should this be? The tax gatherer was honored because of the one very good deed of his life which he was in the very process of accomplishing when death overtook him. He had planned a banquet for the city councilors. When, however, they did not come, the tax collector had given orders that the poor should come to the feast so that the food not be wasted.[5]

Neither this story, however, nor Luke's parable completely fits the intention of Jesus' preceding teaching. The tax collector and the man in Luke's narrative both first invite the well-to-do. (The excuses in Matthew and the

Gospel of Thomas and at least two of the three in Luke show that the intended guests were individuals of means.) Only after this plan fails do they have the poor and the lame, blind, and so forth brought in. In Luke's presentation of the parable it is anger rather than charity that provides the host's motivation.

Yet it is also true that a concern for the maimed and poor, evident elsewhere in his Gospel, has colored Luke's version, and there is implicit as well the Lukan interest in seeing that those with wealth realize that they should make use of it benevolently in this life. One thinks ahead to the teaching that follows the parable about the unjust steward (16:9) and the story of the rich man and Lazarus (16:19–31). The hearing of Luke's parable is bound to be influenced as well by the stories told in the following chapter which are set forth as responses to the charge that Jesus "receives sinners and eats with them" (15:2). In some sense the banquet parable also provides a defense by suggesting that it is the outcast (among whom are the poor and maimed) who are to participate in the age to come. Luke may have fashioned 14:15 (one of those sitting at table with him says, "Blessed is he who shall eat bread in the kingdom of God") as a *lead-in* to the parable, to make clear that this was a story about the kingdom.

Other hints indicating a semi-allegorical hearing of the parable may also be present. Luke's parable seems more interested in those who are finally included than the guests who refuse to come (although v. 24, where the plural *you* makes it clear that the audience at large is being addressed rather than just the servant, does stress the exclusion of those first invited). There is a double summons to those called to fill the banquet hall, and the notes of urgency found in "go out quickly" and "compel" can be heard to reflect the missionary emphasis of Luke's Gospel.[6] A number of interpreters understand the group summoned out of the streets and lanes of the city to be representative of the Jews and those from the highways and the hedges to be the Gentiles. It is more likely, however (if Luke intends such allegorical precision), that those from the city are primarily the outcast among the Jews who accepted Jesus rather than the Jews generally, since Jews more generally would probably better be represented by the original invitees.

Luke, however, is not as interested as Matthew in using the parable as an allegory about salvation history. His primary concerns are with charity toward and inclusion of the outcast and using the parable as a warning against worldly concerns that lead one to miss what is far more important. Probably this last thought is his major reason for presenting the parable and has been the message most stressed in subsequent Christian teaching and preaching. The matter of priorities is also taken up in the teaching that immediately follows, which speaks of hating even family if family relationships get in the way of discipleship, and of the builder and the king who were wise to assess realistically their circumstances (14:26–33). How easy but dangerous it is to become so taken up by business and family matters that one is unable to hear and heed the invitation to be part of God's eternal purposes (see also Jesus' response to three would-be disciples in Luke 9:57–62). These other interests can have their place in life, though one must renounce them (14:33) and they must always be kept in perspective. Helpful sermons along these lines might well end with Luke 12:32: "Seek God's kingdom and these things [necessary food, drink, clothing] shall be yours as well."

The *Gospel of Thomas*'s rendition of the parable seems to present a similar thought but with its own special message at the end:

> Jesus said, "A man had received visitors. And when he had prepared the dinner, he sent his servant to invite the guests. He went to the first one and said to him, 'My master invites you.' He said, 'I have claims against some merchants. They are coming to me this evening. I must go and give them my orders. I ask to be excused from the dinner.' He went to another and said to him, 'My master has invited you.' He said to him, 'I have just bought a house and am required for the day. I shall not have any spare time.' He went to another and said to him, 'My master invites you.' He said to him, 'My friend is going to get married, and I am to prepare the banquet. I shall not be able to come. I ask to be excused from the dinner.' He went to another and said to him, 'My master invites you.' He said to him, 'I have just bought a farm, and I am on my way to collect the rent. I shall not be able to come. I ask to be excused.' The servant returned and said to his master, 'Those whom you invited to the dinner have asked to be excused.' The master said to his servant, 'Go outside to the streets and bring back those whom you happen to meet, so that they may dine.' Businessmen and merchants will not enter the places of my Father." (saying 64)

This version is even more secular and unallegorical than Luke's. Such is true of many of the parables in the *Gospel of Thomas,* and this has led a number of critics to believe that the writer of this gospel had access to an independent source of early Christian tradition which in some cases he has produced in a more original form than have the canonical Christian Gospels.[7] At least in certain instances this may be the case, although care has to be exercised. Christians influenced by Gnosticism were not much interested in this world or its history, since the divine aspect of human life was meant to escape from the material world and time. Their special gnosis (knowledge) taught that humanity was caught in the corrupt and unimportant world of things and told how one could become free from it. This often esoteric knowledge was not to be revealed indiscriminately and in some sense was already known (it just had to be awakened) within true Gnostics. It was, for these reasons, often unimportant to present stories or sayings in ways that made their interpretation too clear. Frequently instead they have a gnomic or deliberately mysterious character. Eschatological understandings (having to do with the consummation of human history) are of no significance. Or, to put it the other way around, it may have been important for Gnostics, or even Christians just tinged with Gnosticism, to omit or amend certain teachings that had a place in the early churches and that could reach back toward Christian beginnings.

The *Gospel of Thomas*'s rendition of the dinner-party parable is, however, somewhat unusual in that a clear moral lesson is drawn.[8] Three of the four excuses that are presented have to do with financial affairs, and the other might also if directing a marriage banquet involved some financial obligation. Matters having to do with such worldly things distract people from what is of importance. Those who make a business of such matters "will not enter the places of my Father."

Each of the three Gospels has given this story about a man and his dinner party its own emphases and slant. It seems probable that the versions they used already had a distinctive character. There are, however, a number of features in common:[9] the scene is an important dinner of some sort; a servant or servants are sent to call the guests, but those invited all refuse to come, going instead to deal with affairs of the world—primarily, if not exclusively, business transactions.[10] The servant or servants are then sent out to bring people in from the streets. It is likely that all three versions also indicate a two-stage invitation to the original guests. This more customary way of inviting people to an important party is only made obvious in Luke, but it certainly seems to be implied when Matthew has the servant call those "who were invited" (using the perfect participle of *kaleō*, "who have been invited," 22:8) and in Thomas's reference to a man who "had guests" whom he then sent his servant to summon.[11] The fact that Thomas has only one servant throughout his narrative, and that Luke ends with one, suggests an earlier story about a man of somewhat modest means who had a servant through whom he summoned his invited guests to his home for a dinner.

Possibly an earlier story also spoke of the host's anger. It is part of the parable's exaggerated character that none of the original guests came. Perhaps the man could have accepted the excuse of one or two of the invitees, but what happened was at the very least an embarrassment to him in a land where the exchange of hospitality was considered so important. Certainly he would have been quite upset.[12]

Given the nature of such stories, it also seems likely that there was a stress at the end on the fullness of the house for the party, as both Matthew and Luke indicate. Also in the nature of storytelling one would expect that an earlier story described the refusals in at least a little detail. Such would build up interest and concern. (It is typical of Matthew to condense such narrative features when they do not have some other function.) Three would be the usual narrative number,[13] although usually in a story it is the third individual or circumstance that turns out differently from the first two. But this third guest also made an excuse! No wonder the host was exasperated.

What could he do? He would make certain that there was a dinner after all. At this crucial turning point the story focuses upon the man and his determination and ingenuity in seeing that—despite life's disappointments and uncertainties—his efforts, expectation, and food would not be wasted. There was to be a party.

The parable may be heard as something like a joke. A man planned a nice dinner party, but when he sent his servant to call the invited guests, one by one they all had reasons why they could not come after all. There he was with all that food steaming and smelling delicious, the wine opened, maybe even the lamps already lit—and no one to enjoy it!

Likely most contemporary hearers have found themselves in at least comparable circumstances. They have made lists, shopped, polished the silver, baked, peeled, boiled, and roasted. Maybe at the last minute it is the children who do not show up. Or perhaps it is even a catered party and something has come up in the community so that many of the guests that were counted on are suddenly unable to be there. What is to be done with all that work, the bright hopes and party spirit, and the splendid food?

The freezer is not big enough. The food could be quickly shipped to a local soup kitchen or orphanage, but that would only be food, not a dinner party.

Social custom or timidity or something else would probably keep most people from calling around to see who might come. But what a splendid idea! This householder is an extraordinary person. Those in the audience can smile and congratulate the host, and, in that sense, join the crowd around the festive table. They have done nothing in particular to merit this lovely party, but are glad to join in it as the audience for a special occasion.

Only after the story has been heard in a manner like this may metaphorical allusion begin to resound. In what manner does the mystery of God's presence in the world happen in this way? Jesus had spoken of other festive occasions of grace and of the unexpected way things turn out. Israel had long thought of the divine restoration as a banquet.

Not everything is spelled out by any means. It is to be a wonderful time —though different from what many people expect, maybe even from what was planned. No matter how individuals at first respond, the purposefulness and inventiveness of the host will find a way to bring about the festivities. But there seems to be a note of warning here as well as grace—a sense of urgency and crisis along with the good food and partying.[14] This banquet is already begun, and listeners seem also to be in the situation of being asked how they will respond to it.

Here is all this food, music, and dancing; yet, once again, it was not looked for in this way. One can feel sorry for the guests who were originally invited. Their excuses are commonplace enough. How were they to know this was to become an event fraught with such significance? In the context of everyday circumstances the most extraordinary occasion is suddenly present. But it is not people's connections or deservings that in the end get them into this party. It seems to be a matter of luck or grace, or whatever one wants to call it. Reversal indeed! The last have become first. It would not be hard to feel a little like the Pharisee hearing of the acceptance of the tax collector or the townsfolk of Jericho watching Jesus go to Zacchaeus's house, or the all-day workers seeing the one-hour workers receiving the full day's wage, or the elder son finding out from his father's servant what all the happy noise is about. What does one think of a party like this and its guests? Who is this householder?

Once more a parable has overtaken its hearers. It began normally enough with a man calling his guests to his dinner party, but soon there were surprises and seemingly exaggerated circumstances. None of the invited guests would come. The man reacts to this situation in a novel way, and the house ends up so full of people that there could not possibly be plates for them all. What sounded like a relatively small dinner party seems to end up as almost a mob scene. Hearers are not so much asked to interpret what happens as they are interpreted by their response.[15] The parable draws them in and, while refusing to supply its own interpretation, asks them what they think of this man and what he does. Do they want to be part of the party on these terms? Are they willing now to be part of a community the membership of which seems meant to have no basis in class or merit and which—especially in the early life of the churches—was hardly representative of those whom one would probably most like to have to dinner or as sister and brother parishioners?

Jesus may have most surprised a number of those in his audience by describing the party as already going on. In his introduction to the parable Luke catches the thought that would have been in many people's minds about the banquet that is to take place: "Blessed is the one who shall eat bread in the kingdom of God!" exclaims one of those sitting at table with Jesus. In this parable and through many of his other stories and teachings, the traditions say that Jesus sought to share his conviction that it was even now possible to experience God's love and justice and the joy as well as the challenge to human judgments that were part of the kingdom's happening. It would take place. It was taking place no matter what the initial response of some who might have been thought to be participants in it.

Elsewhere in the reminiscences about Jesus and in his teaching he is pictured as offering the opportunity to be part of this experience to the kind of people who were often regarded as divinely disfavored because of their circumstances and so as outside the kingdom of God.[16] They also may have been made to feel, and thus likely often thought of themselves, as excluded from the fullness of God's peace. In the parable Luke portrays these people as the "poor and maimed and blind and lame." As has been seen, this might well be his wording, but in so characterizing them he may also be drawing out what was implicit in earlier versions of the story. The only kind of people whom listeners would think of as being able and willing to come on such a last-minute basis would be those who would not normally be invited to such a party.[17]

It should be remembered, too, that Luke did not invent the significance of the categories of the poor, lame, blind, and so forth. Hope for them is part of the prophetic end-of-the-ages vision of Israel and is taken up in a saying of Jesus found in both Luke and Matthew and often thought to reach back to Jesus (Luke 7:22; Matt. 11:5).[18] Jesus' healing ministry and his reaching out to and associating with the sick, maimed, and poor were ways of making the advent of the kingdom known and anticipating the final scene of the parable of the dinner party.

With Luke's description of that scene, and at least in consonance with what is known of Jesus' ministry and teaching, the parable ends with a dramatic reversal of affairs for the poor and maimed of the town. The fullness of the house adds to the joy and the sense of the kingdom's purposes being abundantly fulfilled. One pictures the amputees, with their wooden legs propped up on pillowed chairs, feeding delicacies to the blind as they all join in the singing with the dancing poor. Whatever other meanings and challenges are to be found in the story, it concludes in high and holy humor, offering new hope to all who might otherwise feel uninvited to the party.

6

ONE OUT OF A HUNDRED

The Lost Sheep

What do you think? If a man has a hundred sheep, and one of them has gone astray, does he not leave the ninety-nine on the hills and go in search of the one that went astray? And if he finds it, truly, I say to you, he rejoices over it more than over the ninety-nine that never went astray. So it is not the will of my Father who is in heaven that one of these little ones should perish.

Matt. 18:12–14; see Luke 15:4–7

This is one of the most loved of the little stories in the Bible. The picture of the shepherd bringing home the lost sheep has touched countless hearts and has a place on many a church-school wall. There is, as a result, a tendency to take the imagery and the story very much for granted, and to answer the seemingly rhetorical question about what a man would do if one of his sheep went astray with, "Of course, he'd go after it. Isn't that nice? What a good and caring shepherd." Here is an image of the divine compassion and a model for all Christian pastors.

But just a minute! What about the ninety-nine? How do the other parishioners feel when the pastor leaves them to try to bring back one probably malcontented stray? Or when the pastor is away ministering to those who are in a mental hospital or in prison? In terms of the story, what might happen to the whole rest of the flock when the shepherd leaves them unattended in the hills? Everyone who has any knowledge of shepherding and sheep knows that this would be strange, even irresponsible, behavior. Various predators are about, and sheep are not exactly the most intelligent of animals when it comes to caring for themselves.

Attempts have been made to read some action between the lines that would make the man's behavior more plausible and responsible. Perhaps he handed the flock over to the protection of another caretaker or, as shepherds of that era would occasionally do, herded them into a cave, where they were temporarily safe.[1] But the story, of course, says nothing of this and, since other of the parables that may come from early tradition appear to have a surprising and even outrageous character, one may at least suspect that silence with regard to the care of the ninety-nine was deliberate. "What do you think? If a man has a hundred sheep, and one of them has gone astray, does he not leave the ninety-nine on the hills and go in search of the one that went astray?" The expected answer to that question is probably "Not if he is being sensible." Yet even if one insists that some provision for the ninety-nine is presupposed, the story still more than suggests an unusual bias of concern on the part of the shepherd in favor of the one that is lost or strayed.[2]

The *Gospel of Thomas* (saying 107) seeks to account for the man's behavior in another way:

> Jesus said, The kingdom is like a shepherd who had a hundred sheep. One of them, the largest, went astray. He left the ninety-nine and looked for that one until he found it. When he had gone to such trouble, he said to the sheep, "I care for you more than the ninety-nine."

The size of this particular animal evidently makes it more valuable, and the significant point for Thomas's readers is perhaps that its bigness (so also the large fish in saying 8) makes it representative of the true wisdom or knowledge for which the genuinely wise individual would be willing to abandon all else.[3] Hearers are to notice the manner in which the shepherd was ready to tire himself in the search and the superior love he has for this special sheep.

There are a number of features that Luke's presentation of the parable has in common with both Matthew and Thomas and with each independently, but he has again made the story very much a part of his Gospel. Once more the chief way he has done this is through its setting. Jesus, it is said, told this parable in response to the murmuring of the Pharisees and the scribes who complained, "This man eats with tax gatherers and sinners." This story, along with the linked parables of the lost coin and the prodigal son, are Jesus' defense and rejoinder to them. Major themes of the evangelist are articulated in v. 7: ". . . there will be more joy in heaven over one sinner who repents than over ninety-nine righteous persons who need no repentance."

Luke's stress on the importance of repentance[4] does not, however, clearly follow from the story itself. Nothing is suggested there about the sheep's repentance (do sheep repent?) or even about its being in the wrong, unless one wants to read that into its becoming lost. The evangelist has also rather oddly developed the motif of joy. This is a distinctive emphasis in his Gospel, although its presence in Matthew 18:13 indicates that Luke has probably not imported it into this story. Surely what this parable intends, however, is to focus on the immediate joy of the shepherd. The joy shared with friends and neighbors seems to have been shaped as an earthly parallel to the joy that is to take place in heaven, and in anticipation of the similar conclusion to the next story, about the lost coin (Luke 15:8–10).

The linking or adding of similar stories or sayings to make doublets is a common practice in the passing-along and developing of traditions. The parable of the leaven with the mustard seed and the stories about the treasure and the pearl of great price would seem to be similar instances. The parallels between the parables about the lost sheep and the lost coin are, however,

more on the surface than in the force of the stories. A major difference is that
the woman is running no risk of losing the other nine coins when looking for
the one that is lost. The story more naturally concentrates on her dedication
and single-mindedness in this task and then on the joy that she shares in
finding the coin.

Luke has probably given special emphasis to the word "lost," which he
uses three times to tell of what happened to the one sheep. Along with
"found," the word also has an important place in the stories of the lost coin
and the prodigal son, and the theme is summed up at the conclusion to the
story of Jesus' acceptance of Zacchaeus and that tax collector's repentance.
"For the Son of man came to seek and to save the lost" (Luke 19:10). The
Greek word *apolōlos*, "lost," literally means "on the way to destruction" and
would almost surely have evoked in the memories of hearers of that time the
description of the mission of another shepherd, the God of Israel, who prom-
ises, "I will seek the lost and I will bring back the strayed" (Ezek. 34:16). The
place of the theme word in the lore of Israel and the fact that Matthew uses
the same basic word when summing up his presentation of the parable indicate, however, that Luke could have found it already present in the tradition
he used.[5]

Luke's way of telling the parable, together with his stories of the prodigal,
Zacchaeus, and the woman forgiven of her sins, suggests that hearers are
also to put themselves in the position of the sheep that is saved. His picture
of the sheep being carried on the man's shoulders (a very difficult burden if
the animal is full-grown) describes the only way a shepherd could bring
home a lone stray that would likely have been tired, afraid, and unwilling to
move.[6] Those who have lived with sheep know that one should not, however, become romantic at this point. Fluffy and endearing they may appear,
but up close they are not the cleanest of animals. Nonetheless, it is the shepherd's calling to be this intimate with sheep when necessary. The motif and
sense of intimacy are developed in the Fourth Gospel ("I am the good shepherd; I know my own and my own know me . . . and I lay down my life for
the sheep," John 10:14–15) and have understandably had a profound effect
on and through Christian art.

When Luke tells his listeners that the man will search for the lost sheep
"until he finds it" (similarly in the *Gospel of Thomas*) and depicts the shepherd sharing his joy with friends and neighbors, there is heard a note of the
universalism that is sounded elsewhere in the Gospel. The hope is that this
rescuing will (it is still being and to be accomplished; "there will be more joy
in heaven . . .") come to all.[7]

Whereas in Luke's Gospel the Pharisees and scribes are Jesus' stated audience, in Matthew's Gospel Jesus is addressing his disciples. Matthew's
version is set in the context of advice regarding relationships within the
Christian community and, in effect, is instructing church pastors that they

should care similarly. Matthew wants hearers to learn from the shepherd. At other points in his Gospel Matthew recognizes that the existing church is what might be called a mixed community.[8] It is God's responsibility to do the sorting-out at the last judgment; pastoral concern for all must be exercised in the meantime. The evangelist then introduces the parable with the admonition "See that you do not despise one of these little ones" and concludes with the message that it is not the heavenly Father's will that any of the little ones should perish. He continues on with instruction about how to deal with a community member who has fallen into sin.

Although this setting strongly influences how the parable is heard, and the introduction to the story and its interpretation in v. 14 appear both in vocabulary and message to be largely if not entirely the result of Matthew's creativity, the evangelist seems to have done relatively little otherwise to adapt the parable. His version appears to leave a little more open the genuineness of the question as to whether a shepherd should leave the ninety-nine to go in search of the stray, and the uncertainty implied in "if he finds it" can be seen as closer to a real-life situation. The shepherd's joy is clearly centered in the moment of finding the wanderer. Possibly, too, Matthew has retained an earlier idea of the sheep going astray rather than being lost, although this might well be Matthew's way of stressing the tendency of "little ones" as church members to go astray.

All three versions of the parable tell of a shepherd whose behavior would have to be regarded as extravagant. The ratio of one to ninety-nine and the greater joy over or love for the one should cause all hearers of the parable to recognize that the parable is telling about extraordinary behavior. Few if any shepherds can afford to (nor perhaps should) act in this way.

If, however, this is not normal, sensible behavior, to what is it alluding? What other story or stories is it gesturing toward? Thomas's suggestion about this being a special sheep does not seem indigenous to the parable. The only thing special about this particular sheep is that in one way or another it becomes lost. What is distinctive in the parable is the evidently profligate readiness of the shepherd to leave the flock in search of the one, and the core narrative then focuses on his joy when he finds the stray.

One is probably first reminded of the father's behavior in the parable that tells of the prodigal and the elder, stay-at-home son. The returning son has done nothing to merit the lavish reception by the father. How does it feel to watch such an elaborate reacceptance into the family taking place?

But such in a way is true to life. An old friend who has not been seen in many years moves back to town, and one goes to uncommon lengths to reestablish the friendship and perhaps heal some old wounds. Seventy-five people are invited to a lovely reception and supper party for the recently returned friend. "Well," another friend who has been around for years might say, "who was it that took care of the kids when she was sick and talked to her for days on end when her husband wouldn't? But she never even thought of giving a party for me. Maybe I should move away for a while, or get hit by a car, or something, so someone will pay attention to me."

Or the teacher seems to display extraordinary favoritism toward a rather slow and lazy kid. She gives special attention to his homework and praises him in front of the class for getting today's answers right. *What's the big deal? Some of the rest of us have been doing practically A work all year— even doing extra assignments. But here the teacher is making a big fuss over a guy whose major preoccupation seems to be basketball.*

Of course, in one sense listeners do understand. It is not that the prodigal or the returning friend or slow student is more lovable than the others. Such a person is not better, or more repentant, or worth more. But love has a way of trying to bend itself toward those in need, and it will at times go to extra-ordinary—what may seem unreasonable and unfair—lengths to express that bias. Most listeners to the parable probably recall so contorting themselves toward a child or friend or neighbor who needed their special care.

One major scholar maintained that it is now impossible to know whether the earliest form of the parable was told to console sinners or in response to the accusation of the Pharisees.[9] Was the audience, in other words, to iden-tify with the one or to be in the place of the ninety-nine? As has been seen, the several versions offer both these opportunities and also the suggestion that one might play the role of the shepherd. In developing these possibili-ties the evangelists are following the way of parable. It may be that the first telling of the story had particular hearers in mind. It would be congruent with other of Jesus' parables if the story of the lost sheep was once told to those who found it difficult to appreciate the apparent bias of Jesus' teaching about the kingdom toward those who seemed so little worthy of it. With this background in mind, it is possible that Luke has given the story a historically instructive general context.[10] But it is part of coming to realize the reason for this bias also to identify with the strayed sheep and the searching and re-joicing shepherd. The parable allows listeners to choose the role they find most helpful or suitable or challenging. Most individual hearers and most communities probably think of themselves as needing each of the parts, at different times in their lives.

In the context of Jesus' teaching and ministry the parable would likely have had a surprising—even shocking—impact. The straying sheep is not worth more, nor is it more righteous or more repentant. Jesus' stress would not have been any different from that of many of the Pharisees and other Jewish teachers had he been emphasizing the great measures to be taken to bring back a repentant sinner. Judaism has always been a religion of grace and still today has much to teach Christians about divine mercy. The chal-lenge of the parable, then, is not just to Judaism but to every form of religion which requires repentance or some other way of preparing for God's acceptance before that acceptance can come. If the former message was, Repent and then be accepted, the new message is to the effect, You are accepted; you are already included; now you can change your life. ". . . repentance comes by means of grace."[11]

Not just in religious communities but in most societies and groups such a basic understanding—to the extent that it is put into practice—can be worrisome if not threatening. The radical challenge of Jesus' ministry was not only in his words but in what he did and taught his disciples to do as well. All kinds of people—especially the strays—were being included. Yet, if people are not required in some way to toe the line before being fully accepted, how is any order to be kept? Not only will people not know who is in and who is out, but the very basis for being in or out will be taken away. In Jesus' ministry and in his teaching about the kingdom now coming for a restored people everyone is included already. As in a good family all members are already and always a part. It is true that one can refuse to recognize and accept that inclusion, but the offer of acceptance is there in any case.

A probing question the parable puts before hearers is whether and to what extent they find this good news. It seems to upset the moral order. But that is what, Jesus claims, the inbreaking kingdom is doing. To rejoice in the hearing of the parable one must change one's idea of what God is up to. It is interesting that in the churches of the east, where—unlike in the west—the importance of community is often stressed more than individualism, the parable is frequently heard as a story about the reuniting and completion of the group. Thus, although the pastor's searching may cause the ninety-nine some problems, in the end they can be happy that the community is again unified.

Probably, as we have recognized, no one in the earliest audiences of the parable could have heard it without recalling the divine words spoken through Isaiah, Jeremiah, and Ezekiel:

> He will feed his flock like a shepherd; he will gather the lambs in his arms. (Isa. 40:11)

> He . . . will keep Israel as a shepherd keeps his flock. (Jer. 31:10)

> I myself will search for my sheep, and will seek them out. As a shepherd seeks out his flock when some of the sheep have been scattered abroad, so will I seek out my sheep; and I will rescue them from all places where they have been scattered. . . . I myself will be the shepherd of my sheep. . . . I will seek the lost and bring back the strayed. (Ezek. 34:11–12, 15–16)

To this shepherd every reader of the Psalms cries, "I have gone astray like a lost sheep; seek thy servant" (Ps. 119:176). The parable does not identify the shepherd as God, but the God of Israel is being gestured toward and will on some hearings be sensed as present in the story.

The full implications of what the parable is suggesting about Jesus' relationship to God are now felt. Luke represents Jesus as telling the story to explain and defend his associating with the outcast and down-and-outers, many of whom seem to have had very little concern with religion or the ethical life. In and through the parable, Jesus maintains that the searching-out of the "lost" is a major activity of the inbreaking kingdom of God. He is engaged in this ministry as God's agent. Moreover, to the extent that hearers then perceive Jesus himself as the shepherd, he is glimpsed as acting not only for but as God. One begins to see the shepherd in a kind of stereoscopic manner, with even three pictures—of a shepherd with his lost sheep, of Jesus, and of the divine character—at times almost merging. There are good reasons for the development of the figure of Jesus as the good shepherd in John's Gospel and for the picture on the church-school wall.

The danger remains, however, that mere sentiment will so heavily color that portrait as to dull the surprise of the parable. This shepherd's way is not the way of the world. It is not even the way of religion in the manner in which it is often presented and more usually practiced. Not only does the story offer acceptance and inclusion without first requiring something of the lost but it once again expresses the divine bias toward those in greatest need which is one of the Bible's consistent themes.[12] This preferential attitude Jesus also maintains when he asserts that "the well have no need of a physician, but those who are sick; I come not to call the righteous but sinners" (Mark 2:17; Luke 5:31–32; Matt. 9:12–13).

That bias, too, can be treated very sentimentally and may feel only good to those who see themselves as included within that bent. Yet there is always someone still more in need, and when God's preferential concern seems to be more interested in others, religious folk can feel left out, uncared for, and then resentful of the challenge that calls them to act in the role of reckless shepherd to others.

The continuing community of Jesus' disciples is supposed to be an institution existing primarily for the sake of others. The nurture, the Christian education, the worship and pastoral care are intended to equip a people to reach out to others while accepting the sacrifices that this effort requires. The all too human tendency, however, is to make the nurture a kind of end in itself—to view it as the real ministry and activity of the church, with mission and service an occasional byproduct. It is that understanding of the church and of whom Jesus is ministering to that so heavily colors the picture of the good shepherd and blurs the surprise and challenge of the parable.

To all who share many of the values of a modern society, so influenced by ideas and processes of evolutionary progress, the parable is also a challenge. Indeed, the faith that highly competitive and selective processes will gradually build a better world may well still derive some of its support from Protestant theologies that baptized their understandings of Darwinian insights and interpreted them as revelatory of God's purposes and plan for the world.

This has lent a kind of covert divine sanction (the invisible hand of capitalist economics?) within secular society for the highly developed individualism, the way many educational systems operate, and the measures of ruthlessness which can seem necessary in business, politics, and international society. They may not always appear good in themselves (those who espouse their practice may say), but they provide the priorities for building a better society. They require a kind of triage through which resources go to those who have the skills (and the power) to make use of them. Those on the fringes unfortunately have to suffer, but that is the price that must be paid. The insight that the divine preference is bent the other way and that to follow that way means first to care for those most in need seems not only jarring and extravagant but wasteful and even silly. It presents a quite different understanding about what should be the priorities in the fashioning of a better world—and even what a better world would be. To hearers today, as well as those of the past, the parable of the shepherd leaving the ninety-nine to seek the one that is lost does not make good sense.

7

AS AN INJURED STRANGER

The Good Samaritan

And behold, a lawyer stood up to put him to the test, saying, "Teacher, what shall I do to inherit eternal life?" Jesus said to him, "What is written in the law? How do you read?" And he answered, "You shall love the Lord your God with all your heart, and with all your soul, and with all your strength, and with all your mind; and your neighbor as yourself." And he said to him, "You have answered right; do this, and you will live."

But he, desiring to justify himself, said to Jesus, "And who is my neighbor?" Jesus replied, "A man was going down from Jerusalem to Jericho, and he fell among robbers, who stripped him and beat him, and departed, leaving him half dead. Now by chance a priest was going down that road; and when he saw him he passed by on the other side. So likewise a Levite, when he came to the place and saw him, passed by on the other side. But a Samaritan, as he journeyed, came to where he was; and when he saw him, he had compassion, and went to him and bound up his wounds, pouring on oil and wine; then he set him on his own beast and brought him to an inn, and took care of him. And the next day he took out two denarii and gave them to the innkeeper, saying, 'Take care of him; and whatever more you spend, I will repay you when I come back.' Which of these three, do you think, proved neighbor to the man who fell among the robbers?" He said, "The one who showed mercy on him." And Jesus said to him, "Go and do likewise."

Luke 10:25–37

The parable of the Good Samaritan is a story within a story.[1] It is like a jewel mounted in the setting of the dialogue between Jesus and the lawyer. Many careful readers have noticed, however, that the jewel may not quite fit in the setting. The lawyer asks, "Who is my neighbor?" and Jesus responds with a story about a man who acts as an extraordinarily gracious neighbor. The specific question does not seem to be answered, or it is answered only indirectly.

One may also remember that both Mark and Matthew record a similar dialogue between Jesus and a scribe or lawyer (Mark 12:28–31; Matt. 22:34–40) but do not then go on to relate the parable. These observations have led to the suggestion that the parable of the Good Samaritan may once have circulated separately in the tradition; perhaps it was told by Jesus on a different occasion. Thus it can be intriguing to remove the jewel from its setting and see it on its own. When it is viewed apart from its setting in the frame story, it becomes more clear who the central character in the parable is. The central figure in most stories is the one with whom everyone else in the story comes into contact. In this story that character is the beaten and injured man.

Listeners are meant to identify with him in the story. They are to taste his fear, to feel his pain and then his terror at being left, perhaps to die. They can share his desperate consternation when two of his countrymen—two obviously religious persons, from whom he had a right to expect help—pass him by. Then they are to feel all his mixed emotions when a stranger, a schismatic, stops to help him.

The Fourth Gospel reflects the distaste and disdain many Jews felt toward Samaritans during this period: "Jews have no dealings with Samaritans" (John 4:9). The Samaritans were despised by the Jews of Judea as at best half-breeds whose religion was a strange mixture of the ancient faith of Israel and idolatries.[2] They were not good people. Yet in the story along comes a Samaritan who is very good. The narrative emphasizes his remarkable goodness. The story invites its audience to share in the injured man's confusion and surprise. Should he—could he—let this unclean foreigner help him?

Every hearer of the parable of the Good Samaritan has at one time or another been the injured person—dealt some cruel and agonizing blow, whether physical or emotional or both. One's life's companion dies. Job or reputation is lost. One is mugged on a dark night, becomes terrifyingly ill. Depression overwhelms. One is fearfully alone. Will there be help? Can there be help? Might God's graciousness come again by unexpected means? Maybe it will suddenly be present in another whose religious or political views seem deficient and tainted, even intolerable.

The parable asks whether its hearers are able to accept such graciousness. Or perhaps the act of grace happens in any event. At some time one may be so sick or injured as to be unable to prevent the help. Having received such goodness from another on whom one had no claim—whose kindness was in no sense deserved or merited on account of who one is or what one has done—how does one respond? Having experienced the care of another who has no obligation to act as a neighbor, what will go through one's thoughts when next someone is seen in need? Might listeners discover a new capacity to empathize with and have compassion upon those whose lives are quite unlike theirs? "Just so does the Kingdom of God break abruptly into a person's consciousness and demand the overturn of prior values, closed options, set judgments and established conclusions."[3]

Once the parable has been heard on its own, however, it can usefully be returned to its setting in Luke's Gospel. There are subtle ways in which the dialogue with the lawyer and the parable are closely linked, and one can perhaps now see more clearly who it is that the lawyer is most to identify with.

As insight is gained into this interaction, one may come to believe that a context like this could, after all, have been the original setting for the telling of the parable.

Hearers' imaginative powers are stretched by this play within a play. They can see themselves as the audience watching the lawyer's reactions and observing the other characters as the drama of the Good Samaritan unfolds. They may step forward to play the part of the lawyer. They are then asked to be themselves being the lawyer being the injured man—seeing through his eyes the priest, the Levite, and the Samaritan, while also trying to imagine their feelings. Hearers are also asked to be themselves being the lawyer acting in the parts of the priest, the Levite, and the Samaritan. They are pulled well out of themselves into the lives of others. Then suddenly, when the whole story is over, they are to be just themselves again, trying to interpret in the stories of their lives what they have experienced.

A lawyer stands up to ask Jesus a question. The audience is told little more about him but is meant to understand that he would have been regarded as a kind of teacher, an expert in his knowledge of the law of Moses along with the other traditions and their interpretations. At that time there would have been no sharp distinctions made between what today would be regarded as religious law and civil law. The whole of the law not only spoke to what people were required to do and not to do in society but set out before them what ought to be done if they were to fulfill all God's will for God's people.

This lawyer, one is led to believe, has more in mind than an interesting discussion. He intends to test (*ekpeirazō*; cf. 4:1, 13) Jesus. Although one can only speculate on his motives, the suggestion is certainly present that he would like to sound Jesus out. Though the lawyer's opening question does not specifically ask about Jesus' understanding of the law, that would have been the context and presupposition of the initial inquiry. Perhaps he wants to show that Jesus is unlearned, insufficiently trained in knowledge of the law and methods of argumentation and application, and so discredit him as a legitimate teacher of the people of the torah.

The lawyer's question sets out a big net and invites Jesus to become entrammeled in it. "Teacher," he asks, "what must I do to inherit eternal life?"[4] For the lawyer, this is another way of asking which are the most important features in all the law.

In the story Jesus shows himself adept at this form of testing debate. Since the lawyer has put the question in personal terms, Jesus turns the question back to him: "What is written in the law? How do *you* interpret?"

There is, however, now more going on than rabbinic gamesmanship. Jesus has altered the tone of the discussion. By assuming the lawyer's personal concern, Jesus has considerably deepened his involvement. The lawyer's question is heard as a way of expressing the heart of human longing: "What do you feel to be the true and enduring meaning of life? Which are the purposes and values that are lasting?"

The lawyer gives an excellent answer. Although not definitively codified as such at the time, this double commandment represents the highest aspirations of Jewish life and summarizes the spirit that undergirds all ethical issues. "You shall love the Lord your God with all your heart, and with all your soul, and with all your strength, and with all your mind; and your neighbor as yourself." As far as putting it into words is concerned, it could not be said any better. "You have answered quite rightly," Jesus responds. "Do this and life is yours."

Presumably they could leave the discussion there, but as both the lawyer and Jesus realize, this summary of law leads directly to the next and more practical question. How does one *do* this? Here is the challenge. How can one attempt to enact such lofty ideals?

The lawyer seeks a way to frame this practical concern and also to put the pressure back on Jesus. Listeners are told, in addition, that he now feels the need to justify himself—to demonstrate that he knew he was posing no simple or quickly answered issue when he asked about gaining eternal life. It is difficult enough to know how one is to love God, but this love is at least more easily claimed since it is so hard to evaluate. One can maintain that one loves God, but amid the exigencies and ambiguities of daily life it is far more difficult to show that one loves one's neighbors.

The lawyer appears to be caught up in the personal participation that Jesus invited. He wants to know about values that both transcend and give meaning to life. He also shares with others the need to rationalize and justify his behavior. How can I love others as myself? To begin with, "Who is my neighbor?"

Jesus now seems to hear the question behind the question. As has been recognized, the parable of the Good Samaritan does not appear directly to answer the lawyer's question, but Jesus realizes that out of his need to justify himself the lawyer is really asking the opposite of what he seems to ask. His is not a positive concern—wanting to know who it is that he might reach out to and love. The lawyer's real question is, Who is *not* my neighbor?

Again hearers are invited to be the lawyer. His real question is a question all feel forced upon them. Think of the daily demands that other people are ready to make on limited resources of time, energy, and money. Who can be excluded from neighborly care while we still maintain a clean conscience?

Every day, for instance, I meet people who want at least a little bit of my attention and sometimes my money. In my present work I have relationships with students, faculty, staff, trustees, friends, graduates, benefactors. I may be encountered by panhandlers whose lives seem wasted. Now and then, with a good night's sleep and someone's pat on the back, I might dare to feel I can manage it all. But most days I realize I would be overwhelmed if I tried to share myself or my worldly possessions with all these people. And if I did, and others heard about it, there might be no end to the stream at my door.

And beyond them, what about all the others? The hundreds of thousands, the millions? One sees their empty stares in the newspapers and on television. How many of them starve to death every year? How many will lead impaired lives just because they will not receive basic nutrients during the first few months of their existence? I cannot help all of them—hardly even a few of them. Yet one does not want to go around every day and all day feeling guilty. Yes! Lines do need to be drawn. And this is the role of law: to help one understand ethical definitions. Whom can one set outside the limits of one's neighborly concern without forfeiting claim to be an ethical person?

Jesus, as he so often is said to do, responds with a story. The method reminds hearers that it is in life itself—in the actual circumstances of daily living—that the questions become most real and one may begin to glimpse the possibility of God's presence in the world.

A man was going down the steep and rocky road from Jerusalem to Jericho. Alone on the road he was easy prey for robbers who took everything he had, even his clothes. As muggers will, out of an overspill of their own anger and self-hatred, they beat him severely and left him half dead by the roadside.

Hearers should probably pause for a moment and not neglect the role of these robbers. When this story is presented dramatically, I have often noticed how readily the assigned actors enter into the role of the robbers. Not only does this suggest a tendency to violence which may lurk just beneath the surface of many lives but it is perhaps also a recognition that all bear some responsibility—even if but indirectly—for much of the pain and violence in the world. It is not just others that cause suffering.

But now two supposedly ethical people—a priest and a Levite (an individual who would have had hereditary privileges and functions in the temple) —passed by without stopping. From time to time hearers of the story have been interested to speculate about why they did. There is no reason to believe that they were not good men, and it is not hard to invent creditable moral reasons. Maybe they were hurrying to their temple duties, which they regarded as ultimately more significant than helping a single injured person. The injured, the poor, and the sick would always be in the world, but the praise of the Creator and Sustainer of all things living must never cease. Unless there is worship of that which is greater than self, men and women would not be able to continue on and find the strength to help one another. Or they may have thought that the man was dead and were concerned that by touching him they would make themselves legally unclean and so unfit for their responsibilities.[5] It is not inconceivable that they knew of someone even more desperately ill—perhaps a friend or relative—who they felt had a greater claim upon their help.

Hearers should probably reckon with the most likely possibility, that they were afraid. I would have been. I have passed by people lying on the sidewalks in the slum areas of our cities. Maybe they were drunk or dead. I was afraid to become involved. It was a job for the police.

And maybe it was a ruse. Out there on a lonely road—maybe that was how the robbers tricked one into stopping. And then, when one dismounted[6] and bent over to see how one could help, the man on the ground grabbed you and others jumped out from behind a little mound and *wump* on the back of the head! Then you would be the man in the ditch! Better to find some other neighbors to love, try to forget this one, and make up for it by being extra kind to someone else.

Listeners are not given many details about the third individual to come down the Jerusalem-Jericho road. What they are surely intended to notice, however, is that he was a Samaritan. Since the injured man had been stripped and was at best semiconscious, it was probably difficult to be sure of his ethnicity, but there in the heart of Judea this Samaritan certainly had cause to maintain, "This is no neighbor of mine."

Yet it is the Samaritan who has *compassion* (the Greek verb *splagchnizomai* suggests a deep "gut level" emotion). If the injured Judean was to be considered his enemy, the Samaritan exemplifies Jesus' bidding that the disciples' love is to emulate the love of God by loving one's enemies (Matt. 5:44–45). He interrupts his own journey in order to bind up the man's wounds, using wine to cleanse and oil as balm. He puts him on his mount and takes him to an inn. There he ensures his care for however long it will take him to become well.

At this point hearers return to the frame story, where they are meant to share in the lawyer's response as Jesus asks, "Which of these three, does it seem to you, showed himself a neighbor to the man who fell among the robbers?" "The one who showed mercy on him," the lawyer replies. Jesus closes the conversation by saying to the lawyer, "Go and do likewise."

How well had Jesus met the lawyer's concern? The lawyer, one remembers, had really been asking, Who is not my neighbor? Whom can I not treat with neighbor-love while still managing to see myself as a law-fulfilling and respectable person?

More than this, he also wanted Jesus or the law—someone or something else—to answer his question for him. On the surface it might appear that Jesus was shifting the grounds of the discussion, but at a deeper level he really was insisting that the subject stay the same, in both senses. The question belonged to the one who asked it, and the real focus of concern was with whether and how law might provide limiting definitions for ethical behavior. Jesus' response by way of parable puts another question to all who are that lawyer. His story allows the lawyer to be in the position of an injured man who was graciously befriended by someone who had no reason to help him but who evidently did not have to ask the lawyer's question. What does that now do to your understanding of why you would help another? hearers are effectively asked. And why do you need to know who is or is not your neighbor? What does your asking of this question tell you about your reasons for caring for others? Why are you not content to help those you find you can help and leave it at that?

The response, of course, is that it is very difficult to leave it at that, for anxious insecurity prompts one to keep trying to shore up a slipping sense of moral worth. Continually people find themselves striving to define and limit situations, interpreting life by law. Since they cannot help everyone, they want definitions that will tell them whom they can legitimately set outside their concerns. This is what ethical law is for! This is what religion is about —to help people escape their guilt feelings! But into that losing struggle goes so much of the energy that might have been used to embrace one's own humanity and to reach out to others.

The parable tells of another way. Not only do hearers learn that they are to love God and their neighbor but they begin to see how this can be done. The use of the word "do" four times in the story ("what shall I do to inherit eter-nal life?"; "do this and you will live"; "the one who did mercy"; "do likewise") now assumes its full force. The story moves beyond speculation and inter-pretation on the subject of neighborliness. Freedom for a new kind of life and for a new relationship with God and one's neighbor is offered.

For the disciples, much of the power of this parable came from their awareness that Jesus did not just tell the story. He stood in and behind it. In one role he is the beaten and friendless man (he who himself will be cruci-fied), whose need calls to those who pass by, offering them the opportunity to give a neighbor's care. In another role in his followers' memory and expe-rience, Jesus is the one who does not need to ask the lawyer's question. It is he who stops to help; he is the unexpected Good Samaritan to the dumb man, the paralytic, Legion, Zacchaeus, the Syrophoenician woman, Barti-maeus, and Mary Magdalene. And then in a sense he is both the injured and the helping one; he is the wounded healer who is able to come to the aid of others because he knows their hurt.

Yet the parable threatens to unnerve its hearers even as it exhilarates them. Does one dare to be, does one even want to be, this free? Probably all people have known moments when they have felt this power and freedom, when they have ventured beyond their self-limiting boundaries toward that frontier where Jesus proclaimed the kingdom of God to be breaking in. They have realized what it can mean to stop trying to be merely ethical (observers of the law) and to start being good—to allow a positive love rather than a de-fensive concern with morality to be their guide. They begin to sense what Jesus meant when he insisted that "unless your righteousness exceeds that of the scribes and Pharisees, you will never enter the kingdom of heaven" (Matt. 5:20). But they have also seen themselves shrinking back.

Now it can be realized just how well Jesus can be said to have heard the initial question: "What must I do to inherit eternal life?" By his questions and the lawyer's answers the story with its dialogue leads listeners to that arena where their deep desire to stretch the borders of self and to reach out is fiercely guarded by a fearful anxiety that wills to maintain and fortify its defenses at all costs. In the midst of that struggle they are told of one who found life beyond those fortifications, and shown something of the road that he walked.

8

DO YOU WANT US TO GATHER
THE WEEDS?

The Wheat and Weeds

Another parable he put before them, saying, "The kingdom of heaven may be compared to a man who sowed good seed in his field; but while men were sleeping, his enemy came and sowed weeds among the wheat, and went away. So when the plants came up and bore grain, then the weeds appeared also. And the servants of the householder came and said to him, 'Sir, did you not sow good seed in your field? How then has it weeds?' He said to them, 'An enemy has done this.' The servants said to him, 'Then do you want us to go and gather them?' But he said, 'No; lest in gathering the weeds you root up the wheat along with them. Let both grow together until the harvest; and at harvest time I will tell the reapers, Gather the weeds first and bind them in bundles to be burned, but gather the wheat into my barn.'"

Matt. 13:24–30

Shortly after I became an ordained minister, I was appointed the assistant for a fair-sized congregation. It was in many ways a typical company of Christian disciples—a core of dedicated individuals, quite a few others who were reasonably active and trying to be serious about their faith, and then a number of people who at best attended occasionally, including some who did not seem very interested at all. Full of ideas, I thought that one way to strengthen the congregation would be to weed out those with little commitment. This would allow more attention and resources to be concentrated on those who were ready for growth, and their impact in the community would not then be weakened by those others who bore so little fruit. Since it was part of my job to visit all members of the congregation in their homes, I thought I had a pretty good idea of who was producing, who might yet give some yield, and who was just taking up space in the church directory.

Armed with that directory I went several times to the senior minister to try to convince him of the obvious benefits of my plan for thinning out while strengthening our band of Christians. I had a hard time understanding his response. It was to the effect that these other people would continue to need us from time to time and that, in his experience, some of them might well turn out one day to be more active Christians, if not in this congregation, then somewhere else. Besides, he maintained, people differed in their talents and energies and maybe some of these individuals were serving in the world in their own ways. It was not that easy to tell who could or would bear fruit.

I am not sure how much I learned from that minister's forbearance. I suspect at the time I thought that, like most ministers, he was too concerned with having a large number on the rolls. I kept thinking of what might be accomplished if the rest of the community could see the congregation as a smaller but much fitter and more dedicated company.

In the years that have followed I have heard that debate carried on in a number of groups and organizations. In one way or another a good argument can often be made for making a particular body sturdier and more effective by thinning it. In terms of the Christian gospel it seems hard for the church to "let your light so shine before others that they may see your good works and give glory to your Father in heaven" (Matt. 5:16) when a fair part of the company goes around with uncharged batteries—or worse, if they are not reflecting basic moral values. Too often, it seems, churches try to spread their influence by adapting themselves to the values of society at large rather than first concentrating on the genuine conversion of members to Christian virtues in order that they might then live so as to help change the society.[1]

One can still hear the dialectic in Paul's advice to the church in Corinth. He is shocked to learn that this new congregation is tolerating in its midst a man who is living with his stepmother. "I wrote to you in my letter not . . . to associate with any one who bears the name of brother if he is guilty of immorality or greed, or is an idolater, reviler, drunkard, or robber—not even to eat with such a one. . . . Drive out the wicked person from among you" (1 Cor. 5:9–11, 13). A fragment of the letter referred to may be preserved in this admonition from Paul: "Do not be mismated with unbelievers. For what partnership have righteousness and iniquity? Or what fellowship has light with darkness? . . . Let us cleanse ourselves from every defilement of body and spirit, and make holiness perfect in the fear of God" (2 Cor. 6:14; 7:1). Yet, when it seems this matter was resolved, the apostle adopted a quite different tone. "So I beg you to reaffirm your love for him. . . . Any one whom you forgive, I also forgive" (2 Cor. 2:8, 10). Elsewhere Paul counseled, "Do not pronounce judgment before the time, before the Lord comes, who will bring to light the things now hidden in darkness and will disclose the purposes of the heart. Then everyone will receive commendation from God" (1 Cor. 4:5).

Several centuries later one group of Christians wanted to make sure that those who had denied their Christian profession when threatened with death during a persecution would no longer be allowed to minister in the company of *real* Christians. Augustine, however, used the parable of the wheat and weeds to argue for the inclusiveness of the church.[2]

Forms of this dialectic are found in Matthew's Gospel. The evangelist has pulled together a number of Jesus' parables in chapter 13 and used this collection to signal a turning point in Jesus' ministry.[3] Formerly Jesus had taught everyone, but now it has become clear that a number of people in the crowds are unable really to hear and understand the parables. A division grows between the disciples to whom Jesus explains the parables and those to whom it has not been given to understand the secrets of the kingdom of heaven. Every disciple who does understand can be said to be a "scribe who has been trained for the kingdom of heaven [who] is like a householder who brings out of his treasure what is new and what is old" (13:52).

The parable together with its interpretation which immediately precedes the story of the wheat and weeds tells of a sower who sowed seeds. Some of them were devoured by birds. These circumstances represent individuals who do not understand the word of the kingdom, allowing the evil one to come and snatch it away. Other seed falls on rocky ground and has no root when trouble and persecution arise. Still other seed is choked out by thorns, representing the cares of the world and delight in riches. But some seed is sown on good soil. This is the good earth of those who hear and understand the word and bear fruit and yield "in one case a hundredfold, in another sixty, and in another thirty" (Matt. 13:3–8, 18–23).

This description could seem to present a rather exclusivistic view of the early Christian community, and one is at least reminded of highly separatist Jewish groups of the time like the sect that formed a community at Qumran which was continuously being purified. One of their documents viewed humanity (and the divine realm) as including those who could be described as the sons of light, at war with evil ones known as the sons of darkness. Similarly minded groups are found in just about every religion and certainly among Christians past and present. The extent to which this viewpoint has affected the teaching in Matthew's Gospel is reflected in the frequent pairing of opposing images—good and bad trees, fruit and fish, houses built on rock and sand, God and mammon, dogs and what is holy, pearls and swine, the narrow and wide gate, sheep and goats, and here wheat and weeds. The ending of this parable closely parallels John the Baptist's powerful description of the activity of the one who is to come: "His winnowing fork is in his hand, and he will clear his threshing floor and gather his wheat into his granary, but the chaff he will burn with unquenchable fire" (Matt. 3:12; Luke 3:17).

Yet it is also clear that Matthew recognized the ongoing Christian body in which he lived to be what has been called a *mixed* community. One scholar summarizes Matthew's portrait of the church with respect to moral matters in these terms:

As a relatively wealthy congregation in a heathen environment, materialism and secularism are immediate problems cropping up in the ranks of the faithful. In addition, there is spiritual slothfulness in regard to participating in the work of the Church; there is hatred among Christians; there is lovelessness, as exemplified, for example, by a lack of generosity or an unwillingness to forgive the brother; there are cases of apostasy, an evil compounded by the fact that even

Christians, and not merely non-believers, make themselves guilty of effecting the spiritual ruination of other Christians; and there is a certain prevalence of lawlessness in general which may be defined as disobedience of all kinds toward the law of God.[4]

The existence of so many problems may have caused Matthew to become somewhat pessimistic about the numbers who bear the fruit of discipleship, which may be why he inverted Mark's thirty, sixty, and a hundredfold at the end of the parable of the sower. It is also why the Gospel is replete with stern warnings about the judgment to come and why the evangelist frequently exhorts the disciples of his community to do the will of God. The theme that "many are called, but few are chosen" (Matt. 22:14) is repeated in a number of keys in this Gospel.[5] It is also the case, Jesus responds upon learning that certain of the Pharisees are offended by one of his sayings, that "every plant which my heavenly Father has not planted will be rooted up" (Matt. 15:13). There seems, of course, to be a contradiction here, or at least a paradox that is often found in Christian teaching. Why bother to exhort people to righteous living if it has already been determined who will be saved and who not? This judgment, however, is yet to be made known, and now, Matthew evidently believes, is the time for those who are of the community of Christians to do all in their power to show that they are among those who will be pronounced righteous (*dikaios*) on that day of judgment.

In the meantime the church must evidently be a predominantly inclusive community. At the conclusion of this Gospel's parable of the marriage feast, after the servants have been told to invite to the feast "as many as you find," the hall is said to be full of guests, "both bad and good" (Matt. 22:9–10). Only afterward will the unprepared individual without a wedding garment be excluded. Matthew uses the parable of the net to develop similar themes (Matt. 13:47–50). The large dragnet, pulled to shore between two boats or swung in a semicircle by a single boat with the other end held on to or tied at the shore, would enclose whatever was in the area—"fish of every kind." Only later would there be a sorting-out of the clean and unclean fish, just as the sheep will be separated from the goats in the great judgment scene (Matt. 25:31–46).

Before that time of judgment the church and its pastors must exercise great care not to lose those who might be saved. That concern, as has been seen, is important to Matthew's presentation of the parable of the lost sheep (18:10–14; see chap. 6) and is behind his use of "Judge not, that you be not judged" (7:1). "Why," his Gospel goes on to admonish, "do you see the speck that is in the eye of a brother, but do not notice the log in your own?" (7:3).

It is, of course, not possible for any community to exist without making some discriminations. After the parable of the lost sheep, Matthew offers his community a rather elaborate four-step process for dealing with a recalcitrant sinner. But, after all else has failed, the sinner is to be shunned. Matthew next tells of Jesus reassuring the church that whatever it binds or looses in this regard will be similarly determined in heaven (18:15–18). The whole procedure is then, however, seemingly undercut when the evangelist reports Jesus' answer to Peter's question about how often he should forgive a brother (i.e., another disciple) who sins against him. As many as seven times? "I do not say seven times," Jesus responds, "but seventy times seven" (18:21–22). Forgiveness for Christians seems beyond calculating.

It is in this overall context of concern and advice for the community and of counseling forbearance and forgiveness, while frequently reminding of the certain judgment to come, that Matthew relates the parable of the weeds and wheat. Heard by itself, the parable seems to make two major points and to retain the tension between the notes of waiting and inescapable judgment. On the one hand, human beings cannot safely make the kind of judgments that would discriminate between the good and bad plants. To endeavor to do so before the harvest would result in the loss of at least some of the wheat. But the day will surely dawn when that separation will take place.

Perhaps somewhat surprisingly, however, the interpretation (which follows after the parables of the mustard seed and leaven, and which is presented privately to the disciples) gives almost all its attention to the judgment from a dualistic perspective that has already sharply distinguished between the "sons of the kingdom" and the "sons of the evil one" (13:36–43). This heavily allegorical explanation of the parable appears to have little or no concern with themes of patience and the dangers involved in human decisions about who is good and who is not.

In one sense this stress on judgment sure to come corresponds with the evangelist's emphases elsewhere in his Gospel. As was true of other Christian communities, Matthew's church experienced problems with knowing how it should believe and live in the light of the prophecies that this present age would end. If one knew that that termination was coming tomorrow, there would not seem to be much point in thinking about mission and guidelines for community life. Yet these are of great significance to Matthew— culminating in the missionary charge at the end of the Gospel to "make disciples of all nations, baptizing them . . . [and] teaching them to observe all that I have commanded you" (28:19–20). The Gospel "will be preached throughout the whole world, as a testimony to all nations; and then the end will come" (24:14). With this mission in mind, however, it may then become all too easy to think of the close of the age as a far distant time with only a hazy relevance to present life. Matthew's response to this tendency is to describe the judgment scene in a kind of technicolor. Here and elsewhere one can almost feel the flames in his word pictures and hear the gnashing teeth. No hearer of the Gospel should think of the impending judgment as without immediate relevance.

This similarity in emphasis and language with other parts of Matthew's Gospel has understandably made scholars think that it is the evangelist who has fashioned the interpretation for the story of the wheat and weeds, along with the closely parallel explanation of the parable of the dragnet (13:49–50).[6] That the evangelist, or his immediate tradition, did most of this interpretive work seems quite likely, although it has been suggested that certain elements—especially the interpretation's beginning by seeing the field as the world rather than just the church—may reflect earlier understandings of the parable proper.[7]

One should probably not conclude, however, that it was an opportunity to stress the final judgment that was Matthew's only or even primary reason for presenting the parable. The story seems to be already partly an allegory and easily lent itself to a more developed interpretation focusing on the culminating scene, but that Matthew fashioned or used such an explanation need not mean that he had here lost that other pole of the tension otherwise found in his Gospel—the concern with forbearance in human judgments.

Hearers may detect still another interest present both in the telling of the parable and the interpretation: "Sir [or "Lord," for *kyrios*], did you not sow good seed in your field? How then has it weeds?" Why are there weeds and "causes of sin" and "evildoers" in the world and church? How could this be if God is the ruler of the world—and, especially, Lord of the church? The answer here given to the question, which is in one way or another fundamental to all religions, is that there is also present an enemy (said to be the devil [*ho diabolos*] in v. 39, and similarly referred to as the evil one [*ho ponēros*] in the interpretation of the parable of the sower [vv. 19, 38]). On this view neither God nor human beings desire or are fully responsible for much of the evil in the world. It is the activity of their enemy who must be opposed. And, indeed, the work of the enemy (resulting in weeds in the field and evil in the world and/or church) will in the end not prevent the harvest in accordance with God's purpose.

It has been suggested that several features of the parable which are interpreted allegorically in the interpretation were not part of an earlier form of the story. The interpretation has, in other words, affected the telling of the parable proper. This could be particularly true of the figure of the enemy and perhaps the stress on the harvest and the separate group of "reapers" who appear at the end of the story. A radical form of this theory maintains that Matthew has completely rewritten from Mark's Gospel (a source he seems otherwise to be following in his presentation of seed parables) the story of the seed growing secretly (Mark 4:26–29).[8] He has done this because he did not find Mark's story instructive (perhaps he even found it misleading in that it might suggest a rather lengthy period of unknown duration before the judgment) and because he saw this as an opportunity to emphasize themes that were important to him.

The question as to why Matthew may have omitted the parable of the seed growing secretly is not easily answered.[9] It would seem, however, more rea-

sonable to contend that Matthew has substituted the parable of the wheat
and weeds for it than that he virtually created the wheat-and-weeds story
from a few similar elements. Matthew is evidently also using his own source
of parables at this juncture in the writing of his Gospel, from which he could
have drawn the story of the wheat and weeds.

Unless the *Gospel of Thomas* (saying 57) has used and rewritten Matthew's presentation of the parable, it is also witness to a story in the traditions along these lines.

> The kingdom of the Father is like a man who had [good] seed. His enemy came
> by night and sowed weed among the good seed. The man did not allow them to
> pull up the weeds; he said to them, "I am afraid that you will go intending to pull
> up the weeds and pull up the wheat along with them. For on the day of harvest
> the weeds will be plainly visible, and they will be pulled up and burned."

Thomas, as seems to have been his tendency, may have abbreviated the
story, especially with respect to the dialogue between the man and servants,
but otherwise offers the same basic narrative, which includes the figure of
the enemy and the harvest at the end, although the latter is given somewhat
less stress.

The presence of these features in Thomas is important because there has
naturally been speculation that an earlier version of the parable was much
more secular and still less semi-allegorical. It would tell of the planting of a
field in which evidence of weeds was found and would follow with the advice
that the weeds not be pulled up lest some of the wheat also be torn up or
otherwise damaged along with it. One can imagine such a parable in the context of Jesus' ministry, perhaps used to reflect on the radical inclusiveness of
God's activity and the dangers involved in human judgments about who is or
is not to be reckoned acceptable. The story would arise out of observation of
an everyday situation, for the darnel weed does look very much like wheat
(with a similar bearded appearance) until the plants begin to mature. This
was an unpleasant fact of life for farmers but one with which they had to deal.
Jesus offers a lesson from their experience.

The full appreciation of such a parable would probably have to add, however, that a reference to the harvest was at least not absent from it. The story
naturally leads to this conclusion, and the harvest was, of course, a basic and
well-understood figure for the time of judgment. There is to be a judgment,
but again the point may be that this is to be God's work, not that of human
decision. Once more one can imagine Jesus telling the story, perhaps also directing it to disciples or others who were all too eager to try to anticipate the
judgment and to form an exclusive company of those already known to be
part of the kingdom of God.

It is more difficult to surmise whether the enemy should be regarded as
integral to the story. If he is given no allegorical reference as representative
of greater forces of evil, one can wonder about his motivations and relation-

ship to the man who sowed good seed but view his place in the story as providing little more than a brief explanation for what has happened. Probably, however, from its first use the word would have had at least additional nuances, and since no similar figure is found in other Gospel parables, it is not difficult to imagine him creeping in, as it were, at some point in the tradition to help explain the presence of weed and evil. On the other hand, there is evidence indicating that Jesus viewed the kingdom of God's activity and himself as its herald to be engaged in an intense and personal struggle with the forces of evil.[10] Not only does he do battle with demons when healing people but his exorcisms represent a defeat of their leader. "No one can enter a *strong man's* [*ischyros*, here a figure for the prince of demons] house and plunder his goods, unless he first binds the strong man; then indeed one may plunder his house" (Mark 3:27; Matt. 12:29; Luke 11:21–22).[11] This saying more than suggests that Jesus has bound or is in the process of tying up that strong man.

Whether a figure representative of evil purpose in the world had a place in an early version of the parable or not, one recognizes that belief in such a one provides a kind of answer to deeply felt human questions even though there are moral problems with efforts to explain evil as being caused by a supernatural force. These efforts raise still more difficult questions about the power, character, and purposes of God, and the nature of creation, and can too easily absolve human beings of responsibility for wrong and evil. That being said, however, such a figure is an understandable way of trying to wrestle with the problem of evil while retaining the understanding of a God who is good and who also battles against wrong and wickedness.[12] These issues are central to every religion and many philosophies, and the pained voice of a wondering humanity can be heard at many points in the Bible, asking, in effect, why there are weeds and why they seem to prosper.

O Lord, how long shall the wicked,
    how long shall the wicked exult?
                    (Ps. 94:3)

Why does the way of the wicked prosper?
    Why do all the treacherous thrive?
                    (Jer. 12:1)

The concern with why evil so often appears to flourish while goodness withers seems also to be at least implicit in two of the other seed parables (those of the sower and the seed growing secretly) and in this sense is present in the story of the wheat and weeds even without the activity of the enemy. The presence and power of evil in the world remain a mystery. Attributing the responsibility for it to a Satan does not, however, finally resolve the problems, and a more fully developed theological perspective must find a way to view God as the creator who in the beginning and the end is responsible for all the creation, working within it to overcome and even to transform evil.[13]

This last possibility may be hinted at in the parable when the owner of the field tells the reapers to gather the weeds and bind them in bundles to be burned. Darnel was used for fuel in Palestine. In the end the enemy is out-smarted,[14] and even evil is given a purpose.

Is the parable concerned with this problem and mystery of the presence of evil in the world or primarily as it is found in the church? As has been seen, the evangelist had his reasons for focusing the issue in the growing Christian community—composed of good and fruitful individuals and others who at the least did not seem to be bearing fruit. In the interpretation Matthew appears to narrow the harvest down to the kingdom (presumably meaning the church) out of which shall be gathered all causes of sin and evildoers. Earlier in the interpretation, however, "the field is the world." The parable itself does not define its perspective in this regard, but one should probably not think of it as any more limited than a number of the other Gospel parables in this respect. The situation described is itself specific, but the application is thereby left much more open.

Perhaps the most important question to ask in the hearing of the parable is whether this situation and the man's response are normal and natural or unusual and so meant in this regard to draw the audience's attention. The presence of weeds in the field would certainly seem to be natural enough. Any farmer or gardener would probably suspect that much in any case, and the growth of the look-alike darnel was a phenomenon of the time that caused comment and complaint as well. The rabbis made a play on its name which meant "to commit fornication."[15] Normally, however, the darnel would be weeded out, usually several times during the growing season. No doubt some of the good plants would be damaged or mistakenly pulled up in this process, but the weeding made for a better harvest.

It has been suggested that the situation presented in this parable was unusual in that there must have been an exceptionally large influx of darnel. This is perhaps the reason that a special explanation is required to account for so much weed. Yet one would think that such a problem would, in a wise farmer, call for a still more vigorous response. Maybe what he does is smart, but most agricultural experience suggests that he is headed for a difficult harvest with a lower than usual yield of wheat. He is risking a lot of good wheat by not doing the weeding.

The servants come to the man with what is both a question and a proposal: "Do you want us to go and gather the weeds?" One suspects that to hearers of the time this plan made the best sense, and, while perhaps not as surprising and radical as what the shepherd did by leaving the ninety-nine to go and search for the one lost sheep, this farmer's response could well remind listeners of that shepherd, along with the man who filled his dinner party with all kinds of guests, the father who took back his prodigal son as if he were some kind of hero, the vineyard owner who paid everyone the same wage, and so forth. It again could well seem to be odd, extravagant, and wasteful behavior—not a good model by the world's normal standards.

Of course, if one is rather indolent or indifferent, this could seem to be rather pleasant advice. But if one is trying hard to help God make the kingdom appear and/or to build a better world, it is not easy to find wisdom in this kind of patience or tolerance, or whatever it is to be called. I still think I could have strengthened that congregation by some kind of more selective process that made clear that church membership involved more than having one's name in a directory and showing up at Christmas eve or when a daughter was to be married. Some more sectarian churches, and a lot of educational institutions and other organizations, as well as farms, are run on that selective basis—often with good results. If the parable is suggesting that in the activity of the kingdom of God there is a different perspective and attitude, I do not very often find that perspective easy to appreciate or adopt. Probably the narrative is alluding to the insight that in this world what is good and evil, and valuable and invaluable, may involve a more complex interrelationship than is often realized. Learning to live and let live in such a mixed world is not easy for religious and ethically minded folk. They keep asking, "Do you want us to go and gather the weeds?" Hearers of the parable are, however, evidently to wait upon the judgment of the world's Creator with respect to what is to be kept and what burned away. That harvest is to come!

9
READY OR NOT!

The Wedding Garment

But when the king came in to look at the guests, he saw there a man who had no wedding garment; and he said to him, "Friend, how did you get in here without a wedding garment?" And he was speechless. Then the king said to the attendants, "Bind him hand and foot, and cast him into the outer darkness; there men will weep and gnash their teeth." For many are called, but few are chosen.

Matt. 22:11–14

The Ten Maidens

Then the kingdom of heaven shall be compared to ten maidens who took their lamps and went to meet the bridegroom. Five of them were foolish, and five were wise. For when the foolish took their lamps, they took no oil with them; but the wise took flasks of oil with their lamps. As the bridegroom was delayed, they all slumbered and slept. But at midnight there was a cry, "Behold, the bridegroom! Come out to meet him." Then all those maidens rose and trimmed their lamps. And the foolish said to the wise, "Give us some of your oil, for our lamps are going out." But the wise replied, "Perhaps there will not be enough for us and for you; go rather to the dealers and buy for yourselves." And while they went to buy, the bridegroom came, and those who were ready went in with him to the marriage feast; and the door was shut. Afterward the other maidens came also, saying, "Lord, lord, open to us." But he replied, "Truly, I say to you, I do not know you." Watch therefore, for you know neither the day nor the hour.

Matt. 25:1–13

Some years ago in the Book of Common Prayer of the Episcopal church there was printed out in full as the Gospel reading for the twentieth Sunday after Trinity Matthew's linked stories of the marriage feast (22:1–10) and the man without a wedding garment. In so presenting them the prayer book was being faithful to Matthew's emphases and concerns, but nothing else in the prayer book caused quite so much immediate commentary from parishioners as did that reading every time this particular Sunday rolled around. Even after a quick hearing there seems to be an obvious unfairness involved in sending servants out into the streets on the spur of the moment to invite as many as they could find to fill up the wedding hall and then throwing one poor soul into the outer darkness because he did not have a wedding garment. How could he? He did not have time.

The usual answer to the questioning of the parishioners was to point out that Matthew has probably combined what were originally two parables into one.[1] He may have begun to do this as early as verse 22:2 by describing what was once a dinner party as a marriage feast in order, in part, to prepare for the story of the wedding garment which follows. In so doing the evangelist seems to ride roughshod over what appears to be common sense and fairness, but he accomplishes his own purpose of starkly emphasizing the need to be ready at all times for the consummation of the kingdom of heaven. He may have been worried that by itself the story of the marriage feast and the invitation to all kinds of people "both bad and good" could leave the impression that behavior and response to the opening of the kingdom made no difference. Not so! Both the bad and good are invited, but not all enjoy the feast. "Many are called, but few are chosen."

It does seem, however, that the story about the wedding garment was at one time an independent parable in the tradition, told to underscore the importance of readiness to respond to the new opportunity of God.[2] That earlier story would not have had allegorical overtones regarding the return of Jesus and might have been drawn from everyday observation. Though a white festal garment could readily also be a sign of purity and salvation,[3] the earlier understanding may more simply have referred to the clean robe that one was supposed to keep ready for an important occasion. If someone turned up at such an event dressed in garb dirtied by everyday labor and activity, it would have been considered an insult to the host and the event.[4] A story of this kind would have much in common with the basic thrust of other short parables in the tradition, like that about the thief and the householder (Matt. 24:42–44; Luke 12:39–40) and stories about the master who suddenly returns (Matt. 24:45–51; Luke 12:42–46, 35–38; Mark 13:35–36).

This brief analysis of Matthew's use of the story of the wedding garment and its likely place in earlier tradition may or may not satisfy the questions of the casual reader of this Gospel passage, but it certainly does not resolve a tension, and even a kind of contradiction, that is deeply implicated in the Christian message. Matthew has only highlighted it, not created it. Understandably some teachers of the Bible (including this one) and some religious traditions want to try to relax this tension by lessening the pull from one pole or the other, but it persistently snaps back to the surface. It may be better to begin with the understanding that creative religious insight is not at first concerned with consistency and harmony. That usually comes at a later stage. Insight and revelation often point up life's paradoxes and mysteries. They are in touch with those mysteries and make use of them. They may seek to heighten tension rather than resolve it. Parables, as has been seen, are a way of giving voice to such tensions and the mysterious aspects of life which are their coils.

On the one hand, the parables tell of surpassing and almost unbelievable graciousness. They allude to the openness of the kingdom to all manner of people without any kind of precondition. On the other hand, there seems to be an insistence on readiness and response when that offer comes, which, if not given—and given on time—results in utter rejection with no second opportunity. To the extent that hearers find God's activity present in the parables they may feel confused. Is it forgiveness, mercy, and inclusiveness the parables are primarily emphasizing, or the need for preparedness and decision, with its consequences one way or the other?

Certain features in the descriptions of the rejection of those who do not properly respond to the kingdom's opportunity may well be the work of early Christian teachers and preachers. Not a few preachers since that time have been known, when seeking to emphasize the importance of repentance and the consequences of the failure to repent, to develop in lurid colors what that rejection is to be like. Supposedly one parson was doing just that with this story of the wedding garment and stressing the part about the gnashing of teeth, when an old gentleman called out from the congregation, "But what if we no longer have any teeth?" "Teeth will be supplied," shot back the parson. Dante's dramatic descriptions of the circles of hell are the brilliant literary expression of this penchant for detailing the severity of judgment.

It would, however, look to be a mistake to ascribe all of this interest to later development in the life of the churches. A concern—even a passionate concern—with the importance of responding to the kingdom and of deciding now for its opportunity is of the very texture of the earliest Christian message. Something of great significance is happening in the midst of life. Not to recognize it, to be ready for it, and to act decisively would be tragic.

The parable of the wise and foolish maidens was certainly used to stress these themes. At one time it may have given more place to the joy of the smart young ladies as they were able to participate in the long-awaited marriage feast. In its present version, however, the emphasis of the rhetoric falls upon the sad outcome for those who brought no extra oil.[5] It is a tragic conclusion, although one should probably not miss touches of comedy in what is also a highly stylized and exaggerated narrative.

The fact of the matter is that neither set of the neatly divided group is very attractive. Everyone knows the types and would not want to have either of them for roommates. Those who did not bring extra flasks of oil are the silly people who never seem to think ahead and then want to sponge off others to the detriment of everybody's efforts. They always imagine that by running around at the last minute, and borrowing a little here and making an excuse there, they can get the same results as everyone else. In this story one sees them charging out in the middle of the night to get more oil. Apparently they are successful in that venture, but this time around it is too late for them. By the time they return, the door is shut.

One can make out a good case for the wise maidens' refusal to lend them any of their oil. As they themselves argue, "Perhaps there will not be enough for us and for you." The festive occasion requires light both symbolically and in order to see by. In the long run it would be neither intelligent nor charitable to risk the possibility that this one-time event of the reception of the bridegroom take place in darkness. Perhaps in other situations sharing or lending might be the fairest response, but not this time. Not this most important time!

This understanding has, however, not prevented a number of preachers from agonizing over the conduct of the prudent maidens. If one fastens on the details of the story and tries to moralize them, the narrative does not appear to provide the proper object lesson in Christian behavior. And there also seems to be a certain haughtiness and tone of superiority in the wise maidens' words. One knows that kind of roommate too, always getting the work done on time, followed by advising, "It's really better for you to do your own work. You've got to learn sometime." But could they not have figured out some way to share at least a little, or have promised to keep a side door open for the others when they got back?

Such a concern, of course, misses the force of the parable with its insistence that there are some life situations in which one is either ready or not. Right then and there is the moment, and what is needed cannot be borrowed or shared. One either has it and uses it or the moment forever passes by. It can be true in sports, in having the knowledge of a language or a scientific discipline, in the love and care of others, in forgiveness, in responding to a cry for justice, in being able to rejoice.

The evangelist Matthew has, as in other instances, made use of a parable to speak to the needs and concerns of the Christian community of his time. That community, as has been seen, was a mixed church composed of committed individuals and others whom Matthew worried over. In his community there were both the zealous and the lax—those who knew that there would be a day of reckoning and tried to prepare themselves and those who spent rather recklessly against their moral credit, thinking of the judgment as a time far in the future.

It is to this latter group that Matthew has particularly directed the parable. It comes toward the end of his Gospel and is surrounded by other parables (the marriage feast filled with guests and the man without a wedding garment, the faithful and wise servants whose master returns suddenly, the servants judged on the use of talents, and the scene in which the peoples of the nations are divided as a shepherd separates sheep from goats), along with sayings and dialogues having to do with the end of the ages, judgment, and the coming of Jesus as the Son of man.[6] One of the most difficult questions in Matthew's church, as in other Christian communities, addressed the "delay" in Jesus' coming. Matthew's Gospel offers a double response. The delay is a divinely given opportunity to teach and preach the Gospel to all nations and to build up the community of Christian discipleship. On the other hand, although no one can or should try to predict when it will happen (not even angels nor the Son knows! Matt. 24:36), the time of judgment is not off in the never-never. It will take place and will come with a suddenness and finality that will catch many unaware and unprepared. In the immediately preceding story the returning master rewards the faithful and wise servant who has taken good care of his household. But the wicked servant who says to himself, "My master is delayed," and begins to beat his fellow servants and eat and drink with the drunken—that servant will catch it in full. The master will come on a day he does not expect him and in an hour he does not know and punish him fiercely. Again there will be weeping and that gnashing of teeth (Matt. 24:45–50).

This context, understandably, strongly influences the telling of the parable of the wise and foolish maidens in Matthew's Gospel and makes inevitable its hearing as an allegory about the Parousia or return of the Lord of the church. The marriage feast is the consummation of the kingdom and time of judgment. The delayed bridegroom who comes at the unexpected hour of midnight is Jesus. The wise and foolish maidens are types of Christian disciples.

So heavily has the context influenced the presentation of the parable that the evangelist has woven in some motifs that appear contradictory. The last admonition to "watch, therefore, for you know neither the day nor the hour" (25:13) seems to be borrowed from a saying found at other points in the Gospel (Matt. 24:42: "Watch, therefore, for you do not know on what day your *Lord* is coming") and attaches more directly as a conclusion to the preceding story of the suddenly returning master (Matt. 24:45–51; Luke 12:42–46).[7] In the story of the maidens, however, all ten of them went to sleep! The parable is concerned with preparedness, not watchfulness as such.

One also suspects that the final scene (25:11–12) has been added. Again similar wording is found elsewhere in the tradition (Matt. 7:21–23; Luke 6:46; 13:25–27), and it does not seem to make sense or be relevant to the story that the bridegroom should know or not know various of the maidens. The narrative ends more naturally with the unprepared, now-returning women finding that "the door was shut."

Commentators on the parable have noted other difficulties. The maidens, whom one would normally think of as attendants to the bride, or at least to the bride together with the bridegroom, at first seem to set out as though they were going to accompany the bridegroom (25:1) from one house to another. But when the bridegroom arrives, he appears to have come directly to the house where the feast is to be held (25:6, 10). Although parties that began in the evening and lasted well into the night were customary, the very late hour of midnight (see Mark 13:35) may seem more influenced by Christian allegorizing than what would appear to fit the interests of the story itself.

These and other difficulties with relating the story to what is known of Jewish wedding customs of the time, along with the bent of the parable in the direction of postresurrection allegory, have led to the suggestion that Matthew (or his tradition) has created this story, perhaps out of materials found elsewhere in Gospel sayings and stories.[8] Such a composition is, of course, a genuine possibility, but it seems more in keeping with Matthew's procedures generally to see him taking over a story from his tradition and adapting it as necessary to fit the concerns of his time. While not that much is known of wedding customs of the era, it is not difficult to posit a basic story drawn from everyday life. After partying at the bride's home, and after the attendants have escorted the bride to the bridegroom's (probably his parents') house, they then go out to meet the bridegroom, who is delayed by various details of the marriage which he has had to deal with.[9] The central concern of the parable would then be congruent with emphases found elsewhere in the early tradition. The opportunity to respond to the joy and responsibilities of God's activity in the world can come suddenly and then and there be realized or pass a person by. One does nothing to deserve the opportunity, but preparedness is critical. One thinks not only of other parables, such as that of the wedding garment, the suddenly returning master, the dinner party, the treasure, and the pearl of great price, but of stories like that of Zacchaeus and of the response of the first disciples to Jesus' invitation,[10] along with his teaching about the kingdom and discipleship more generally.

These stories, along with this parable of the ten maidens, were understandably heard by Christians of the evangelists' time in the light of their expectation of Christ's return. After the resurrection they had a more clearly drawn perspective on the gospel message. That postresurrection perspective is in general accord with the stress on the need for preparedness and decision found in the earlier teaching, while it also in some ways relaxes and in other ways heightens the tension. The sure character of the consummation (especially in that it will involve the seeing of Jesus again) is perceived more definitively even as it is now more clearly an event in the future.

The earlier message about the kingdom also looked forward to a future consummation of God's purposes, but the imminence of God's activity was powerfully felt in the present. That which was crucial to the meaning of life was beginning to happen already. In many ways the difference between Jesus and a number of his contemporaries was over this point. In his preaching and ministry the kingdom of God was already breaking in and transforming the way one was to view life, its opportunities and judgments. The acts of power—the healings and exorcisms of unclean spirits that were already taking place—were revealing the kingdom's purpose and character.[11] One could now repent (have a new view of life and its future) because "the kingdom of God is at hand." It is in some sense "in your midst" (Luke 17:21). Now is the time to be ready and to decide for it. If not now, when?

This understanding of the present reality and demand of the kingdom in Jesus' proclamation has been criticized for being too much an existentialist and modernist interpretation that does not take sufficiently into account the futuristic and eschatological view of time and history in Jesus' teaching. That criticism is probably a healthy reminder that the *already here–not yet come* coil is part of the very foundation of the Christian message which cannot faithfully be resolved in any one interpretation.[12] This realization, in its turn, however, may help to make one aware that time itself can be seen from a number of perspectives. Indeed, the harder one looks at time, the less, one realizes, is understood about it.

One must, at least on present evidence, accept the irreversibility of time, but the poet's insight that what appear to be different points in time might, from another perspective, be coexistent, is now accepted scientific theory. Time is relative in a number of senses. There is the time of the calendar and memory time, one's personal sense of the passage of time in relation to what clocks say. There is the time of the individual and time viewed in more societal terms. Time is the context of the individual's concern with death and the possibility of finding a lasting meaning for life. But there is also the time of the race, and the race's historical time can then be seen against the ages of the world, and this world's existence in relation to universal time. "The river is within us, the sea is all about us."[13]

The ancient view of cyclical time (of the ages repeating themselves) was radically altered by the idea of linear historical time, but then humanity asks whether that linear time leads anywhere or might be part of so long a cycle that it only appears linear. In any case, does not time in some important senses repeat itself—if not identically, then at least most similarly, as in a game in which each time is the same though different, over and again?[14] In different lives times happen again. When I am a youth and when I first love another, I am the same age with all others whenever they are having these experiences. So it is when I marry, have children, grow old, and am dying. In the Bible there is what has been called prophetic time—a sense of the meaning and purpose of life breaking into the moment—as opposed to time that would just go on endlessly or time that would come to a single definite end.

When thoughtfully questioned, our understandings of what is past and future are seen to be in many ways fictions that are created by memory and imagination to tell the stories, both individual and corporate, of our lives. We tell stories to gain some sense of identity in the ever-fleeting, constantly ephemeral present. Is our idea of time firmly a part of the way things are or largely a construct of the human mind? In the latter case is it sheer accident or is it somehow given? Is it a clue into how time and life may be given significance?

Stories are a means of shaping and playing with time—beginning here and stopping there, hurrying or slowing, looking at time from different authorial perspectives, warping clock time through flashbacks and so forth, now concentrating on the individual in time, then some larger group.

Through story and parable the Bible manages to frame and ask many questions of time. No one perspective is heard singly, and that is true even of Jesus' voice, perhaps because he himself—especially through story and parable—viewed time in ways that allowed for some of its complexity and paradox, seen from human vantage.

In a number of those stories, however, there is an aura of the urgency about the present moment, the only time in which one lives. An opportunity is here. The "end of time"—at least something of history's meaning and goals—can be realized now. It is not just going on and on, nor does its significance only have a future consummation. Jesus' stories seem to put so much pressure on the eschatological perspective of historical time coming to its end and bringing a new beginning that its chronology takes on a different dimensionality. Its clock becomes so tightly wound that its face can no longer be read through the eyes of usual understanding. The opportunity of the kingdom of God—of a relationship with divine purpose—is there for all kinds of people without condition and begins now. Humans live on the frontier in which this possibility is inbreaking. In some sense it may be always now, but the door both opens and shuts. The boundary is experienced in moments of insight and revelation which provide sudden opportunity to accept the challenge and excitement of that purpose—or not—in the only time in which one lives: now.

10

ON NOT BEING ABLE
TO REPAY

The Unmerciful Servant

Therefore the kingdom of heaven may be compared to a king who wished to settle accounts with his servants. When he began the reckoning, one was brought to him who owed him ten thousand talents; and as he could not pay, his lord ordered him to be sold, with his wife and children and all that he had, and payment to be made. So the servant fell on his knees, imploring him, "Lord, have patience with me, and I will pay you everything." And out of pity for him the lord of that servant released him and forgave him the debt. But that same servant, as he went out, came upon one of his fellow servants who owed him a hundred denarii; and seizing him by the throat he said, "Pay what you owe." So his fellow servant fell down and besought him, "Have patience with me, and I will pay you." He refused and went and put him in prison till he should pay the debt. When his fellow servants saw what had taken place, they were greatly distressed, and they went and reported to their lord all that had taken place. Then his lord summoned him and said to him, "You wicked servant! I forgave you all that debt because you besought me; and should not you have had mercy on your fellow servant, as I had mercy on you?" And in his anger his lord delivered him to the torturers, till he should pay all his debt. So also my heavenly Father will do to every one of you, if you do not forgive your brother from your heart.

Matt. 18:23–35

Everyone enjoys a story about a villain getting his just deserts. Millions of people wait impatiently through the day to return home and see if television's conniving bastard will finally get what is coming to him. In movie theaters audiences cheer as the merciless banker is caught in the same kind of trap he has devised for the poor young widow, or as the spaceship of the cruel overlord of galaxy X explodes in cinematographic fireworks. Although readers of the New Testament may sometimes cringe at the descriptions of punishment especially well detailed in Matthew's Gospel, they do not do so in this case. People do not usually cheer and clap in most churches, but there still can be heard a few muffled words of agreement and heads are seen bobbing in approval as the unforgiving servant is handed over to the torturers. "Good! That's exactly what he deserved!"

Later, however, one might begin to reflect and perhaps even find a crumb of mercy for this hardhearted man. In the dialogue preceding the parable Jesus speaks of forgiving not just seven times but seventy times seven. Maybe even this character should be given just one more chance. One commentator suggests that the parable has in a sense caught the hearer who "is entrapped in a web of evil that results from the attempt to bring justice. . . . This leads to the recognition that the fellow-servants and the reader have behaved just as the first servant. They too have failed to forgive."[1]

Yet, of course, it is part of the purpose of the story to suggest that there is another opportunity to show forgiveness. That chance is now for hearers of the story who know themselves to be the servant forgiven so much. Although Matthew's presentation of the parable is neatly constructed in three scenes of about the same length, with punishment or the threat of punishment prominent in each, it is possible that an earlier version of the narrative had only the first two—simply setting in contrast the forgiveness given to the servant and his merciless attitude toward another, and leaving hearers to draw the appropriate conclusion. In any case, it seems likely that the evangelist has, as elsewhere in his Gospel, developed the theme of judgment— adding to the ending of the story and perhaps also providing the setting at a time of a settling of accounts.[2] And, although torturers (v. 34) were used in some countries as a way of making debtors tell where they had any hidden assets, their more important function in this narrative may be to impress Matthew's audience with the severity of the punishment unforgiving disciples will receive.[3] No one knows when the last judgment will take place, and the church is to do mission and must learn how to live with internal problems in the meantime, but neither should there be any doubts about the certainty and fearfulness of that judgment.

Throughout that section of his Gospel, Matthew is trying to present a carefully balanced message. The little ones (*hoi mikroi*, 18:10) of the community are special subjects of God's care and favor. They are sought out as by a shepherd who would leave ninety-nine others on the mountains to search for the one stray (18:10–14). If a member of the community sins, there is a carefully worked out process for reconciliation (18:15–20). Peter's willingness to forgive as many as seven times is by Jesus stretched virtually to infinity: seventy times seven (18:21–22). Yet there evidently are limits as far as Matthew is concerned, and a time of sure and harsh judgment. "Woe to the one by whom the temptation comes" (see 18:5–9); the sinner who continues to refuse to listen to the voice of the community is to be shunned (18:17), and then there is the ending to this parable.[4]

Matthew has thus found an instructive context for the story of the unmerciful servant, even if it seems at least potentially contradictory.[5] The evangelist is dealing with a tough problem, because, while one might hope that forgiveness could be virtually unlimited and that all would eventually recognize and respond to it, this attitude is very hard to live out in practical terms in a community—especially when some members are being hurtful to others. This parable does not escape that tension, particularly when it is interpreted in relation to the preceding discussion about repeated forgiveness.

Since, however, the parable obviously does not in fact illustrate the theme of repeated forgiveness, it is also helpful to hear it independently. Matthew himself encourages this in his final verse, which clearly echoes earlier words on the subject of forgiveness that follow the prayer Jesus taught his disciples: "For if you forgive others their trespasses, your heavenly Father will also forgive you, but if you do not forgive others their trespasses, neither will your Father forgive your trespasses" (6:14–15). Mark's shorter version of this teaching concentrates on the more positive aspect of the counsel: "And whenever you stand praying, forgive, if you have anything against anyone; so that your Father who is in heaven also may forgive you your trespasses" (11:25). Yet the Markan saying agrees with Matthew's in understanding that human forgiveness is a condition of divine forgiveness, and both versions in this way concur with Matthew's wording of the Lord's Prayer, which asks God to "forgive us our sins, as we *have* [already] forgiven those who sin against us" (6:12).

For obvious reasons the story of the unmerciful servant has been used over the centuries (just as by Matthew) as a kind of cautionary example story illustrating this insight. The awareness that disciples must forgive if they expect to be heard by God is also at least closely paralleled in another teaching from this Gospel. "If you are offering a gift at the altar and there remember that your brother has something against you, leave your gift there before the altar and go; first be reconciled with your brother, and then come and offer your gift" (Matt. 5:23–24). One then remembers still more words of Jesus about turning the other cheek to one who strikes you, being willing to give your inner garment as well to the one who asks for your coat, being ready to go two miles with the individual who asks you to go one, giving to those who beg, and loving even enemies (Matt. 5:39–48). Within the community of disciples there is to be an extraordinary sense of reconciliation and mutuality. Several of the above sayings indicate that this mutual forgiveness, acceptance, and reconciliation are preconditions for approaching God and asking God's forgiveness.

The parable clearly, however, describes something more than this. The neatly structured parallelism of the first two scenes forces a comparison. Listeners hear first of the enormous debt of the servant to the king and then of the significant but relatively minor amount owed by a fellow servant. The king and the servant both express anger and determination to regain their money—the king by threatening to sell the servant and everything he has, including his family, and then that same servant by seizing his fellow servant by the throat. Using almost exactly the same words the two debtor servants make their petitions: "Have patience with me, and I will repay you (everything)." Inescapably hearers are made to compare the two very different and surprising responses. The first scene led one to expect no mercy; instead, there is forgiveness. The second scene ought to have ended with forgiveness; instead, there is no forgiveness. The king not only had patience but in his compassion (again, *splagchnizomai*) he released the servant (the Greek verb *apoluō* suggests he was already in some form of custody) and forgave him the debt; that same servant then had his fellow servant shut in prison until he could get his debt paid. The lesson is clear: those who are treated with great mercy should not act like this servant when they have an opportunity to be merciful.

The theme of forgiveness is reflected upon in a somewhat different way in a little parable found in Luke's Gospel. A Pharisee was critical of Jesus' allowing his feet to be bathed with the tears of a woman known to be a sinner and permitting himself to be anointed by her. Jesus responded: "A certain creditor had two debtors; one owed five hundred denarii and the other fifty. When they could not pay, he forgave them both. Now which of them will love him more?" (Luke 7:41–42). Great mercy, this story suggests, is bound to have its effects—in this case by inducing much love in the heart of the one forgiven so much. With such stories Jesus apparently defended his ministry to sinners and perhaps was also offering a mirror to those who felt in little need of repentance.

These are, of course, rather different points from the one made by the parable of the unmerciful servant, but one can imagine the teacher then going on to use the negative example of the unmerciful servant to illustrate how the experience of forgiveness should reach out to others. This was the experience of many early followers of Jesus. In association with him and in relationship to God's new activity in the world they were as reborn people. They had been set free from their sins. Not only ought they be, they *were*, empowered to share that message of forgiveness with others by enacting it in their personal relationships.

Sometimes, however, the story of the unmerciful servant is criticized for being so wildly exaggerated as to be out of touch with any comparable human experience. The amount of money owed by the servant to the king was hundreds of times more than a person could expect to earn in a lifetime. This has led to the suggestion that the servant was in fact one of the king's chief ministers and that the amount involved represented the income from several provinces.[6] Even then, however, the amount seems very large, and it has also been conjectured that the story presupposes a huge loan from the king that the servant had somehow managed to lose all or a major part of.[7]

The circumstances of the narrative seem to belong more to those of a fable than a realistic story in at least two other ways. Israel knew of no custom of a man being put in jail because of debts, much less the selling of family members to regain part of what was owed. The picture of a king with absolute power over his subjects seems to be drawn imaginatively from ideas about oriental potentates. Such fabled monarchs, however, would be expected to be rather fierce and pitiless—in the way the king reveals himself to be at the end of the parable. Yet this king not only is at first patient with his indebted servant but he forgives him a virtually unimaginable amount.

Obviously the first scene in the story alludes to the spiritual and psychological experience of those who found themselves forgiven in a manner they never expected they could be forgiven. The enormous exaggeration more than implies that the experience is beyond calculation. Any legalistic understanding of forgiveness should be shattered.

The order and direction of movement of the experience of the story is also important in its interpretation. One can forgive others (or should be able to forgive others) what are by comparison relatively small amounts, because one has first been forgiven so very much. This ordering corresponds to what is found elsewhere in the Gospels: the shepherd searching for the strayed sheep, the opening of the banquet to all kinds of guests. It becomes particularly evident in the manner in which Jesus first extends his acceptance to the tax collector Zacchaeus by offering to stay at his house, an act that is followed by Zacchaeus's promise to give to the poor and restore fourfold any amount he has defrauded (Luke 19:1–10).[8] The acceptance and forgiveness offered by Jesus, as he enacts the character of the kingdom of God, give people the power to live by the kingdom's ways. The experience of the coming of the kingdom brings with it the opportunity and capacity to repent, that is, to ask for forgiveness and have a new hope for life.

Yet, as has been seen, this ordering or movement also goes in the other direction in the Gospels. Repentance in preparation for the kingdom is certainly the emphasis in John the Baptist's teaching (Matt. 3:1–10; Luke 3:3–14; Mark 1:4–5) and seems to have been retained in Jesus' message, although there the insights and the experience of forgiveness are more complex. Human repentance and forgiveness provide opportunity for God's forgiveness, but the acceptance and forgiveness realized through the stories and actions generated by the coming kingdom also enable repentance and forgiveness to take place. Though encountered as a spiritual and psychological truth, this experience cannot be stated simply or fully encompassed in any one story. Forgiveness enables forgiveness. In Luke's version of the Lord's Prayer it is set forward as a virtually simultaneous action: "Forgive us our sins, for also we forgive all who are indebted to us" (Luke 11:4).

But if forgiveness enables forgiveness, it is evidently also true that the lack of forgiveness can inhibit forgiveness. In the story of the unmerciful servant the unwillingness of the servant to reenact the mercy he has experienced has the result of taking his forgiveness away from him.[9] That truth may unfortunately also be experienced in life by anyone who will not adopt a forgiving attitude toward others. Those who remain angry and determined to get what they feel they deserve without showing mercy may well find that they can no longer experience the effects of forgiveness in their own lives. In many situations in life people are not so much punished *for* their sins as *by* their sins.

Anyone who has ever tried to forgive an angry neighbor—especially one who is good at keeping count—knows how hard it is for such a person to accept words and actions of forgiveness.

Why? Why can the neighbor not feel forgiven and forgive? Why can this servant not show mercy? Why can I at least sometimes not forgive? It is perhaps all too easy after the hearing of this parable to become sentimental about forgiveness. Of course, once forgiven so much, the servant should be forgiving in a comparable manner. But one can think of at least two reasons why he cannot be.

It is important to recognize how angry he apparently is, as he seizes his fellow servant by the throat. Sometimes being forgiven can make one angry. Especially is this true if one has had nothing to say about the terms of forgiveness and there is no way one can think of of in some sense getting even by forgiving back. Such forgiveness can, in its way, put one in another kind of debt. It may, at the same time, make one far more aware of injury done or what was done wrong. Up until the point of forgiveness, one is often busily justifying one's actions. Forgiveness may make more clear the character and dimensions of the wrongdoing. Only after being forgiven do I really see how badly my careless driving has damaged my neighbors' hedge and that their having a noisy child is not really a comparable offense. Only after being forgiven by prisoners for punishment often far out of keeping with their crimes can one really see what our society's penal system is like. Those who have a sense of moral indebtedness after being forgiven, and who find themselves wishing they could get even, may need to realize that the only way to deal with such indebtedness is to try passing forgiveness on to others.

The other reason that expressing forgiveness even after being forgiven can often be difficult is that one still wants the world to be fair—especially to oneself. If the second scene in the parable can be heard just by itself, it is not difficult to imagine what would go through one's mind when encountering the fellow who owed the equivalent of many days' wages.[10] The lender has worked hard for that money. Perhaps it was to be used for a family luxury or, more important, to help the family be decently fed and dressed. This fellow has been lent the money in good faith—one friend to another, knowing its terms with regard to when and how it was to be repaid. That he has had tough luck or been lackadaisical with it is hardly the lender's fault. Other people all have the right to collect their debts. Why should this lender be the only one expected to be generous? The world of loans and debts cannot really be expected to be run on the basis of mercy. Sometimes the only way people learn the true worth of money is to have its exacting terms pressed upon them! Besides, what would happen if others heard about this mercifulness and wanted to be treated in the same way?

What the servant does to the fellow who owes him a hundred denarii in many ways makes sense. It is, after all, the way the world works. The further one gets from the opening scene of the parable, the more sense it makes. Only when the servant's tough-mindedness is put in the context of the larger parable do new possibilities emerge and are hard challenges presented—to which it is often difficult to respond.

11

TREASURE

The Hidden Treasure

The kingdom of heaven is like treasure hidden in a field, which a man found and
covered up; then in his joy he goes and sells all that he has and buys that field.

Matt. 13:44

Stories about buried treasure are found in the folklore of every culture—
thousands of them altogether, many of them variations on basic plots. Part of
the enjoyment of these stories is no doubt the imaginative opportunity they
provide to put oneself in such circumstances and to ask, What would I do if I
found such treasure? How would I feel? How would my life be changed?

This is one of the things that is maddening about this all-too-brief parable.
Hearers want to know more. Were the evangelist a newspaper reporter, he
would not find that he had a job for long.

Perhaps the comparable story in today's newspapers has become almost a
stock item: the article about the sixty-three-year-old truck driver with em-
physema, or the cleaning woman who is a mother of six, or the young, single
clerk at the grocery store, who suddenly wins three and a half million dollars
in the lottery. The story goes on to tell us why the person took a chance on
the lottery. It answers our questions: Where did the winner buy the ticket?
How many did the winner buy? Did the winner have some special reason for
picking these numbers? Does the winner play the lottery every week? Did
the person have some feeling of being likely to win?

Maybe there is a picture of the elated winner holding the winning ticket.
What is the person going to do now? Will the winner quit work or stay on
working? Will the person pay off debts, buy a new car, go on a vacation, help
friends, give some away, invest it? Perhaps there are some brief comments
from the neighbors. What kind of a person is the winner? Will this change
him or her?

Sometimes, after a few months or even years, a follow-up article can be
found in the Sunday paper. Sam Brown, who won the giant lottery two years
ago, says he is really the same fellow he always was, though he did quit
working and now spends half of each year in his condominium in Florida. Or
Irene Peters has somehow managed to run through almost all her winnings
and now has large debts her income cannot cover. She does not know where

it all went. A lot had to go for taxes; some she gave away. She probably could not really afford the new house and car. The car was in a bad accident anyway.

The saddest story of all is that of Mildred Tomlin, who says the money was the major factor in causing the breakup with her husband and, later, divorce. The only time the children ever come by anymore is to ask for money, and she does not seem to have friends as she used to. Probably all of this has contributed to her bad health. She wishes she had never bought that lottery ticket.

The theme of discovered treasure leading to tragedy is one of the basic plots of treasure stories. Especially is this so if the finder did not seem to be a very deserving person to begin with or if the treasure was illegally or immorally gained. In a number of tales there is an implicit warning about having anything to do with treasure that is buried. The act of digging it up and handling it puts one in touch with deep and mysterious forces of the earth—that unseen arena where precious metals are sometimes found and from which food appears. There in the ground are the secrets of growth, but there is also death, for to the earth all things living return.

Psychologically there is probably some sense that the finder has come into relationship with deep-seated powers within the self—of greed and a lust for power. These in the end turn upon the owner and bring about death. Or it may be that the treasure awakens greed in others (often family members or friends), replacing kinship and good will with devious scheming. In the end there is tragedy for all. Gold in the final scene is recognized to be a kind of root of evil that never should have been dug up. The once-shining metal is at last seen as the "filthy lucre" it always was. In a number of treasure tales the trove is eventually found to be worthless.[1]

Probably this kind of ending actually makes hearers feel better. Maybe they feel better for not having won the prize or found the treasure themselves. See what it leads to anyway! It may satisfy a suspicion that life finally must turn out tragically for everyone, even those who seem to have been very lucky. Fortune is, at best, always two-faced, and eventually all are leveled. The more significant satisfaction, however, probably comes from feeling morally instructed about the dangers of treasure that one has not worked for or otherwise deserved. The imparting of that lesson appears to be one of the important functions of such tales.

There are, on the other hand, many treasure stories that are instructive in other ways. Sometimes, although the finding of the treasure still can be seen as fortunate, the hearer also recognizes it to be a kind of reward for goodness or a lifetime of searching or otherwise preparing oneself for this great stroke of luck. Or the narratives may teach by telling of the wise or charitable things that were done with the treasure. In some traditions it is seen that the treasure is really a figure for *wisdom* that, whether the finder has looked for it or it has been discovered only by chance, is now cherished and used according to the ways of wisdom.

One can recognize the tendency to make a treasure story instructive in these terms in the *Gospel of Thomas*'s versions of the parable of the treasure (saying 109) and of the allied story of the pearl (saying 76):

> The kingdom is like a man who had a [hidden] treasure in his field without knowing it. And [after] he died, he left it to his son. The son did not know [about the treasure]. He inherited the field and sold [it]. And the one who bought it, went plowing and found the treasure. He began to lend money at interest to whomever he wished.

> The kingdom of the Father is like a merchant, who had a consignment of merchandise and who discovered a pearl. That merchant was shrewd. He sold the merchandise and bought the pearl alone for himself. You, too, seek unfailing and enduring treasure where no moth comes near to devour and no worm destroys.

Whether the author of this gospel knew the parables from Matthew's Gospel or another source, it would seem that he has reshaped them from a perspective influenced by Gnosticism and with that interest in mercantile activity found at a number of points in his collection of sayings. Hearers are to learn from the father and son who did not recognize the treasure of life in their midst. The lesson is that "unless you look for the treasure in your own field it will pass to others who will profit from it."[2] The lucky one who here legitimately acquires the field and then discovers the treasure does, however, then recognize it for what it is. His lending of it may indicate a wise use of the treasure and/or a sharing of genuine knowledge with others. True to the folklore pattern of such stories, the finder demonstrates his new wealth.

In the story of the pearl the prudence of the merchant is stressed. The pearl evidently represents wisdom, and Thomas adds his version of another saying from the tradition to emphasize wisdom's unfailing character.[3]

Because the two parables are separated in Thomas, some scholars believe Matthew first brought them together in his Gospel. One can imagine, however, that their similarities caused them to be linked at an earlier point in the tradition. Some critics suggest that Jesus may have used them in tandem to reinforce a similar basic concern.[4] In any event, Matthew would appear to have seen them in this light, and the two short narratives do have much in common.

Although they begin a bit differently, they are both intended to say that the kingdom of heaven is *like this situation*. One may or may not regard the significance of the two stories as self-evident, but they are also similar in that neither offers hearers a lot to go on. Those who probe them are left with a number of unanswered questions. Both move quickly to their conclusions focused by the parallel structure of *finding* and then *goes/went, sells/sold all*, and *buys/bought*. The manner in which the treasure parable shifts to verbs in the present tense as it ends seems to make the action even more dramatic.

Neither story tells what was done with the great find. Some interpreters believe that it is implied that the treasure and highly valuable pearl were sold for great wealth,[5] but that understanding may in fact run counter to the concentrated effect of the narratives. In an important sense one does not do anything with this treasure. One just has it. It is the kingdom—not valuable for what one can sell or trade it for—but wholly for itself. It is treasure of surpassing value.

To his mixed community (consisting of many who were lax and inconsistent in discipleship as well as the more dedicated) Matthew has directed these stories with their examples of "total commitment."[6] They tell of a single-mindedness and an alacrity in willingness to give up all else in life for what is of worth beyond measure. The one who discovers the treasure and the merchant respond with everything they have. They are in some ways illustrations of the saying that follows the warning not to have earthly treasures that rust and can be stolen but to have treasures in heaven: "For where your treasure is, there will your heart be also" (Matt. 6:19–21; Luke 12:33–34). Hearers can contrast the story of the man who asked Jesus about inheriting eternal life and was told to sell what he owned and give to the poor and so have treasure in heaven but was unable to do so because he had great possessions (Matt. 19:16–22; Mark 10:17–22; Luke 18:18–23).[7]

It is, however, rightly pointed out that what is described in these stories is not giving away everything but using all else to purchase what is regarded as of still more worth.[8] In this sense the two parables are not concerned with sacrificial living for the sake of those in need, and that would be the wrong sermon to preach using these stories as texts. Nevertheless, there is a kind of willingness to surrender all other things that is involved in their actions, comparable, for example, to the athlete who goes into strict training in order to win the gold medal. Matthew's audience was probably meant also to remember sayings of Jesus such as "The one who loves father or mother more than me is not worthy of me; and the one who loves son or daughter more than me is not worthy of me; and the one who does not take up a cross and follow me is not worthy of me" (Matt. 10:37–38). The kingdom must be given a priority that is absolute.

The twinned parables of the treasure and pearl are together used by the evangelist to stress this theme, but it is worth recognizing that there are also differences in the narratives. Fortune suddenly presents both individuals with a unique opportunity, but in the case of the pearl merchant hearers are able to reflect on the virtue of the "prepared mind." Lucky he may be, but without the skill he has developed in discerning pearls through preparation and searching, he would presumably never have been able to perceive the true nature of the opportunity.[9] It is not suggested, on the other hand, that the one who finds the treasure is either prepared or searching for anything. This individual is just plain lucky.

There are also aspects of the treasure story that are, as it were, more murky. This is true not only because of those connotations that go along with treasure buried in the ground but because hearers cannot be certain of the morality of the treasure finder's actions. Looking back through sermons and scholarly interpretation of the parable, one can find a fair amount of concern in this regard.[10] It seems probable, however, that the early hearers of the parable would have understood that what the individual did was legal. In a sense ancient treasure belonged to no one by right, and, if the person was a day laborer and not a servant who would have borne more responsibility to the owner, he was within his legal rights in concealing the find and then buying the field.[11] What is not illegal is, however, not always considered morally right, and it is at least difficult to get very excited about the ethics of the treasure finder. It has been suggested that Matthew might not have included the parable in his Gospel were it not already linked with the more aboveboard story of the merchant who had been searching for fine pearls and purchased the one of great value in the open market.[12]

Yet it is in part because the parable does not seem very concerned with advertising practical morality or common-sense prudence, and because the narrative does not fulfill expectations based on similar stories, that it reminds of other of Jesus' parables in their challenge to usual ways of thinking and expecting. The treasure finder "is as unscrupulous in his way as the Unjust Steward himself"[13] who did what he had to do without much apparent regard for the niceties of the situation, in order, in his circumstances, to make the calamity of losing his job into an opportunity for a new life.

Heard in this perspective, the parable is also at least as much a question as advice: What would you do—or what will you do in similar circumstances—in the story of your life? Even more than the story of the pearl, the treasure tale intimates how much luck or, if you will, grace is involved in coming across the kingdom of God—God's presence which in many ways is hidden below the appearances and surface interpretations of life. Coming into contact with that presence puts one in touch with mystery and risk. The one who stumbled across the treasure found without seeking; in a sense he was as much found as finding. But now if one is to seize this opportunity one cannot play it safe. If the individual realizes that the opportunity of this treasure is worth more than all else possessed, present life and the future are utterly changed.

The parable now seems to allude to stories about marriage feasts and dinner parties, and perhaps to still others about finding the unexpected—what one has neither sought nor earned—and thus having everything disrupted. When what counts more than all else in life is suddenly come across, what happens to planning, investment schedules—even concerns about prudential morality and deserving? Whose future is it then?

12

NO WAY OF SAVING

The Talents

For it will be as when a man going on a journey called his servants and entrusted to them his property; to one he gave five talents, to another two, to another one, to each according to his ability. Then he went away. He who had received the five talents went at once and traded with them; and he made five talents more. So also, he who had the two talents made two talents more. But he who had received the one talent went and dug in the ground and hid his master's money. Now after a long time the master of those servants came and settled accounts with them. And he who had received the five talents came forward, bringing five talents more, saying, "Master, you delivered to me five talents; here I have made five talents more." His master said to him, "Well done, good and faithful servant; you have been faithful over a little, I will set you over much; enter into the joy of your master." And he also who had the two talents came forward, saying, "Master, you delivered to me two talents; here I have made two talents more." His master said to him, "Well done, good and faithful servant; you have been faithful over a little, I will set you over much; enter into the joy of your master." He also who had received the one talent came forward, saying, "Master, I knew you to be a hard man, reaping where you did not sow, and gathering where you did not winnow; so I was afraid, and I went and hid your talent in the ground. Here you have what is yours." But his master answered him, "You wicked and slothful servant! You knew that I reap where I have not sowed, and gather where I have not winnowed? Then you ought to have invested my money with the bankers, and at my coming I should have received what was my own with interest. So take the talent from him and give it to him who has the ten talents. For to every one who has will more be given, and he will have abundance; but from him who has not, even what he has will be taken away. And cast the worthless servant into the outer darkness; there will be weeping and gnashing of teeth."

Matt. 25:14–30; see Luke 19:12–27

JESUS
  A
  V
  E
  S   declares the familiar neon cross in front of the rescue mission. If the mission happens to be near a bank, the bank management could hardly ask for a better recommendation. But wait, interposes the hearer of this parable.

The policy recommended by Jesus seems to be more one of investing than saving—and not just putting money into safe operations either. This parable talks about at least doubling one's stake. The parable sounds like both a description and a warm recommendation of a form of capitalism—including even a ruthless willingness to let the devil take the hindmost.

That last aspect is bothersome even to a number of the supporters of capitalism, although some of them would also agree that the acceptance of certain harsh realities is necessary to make capitalism function properly. It is comforting, therefore, to concentrate on the good things that come to the first two servants in the parable and to see what happens to the third as a kind of unfortunate byproduct. Clearly, however, the interest of the parable is mainly in the third servant. The structure and movement of the narrative cause listeners primarily to associate with him. As a result one cannot help feeling questions and even protest well up in one's throat.

Those concerns go back at least as far as Luke's audience, and probably earlier. "Lord, he has ten pounds!" (19:25) protest the servants in Luke's version. Is this a world where the rich only get richer? That servant already has quite a lot, and now the other will have none. And not only will he have none, the Gospels also tell us he is to be punished—cast away as worthless. Survival of the fittest it may be, but the penalty still seems out of keeping. The master, after all, did not in Matthew's story give his servants any specific instructions. Realizing the master was stern, the servant was only being careful with what had been entrusted to him. Is caution that wrong?

Yet, whatever questions they might have had about the parable, both Luke and Matthew found it to be otherwise instructive for their listeners. The number of differences in their two versions suggests that they did not derive the narrative from a common source; the similar structure and many agreements in wording indicate that they were both making use of the same essential story passed on from further back in the traditions.[1] Indeed, basic elements of the story (having to do with a householder or master who goes away, leaving servants in charge of certain matters, and who then returns for a time of reckoning) are found in a number of Gospel stories and seem to have composed an often-used set of circumstances for parables told and retold in the early life of the church.

Luke or his source[2] has also inserted into the parable part of another story about a nobleman going away and returning, which does not seem to fit very well with the rest of the narrative. This account (found in all or parts of 19:12, 14, 15, 27) has strongly influenced the opening and ending of Luke's version and probably the description of the first two servants' future responsibilities as well (being set over ten and five cities, 19:17, 19). This part of the story seems to derive from historical circumstances, probably regarding Archelaeus going to Rome seeking to be named king and later returning to punish those responsible for sending an embassy after him to protest his being given reign in Palestine.[3] Likely this story was at one time woven into the parable to give it a certain historical verisimilitude and probably also to make a veiled allegorical reference ("A nobleman went into a far country to receive kingly power," 19:12) to Jesus' ascension and expected return, although without too much regard for coherence. Particularly confusing is the fact that Luke starts out with ten servants being given ten pounds (evidently one each) but that later one hears (as in Matthew) only of what three servants did with the money.

Along with Matthew, Luke relates the parable to the last judgment, at the same time dealing with the issue of the delay in its coming. In narrative terms Luke's version is addressed to Jesus' contemporaries who "supposed that the kingdom of God was to appear immediately" (19:11). There directly follows the entrance into Jerusalem, and one can imagine all manner of excitement and expectation regarding the possibility that the reign of God was right then to come in its fullness. But there has yet to be the period of time imagined in the parable during which the servants invest or try to conserve what has been given them. The question about how soon the kingdom would come was also a concern of Luke's contemporaries, and the parable is then a way of helping them understand that Jesus himself foresaw a period of time before the kingdom's advent. The story in this way offers counsel and admonition about Christian service in this interval. "Trade with these till I come" (19:13).

By setting the parable after a long series of teachings about the consummation of history and shortly before Jesus' passion, and also between the parables of the ten maidens (five of whom are prepared and five not) and the great judgment scene (when the nations are divided as a shepherd separates the sheep from the goats), Matthew has made certain that the parable of the talents will be interpreted with reference to the last judgment. By beginning the parable, *"For* it will be as . . . ," the evangelist makes the talents story a kind of sequel to that of the ten maidens. He then also shows his community's interest in understanding the delay when he observes, *"Now after a long time* the master of those servants came and settled accounts with them" (25:19). Once again Matthew is concerned to teach that the judgment will come (a time in which some will "enter into the joy of your master" [25:21, 23] and others will be severely punished) but that in the meantime there is much to do as Christ's disciples. Watchfulness and preparedness for the full advent of the kingdom do not involve just sitting around in wedding garments. Matthew wants to warn those in his audience who may be content to "save" their faith that much more is asked of them.

As he has done with other parables Matthew has probably developed the description of the punishment using again references to "outer darkness" and the weeping and gnashing of teeth, although one should recognize that Luke's conclusion is, if anything, even more fierce. Their endings are not out of keeping with what comes before in the story. This parable tells of one very tough master!

It has also been suggested that at some point in the passing-along of the story the saying ". . . to everyone who has will more be given (and he will have in abundance), but from the one who has not, even what he has will be taken away" (Matt. 25:29; Luke 19:26) has been added to help interpret the parable. It is a saying found in other connections in the Gospels[4] and is not fully congruent with what happens in this narrative, since the saying does not refer at all to the second servant, and the third servant does, in fact, have something to be taken away.[5] The last part of that criticism may, however, be too literal minded, for, in another sense, the servant has only what is lent to him and then has that taken as well. In this sense the saying describes fairly accurately what has taken place.[6] It also sums up what can happen in capitalistic situations. Capital flows to the successful investors, and others may lose out entirely.

If, however, there is doubt as to whether Matt. 25:29 is integral to the story, there really should be none with respect to "So take the talent from him and give it to him who has ten talents" (Matt. 25:28).[7] This is the necessary end of the plot and corresponds with the surprise and seeming scandal of unfairness found in other Gospel parables. In this case, because the narrative leads up to and focuses on what happens to the third man, it is a tragic story that requires catastrophe for him.

The dimensions of his catastrophe and the magnificence of the outcome for the first two servants are huge in Matthew's version of the parable. While some commentators prefer Luke's more "realistic" pounds (or *minas*), Matthew's talent, which was worth at least fifty times as much, is in keeping with the extravagance of Gospel stories.[8] A very great deal is at stake! One may recall Jesus' response to Peter, who, when speaking on behalf of the other disciples, reminded Jesus that they had left everything to follow him. "There is no one," Jesus tells him, "who has left house or brothers or sisters or mother or father or children or lands for my sake and for the gospel, who will not receive a hundredfold now in this time, houses and brothers and sisters and mothers and children and lands, with persecutions, and in the age to come eternal life" (Mark 10:29–30). Mark has likely added "with persecutions" to make this saying fit better with actual Christian experience; Matthew and Luke were content more simply to say "a hundredfold" or "manifold" without detailing all that disciples were to get (Matt. 19:29; Luke 18:29–30), for, if one wants to be literal about it, who wants hundreds of houses, brothers, sisters, and mothers? There are enough problems now. But, of course, this is the Gospels' way of saying that in the kingdom disciples will find uncountable new rewards and responsibilities.

In most other respects as well Matthew seems to have better retained an earlier form of the parable. At least he has made a more interesting story of it. The opening scenes are more adroitly set—especially with their description (25:16–18) of what the three servants did. Already listeners are drawn in and asked in some sense to take sides. There is the familiar folkloric pattern of two men who do things one way and then the third another—

pointing attention to the third individual: Why did he do this? What would you have done? What will happen to him? The suspense builds as the audience is made to listen to the little speeches of the first two servants as they present the excellent results of their investments, followed by the master's commendation. But what will happen to the third?

The audience of the time would probably have recognized that what this third servant did with the money was both legal and safe. The angry master will tell him that he at least ought to have invested the money with bankers, but there was no federal savings-insurance program in those days. The most secure thing to do was to bury the money, and, if done carefully, that evidently would have freed the servant from liability were the money then stolen.[9]

The master had not told him what to do or what his expectations were. The only thing the servant knew for sure was that he was a tough master, used to getting not only his own but more. Maybe on this basis the servant should have figured out that he was to do more than keep the talent safe. He is for the moment a comic as well as tragic figure. One sees him coming forward hesitantly from behind the others, already trying to excuse himself and half blaming the master's demanding reputation for his own timidity. Rather pitifully he hopes to get away with handing back the one talent. "Here you have what is yours."[10]

Why not just rebuke him (as in fact is done in a later church retelling of the story)?[11] What has he done that is so wrong that it should become a great disaster for him? A number of commentators believe that the parable was first directed at the religious leaders of the time to the extent that they tried to make sure of their own rightness before God by interpreting law defensively and so understanding goodness to be not sinning and not taking any chances on offending God.[12] Given the guidance of God's torah—with all the opportunities it provided for being of service to others and reaching out with the faith of Israel—some of these officials had instead used the law only to define and defend, to try to keep themselves and what they had pure and safe.

This interpretation of the parable would seem to be in tune with some of Jesus' own concerns and the tenor of other of his parables. One almost inevitably thinks of the priest and Levite who passed by the injured man on the road to Jericho, and wonders what was going through their minds. In general terms it also reflects aspects of Paul's experience with the law which ought to have provided life but instead "proved to be death to me" (Rom. 7:10).[13] Although it would be a mistake in historical understanding to imagine that all Jewish leaders so understood and lived by law, it would also be a mistake not to recognize that the tendency to define being good and ethical primarily or even almost solely in negative ways is an all too human trait. One of the more poignant tales of human behavior to come from the Second

World War tells how the strict morality of a number of Christians interned by the Japanese in China made cooperation with other prisoners in the common life of the camp (and sometimes in just decent caring and charity) very difficult.[14]

The call to "love one's neighbor" and to "keep oneself unspotted from the world" (James 2:27) do not ride together in an easy tandem. One recalls how Paul found himself of two minds in this regard,[15] and a more amusing illustration was passed along by Garrison Keillor in a news item from Lake Wobegon. It seems that, by dint of a misunderstanding between a husband and a wife while camping, a man found himself naked in the countryside one cold October night in Minnesota. Covering himself as best he could with branches, the man came to the house of two sisters who lived together. He knocked on their door. The two ladies looked out an upstairs bedroom window and then quickly snapped the shade shut.

One of them said, "Why let him in, he's naked out there."

And the other one said, "We can't let him in; he's naked. Call the police."

"Well, we gotta let him in; he's naked."

"He's naked; we can't let him in. What's he doing naked out there?"[16]

The recognition of how prevalent and ingrained is the human disposition to try to define being good and having purpose in life by safe and saving ways should keep one from thinking too specifically about the audience to whom the parable of the talents was addressed. In its earlier forms the story may well have had a number of the religious leaders of Judaism within its scope. Yet, while the third servant acts legally in burying his talent, there is nothing in the narrative that would otherwise suggest that the talent is a figure for the law or that the parable speaks only to the attitudes of scribes and Pharisees. The compass can well be broader.

One interpreter of the parable speaks disparagingly of the "unconvincing excuse" of the third servant.[17] Probably in terms of the rhetoric of the story that is fair enough, but listeners had best be careful before being too condescending to his concerns. The first and second servants made piles of money for their master all right, but there were no sure bets out there. Unanswered in the story is what the master would have responded if the third servant had stepped forward and said, "Master, I knew you to be a hard man, reaping where you did not sow and gathering where you did not winnow, so I invested your money with this guy who had a marvelous idea about how to make a real bundle. I checked it out with a lot of people who assured me it was a terrific opportunity. If it had worked, you would probably have got back at least ten times what you gave me to invest. But it didn't pan out and the guy went bust."

It is pleasant to think that the master would have said, "Nice try. You have the right spirit. Let's see how you do next time." But there is certainly no guarantee of that. This master sounds very hard-nosed. Perhaps, for losing his money entirely, one is boiled in oil.

Sometimes, because both stories have to do with buried money, what the third servant does is contrasted with the response of the fellow in another parable who found buried treasure and sold everything to have the field and treasure. He staked all he had on that opportunity. But this servant might reply, "That was fine for him. In similar circumstances, maybe I would do the same, but not everyone can be so lucky."

The maddening thing about the parable (and one may want to say the maddening thing about life as well) is that one is not told enough about its terms. Apparently almost everyone recognizes that the master is tough, but what is that supposed to mean when it comes to trying to invest what one has temporarily been put in charge of? And where has this master gone away to? Is this like the absence of God, who may seem so distant as not to care at all? Or of Jesus, who, despite all the church's hallelujahing, may just be a dreamy, dead carpenter turned preacher who is never coming back? How is one to know?

And what is this talent anyway if it is not really money? Is it the torah of God or the teaching of Jesus? Or is it, as so many preachers have suggested, intended to be a figure for (helped especially by the play on words in the English language) one's God-given talent—perhaps as a teacher or linguist or doctor or worker with one's hands—that is to be developed in life? One thinks of Paul's image of the one body of Christ with its many members and different functions—varieties of gifts and services inspired by the one Spirit of God. "Having gifts that differ according to the grace given us, let us use them" (Rom. 12:6).[18] This interpretation seems to be encouraged in Matthew's version as the several servants are given different amounts, "to each according to his ability" (25:15).

One does, of course, recognize that there is a kind of psychological truth that either is alluded to or can be easily read into the story—a "use it or lose it" message. A muscle that is spared is lost. A capacity for love that is not used in loving (and surely all loving involves risk) after a while becomes empty. Even what one had is taken away. The parable can thus be heard as a kind of wisdom story without any specifically religious message or reference to the last judgment. Its essential teaching in this sense is true with regard to human life—for all people at all times.

One scholar has suggested that the reason the third servant did not invest his talent is that he thought it too small (at least by comparison) to bother with. He may even have been upset, and perhaps angry. Others had been given five and ten times as much. He would not be able to earn very much interest anyway. A lesson to be drawn from the parable might then be that even those who feel they have been given relatively little in life (who may even feel shortchanged) are expected to invest what they have.

Yet then there is the still more mysterious challenge of the gospel: "Whoever would save their life will lose it; and whoever lose their life will save it."[19] This saying has been heard through the Christian centuries as a call to sacrifice. Sometimes that losing of life has been interpreted largely in terms of denial of the world. More positively it has been heard as a challenge to accept the sacrifices that are demanded by lives of caring and service—especially as disciples learn from the dramatic scene that follows this parable of the talents in Matthew's Gospel: they can serve their Lord by giving food and drink to the hungry and thirsty, welcoming strangers, clothing those who have none, and visiting the sick and those in prison (Matt. 25:35–40). In that final judgment scene those who try to save by not caring for people in need do lose everything while those who serve find salvation, and it is understandable that disciples would want to think that they have thus discovered the formula: if individuals do the sacrificial losing called for in service to others, they will find themselves saved for eternal life—or, in more existentialist terms, they will come to experience the true values and meaning of life. This is what it means to lose one's life and find it. Hard—maybe in some ways it is almost impossible to do this—but at least one has the security of knowing what the rewards are to be. The terms are established.

But what if risking and losing one's life means going even one step further —means realizing that to lose one's life "in order" to save it is actually another way of trying to save one's life. As attractive as Christian service and charity often are, the one being helped can still have the feeling that these persons are helping only so that they can gain eternal life, that their present sacrifices are, in fact, long-term investments—a way of saving themselves for greater reward and divine commendation. *I am part of their game plan.*

Maybe being willing to lose one's life means being willing to risk losing eternal life too. The sure thing that is learned from the parable of the talents is that one cannot save anything without risking it. That is a tough and painful lesson to learn which many people probably eventually find out from life itself. It is a message that also is to be heeded by communities of people and societies—churches primarily engaged in serving only their own members and nations that would use military power and economic might to keep their peace, high values, and good life for themselves. The parable can be heard as a challenge to their ideas about saving and preserving and security.[20] In this sense it might even be said to be an "antiwisdom" story—a questioning of prudential ideas about how people finally get and keep what is really worthwhile. Especially does it challenge those who see being religious best expressed in sectarian living—trying to save their own purity and not the world. By way of contrast Jesus himself can be regarded as a model for reckless, unsafe living—careless about his reputation through his frequent association with those regarded as unclean and in his acts of healing on the Sabbath, which some saw as a violation of God's own law. He is a blasphemer, "a glutton and drunkard, a friend of tax collectors and sinners." He is even in league with the prince of demons.[21]

Yet this too might be acceptable if one could be sure in one's heart that a special approved place was being gained in the eternal scheme of things— that even now one was being regarded as more right than others. But being in the shoes of the third servant may be to realize that there are no guarantees. It is conceivable that one is living with a lose/lose possibility. Living so as to conserve and trying to keep for oneself and one's own is a way of losing. It is understandable why people cling to this way, but the end is tragedy. Yet risking and investing life beyond oneself could also lose. One can only find out by trying. Servants are in a tough spot.

13

HELP?

A Friend at Midnight

Which of you who has a friend will go to him at midnight and say to him, "Friend, lend me three loaves; for a friend of mine has arrived on a journey, and I have nothing to set before him"; and he will answer from within, "Do not bother me; the door is now shut, and my children are with me in bed; I cannot get up and give you anything"? I tell you, though he will not get up and give him anything because he is his friend, yet because of his importunity he will rise and give him whatever he needs.

Luke 11:5–8

The Unjust Judge

And he told them a parable, to the effect that they ought always to pray and not lose heart. He said, "In a certain city there was a judge who neither feared God nor regarded man; and there was a widow in that city who kept coming to him and saying, 'Vindicate me against my adversary.' For a while he refused; but afterward he said to himself, 'Though I neither fear God nor regard man, yet because this widow bothers me, I will vindicate her, or she will wear me out by her continual coming.'" And the Lord said, "Hear what the unrighteous judge says. And will not God vindicate his elect, who cry to him day and night? Will he delay long over them? I tell you, he will vindicate them speedily. Nevertheless, when the Son of man comes, will he find faith on earth?"

Luke 18:1–8

"Why do you stand afar off, O Lord? Why do you hide yourself in times of trouble? In arrogance the wicked hotly pursue the poor" (Ps. 10:1–2). "Rouse yourself! Why are you sleeping, O Lord?" (Ps. 44:23). In the time of the psalmist, during Jesus' ministry, and when Luke was writing his Gospel, and certainly during our years as well, God could and can seem very distant and even impassive—a God apparently deaf to human pleas. It is as though, the psalmist suggests, God were asleep. In the twentieth century this sense of God's absence is interpreted by some as God's nonexistence. That idea was not an option open to many people in biblical times, but they could acutely feel a sense of aloneness and helplessness in a scheme of things that did not evidence any special concern with flourishing injustice. God was invisible, and outward appearances often seemed to indicate that indifference and perhaps even evil were dominant. Did God hear the prayers of God's people?

These two stories seem to be a response to that doubt. Both of them look to be drawn from experiences with which almost everyone of the time would have been familiar. Indeed, one can imagine that listeners would have known a widow in trouble and perhaps also an unfeeling judge, or a neighbor who was asked for help in the middle of the night. Or they may have remembered when they themselves were in similar circumstances. Both parables are also rather like jokes—comic stories about the predicaments people find themselves in and how they get out of them. They do not have anything particularly to do with morality, and hearers realize the laugh would be on them were they to think that the stories were concerned with describing a mode of behavior they ought to emulate in their everyday lives. The clue to the way in which they both function as parables is to be found in Luke 11:11–13. "What father among you, if his son asks for a fish, will instead of a fish give him a serpent; or if he asks for an egg, will give him a scorpion? If you then, who are evil, know how to give good gifts to your children, how much more will the heavenly Father give the Holy Spirit to those who ask him!" If one who is not good, not caring, etc. can do what is good, then how much more will the one who is good do!

Luke has set the two parables in contexts having to do with prayer. One of the emphases of his Gospel is the importance and significance of prayer, and hearers are thus inclined to view the petitioners as the foremost figures in these little stories. One can also learn, however, by allowing the friend who was asleep and the judge to have major roles.

The parable of the widow and the judge is followed in the Gospel by the story of the righteous Pharisee and the repentant tax collector and their quite different prayers, but of more influence on the interpretation of the widow-judge relationship is the preceding chapter and the verses that come immediately before and after this parable. Much of chapter 17 is concerned with the coming of the kingdom as the day of the Son of man (known by disciples to be Jesus returning in glory and for judgment) and the need for faith. The question of the Pharisees (17:20) about when the kingdom of God was coming is also a question of Luke's church. In part the answer is that the kingdom of God is already happening "in the midst of you" (17:21), but it is also still to come in a dramatic consummation. That day is not known, but disciples are to trust that it surely will arrive. The disciples ask, "Where, Lord?" *How do we know when and where it is coming?* "Where the body is," Jesus responds, "there the eagles will be gathered" (17:37); that is, as suddenly as the vulture eagles appear (seemingly out of nowhere) when a creature falls in the desert, so will be the sudden advent of the day of consummation.

Then, to illustrate another of the evangelist's concerns (how in such circumstances disciples "ought always to pray and not lose heart"), the parable is told. Its two characters are stock figures, as is the widow's situation, yet they are drawn from common experience.[1] Even today (perhaps in certain countries especially, but also within the judicial system of any society) it is possible to feel this trapped and powerless. If the system works on the basis of bribery or liberal legal fees and one has limited resources, one has little recourse. Hearers are not told what this matter is about (probably it would be understood to be a question of money—perhaps having to do with the widow's inheritance),[2] because that is not of importance to the narrative. Very likely it was a minor matter as far as the judge was concerned, although one can believe it was not insignificant to the widow.

It must be remembered, too, that as a woman the widow would have had little legal standing. Among other things, she would have needed an advocate of some kind to present her case in court. But, of course, she had no husband and probably little money.[3]

One can imagine that the judge was waiting for some form of payment from the more powerful adversary of the widow, but the story itself does not actually describe the judge as corrupt.[4] That may be understood, but what the parable does emphasize is that he is not going to be moved by conscience or what other people think. He even says this about himself. Public opinion or any fear of God will not cause him to act any faster or decide the case one way or another. It will do no good, in other words, for the widow to appeal to morality or the customs and standards of the community.

Without money, influence, or even the help of an appeal to fairness, what is she to do? She uses the only weapon she has: she makes a pest of herself. In a relatively small town it would not be hard to know where the judge was most of the time. Perhaps for more than a week now she has been outside his house when he has left for work, trying to keep up with him as he strode quickly away—plucking at his sleeve, again telling him how unfair her adversary was. When she could get near enough to the proceedings, she popped up every time a case was decided and shouted that she should be heard next. When court recessed and again when the day was done, there the stubborn widow was, sometimes whispering but more often railing. It was getting so that he could hear her in his sleep. She has got on his nerves. Finally he tells himself, Because this widow bothers me I will vindicate her, before she wears me out with her obstinacy.

The introductory verse suggests that Christians are to be similarly persistent and importunate in their prayers. This emphasis is picked up again in the allegorizing summary when it is maintained that God will surely vindicate his elect who cry to God day and night, although there then is the question as to whether people will have the faith to be persistent and trusting until the Son of man comes, he who will be the judge at the end of time and set all things right.

At least as important to the parable, however, is the figure of the unrighteous judge. One can find nothing good to say about him, but as the commentary first implies and then states, if even one such as this will vindicate the widow because of the trouble she is causing, "will not God vindicate his elect?" Moreover, we are told, this vindication—though it may appear delayed in coming—is really not slow in the way that of the judge may well have seemed. "Will he delay long over them? I tell you he will vindicate them speedily."[5] This last word with its sense of imminence again recalls the tone of the previous chapter, in which the kingdom and the day of the Son of man are said to come without warning, perhaps when people least expect it.

So do these final verses (which probably represent the concern of the evangelist mixed with earlier interpretation)[6] offer the assurance of God's vindication before too much longer, while also asking disciples if they have the faith to be persistent in their trust and prayers. The theme of vindication (*ekdikeō*, vv. 3, 5; *ekdikēsis*, vv. 7, 8) joins the story and its commentary first in expectation and then in promise. The emphasis of the Greek word translated as "vindicate" is not on vengeance but on setting things right—making justice. In the story it may suggest that the judge himself will now act as the widow's advocate in court, presenting her case for her. In the commentary God (known in the Scriptures and other traditions as the truly incorruptible and righteous one)[7] is the judge and advocate of the chosen, who will render "justice" and so in this way show that this is the God in whom the faithful are right to put their trust. In tune with the use of a humorous story to encourage this belief, there is also a little play on words: the widow pleads for "justice" to be made against her adversary or opponent (*antidikos*). The judge "makes justice" despite his being not just (*adikia*). How much more will God "make justice" for his elect and "make justice" speedily!

The earlier Lukan story also tells of an individual who makes a request of someone who gives what is asked for only because he feels pressured to do so. The grammar and the translation of one key word in the parable are sufficiently ambiguous, however, that it is difficult to be sure of the story's major emphasis. On one hearing the person asking for the bread is the more central figure, and one would have a rendering along these lines:

> Suppose one of you has a friend, and he comes at midnight and says, "My friend, lend me three loaves of bread, since a friend of mine on a journey has just arrived and I have nothing to put before him." And suppose the man inside replies, "Do not bother me! The door is already bolted, and my children and I are in bed. I cannot get up and give you anything now." I tell you, even if he will not get up and give it to him because he is his friend, because of his persistence he will rouse himself and give him as much as he needs.[8]

On this interpretation the stress seems to fall on the persistence of the caller, and one is reminded not only of the widow but of Luke's introduction to that parable (". . . that they ought always to pray and not lose heart"). This sense of the story of the persistent friend also seems to be picked up by the two following verses, which tell hearers to ask, seek, and knock, for those who do will receive, find, and have it opened to them.

With a bit more strain on the Greek, the story can also plausibly be translated in such a way that the awakened friend emerges more prominently. The story proper is then one long rhetorical question:[9]

Which among you has a friend and going to him in the middle of the night says to him, "Friend, lend me three loaves, for a friend of mine has arrived on a journey and I have nothing to set before him"; and he will answer from within, "Do not bother me; the door is now shut and my children are with me in bed; I cannot get up and give you anything"? I tell you, though he will not get up and give him anything because he is his friend, yet because of his not wanting to be ashamed he will rise and give him whatever he needs.

This hearing of the parable seems then to be picked up in the subsequent verses, vv. 11 and 12, which ask "what father among you" (again a rhetorical question, beginning with quite similar wording to the opening of the parable) would not give good gifts to his children. Then "how much more will the heavenly Father give the Holy Spirit to those who ask him?" One is at least tempted to guess that vv. 11 and 12 (perhaps with the "good things" of Matthew's version rather than Luke's Holy Spirit) were an earlier interpretive commentary for a parable that primarily concerned itself with the friend who in fact would not refuse the request despite the lateness of the hour. That possibility is made more complicated, however, by the fact that Matt. 7: 7–11 has the equivalent two pairs of verses about seeking and receiving and the father's gifts in the same order but without Luke's preceding parable. But it is not impossible that Matthew omitted what seemed to him a rather strange parable and kept the appended sayings of which the words about seeking and receiving are secondary.

In any event, even in Luke's source the parable may well have been in some tension between two rather different ways of hearing the story, and this could account for some of the ambiguity in the Greek text. The translation that focuses on the awakened householder and his giving of the bread because he does not wish to be ashamed seems a better way of rendering the Greek word *anaideia*, which is usually translated as "persistence" or "importunity" and attributed to the petitioner, and early hearers of the story may already have been drawing their lesson from the petitioner's "lack of shame" in making his late-night request.[10]

In other words, whether it is a result of Luke's ways of construing the story or the result of earlier interpretive activity, we have now another illustration of how the churches began to find "many things in parables." Perhaps, in the way of parable, there was a degree of openness built into the story to begin with, allowing for focus on either character or, in a more complex manner, on the event itself and the interchange between them. The evidence tends, however, toward putting the sleepy householder center stage in this humorous vignette drawn from an experience anyone could identify with.

The time is midnight, the setting probably a small town where everyone knows everyone else. A friend traveling in the evening to avoid the heat of the day arrives at a very late hour, and there is little or nothing to give him. The oven cannot be heated until the morning to make the bread essential to the meal.[11] Yet the duty of hospitality is great, and so, despite the hour and the disturbance the host will cause, he goes to call on one of his neighbors. He would know who had recently baked bread and who would have enough to lend the three small loaves to make a good meal. No doubt presuming a bit on their relationship, he calls to him, "Friend," and briefly tells the story of the friend who has come to visit him. Friendship has led him to make this request. Surely, it is suggested, you will understand.

Anyone who has ever been awakened at such an hour by a knock or a call with a similar request knows how one first feels like reacting. In Palestine at that time the householder would have been sleeping on a mat in a one-room building with his family about him. The work of unlocking the door (probably drawing a bar from between two rings fixed to the doors) would have been somewhat cumbersome and noisy—waking the children. One notices that he does not reply, "Friend," in return! Nonetheless, will he say, "Do not bother me; the door is now shut and my children are with me in bed; I cannot [meaning I will not] get up and give you anything"? No, of course not, is the answer to the rhetorical question. These would be flimsy excuses indeed. Not wanting to be ashamed, he will get up and give him whatever he needs.

If then (hearers were probably meant to conclude, and certainly early interpreters and/or Luke did) a half-awake friend would give the needed bread, not because of friendship but in order to avoid shame, how much more will God respond with what is most needed. Most listeners to Luke's Gospel would also remember that just a few moments earlier (11:3) disciples had been taught to pray, "Give us each day our daily bread." This, the parable suggests, God will surely do.

14
SURPRISE!

The Seed Growing Secretly

And he said, "The kingdom of God is as if a man should scatter seed upon the ground, and should sleep and rise night and day, and the seed should sprout and grow, he knows not how. The earth produces of itself, first the blade, then the ear, then the full grain in the ear. But when the grain is ripe, at once he puts in the sickle, because the harvest has come."

Mark 4:26–29

The Mustard Seed

And he said, "With what can we compare the kingdom of God, or what parable shall we use for it? It is like a grain of mustard seed, which, when sown upon the ground, is the smallest of all the seeds on earth; yet when it is sown it grows up and becomes the greatest of all shrubs, and puts forth large branches, so that the birds of the air can make nests in its shade."

Mark 4:30–32; see Matt. 13:31–32; Luke 13:18–19

Even after studying plant biology (perhaps especially after studying plant biology) one finds something mysterious about putting seeds in the ground and then waiting for them to germinate and grow. For days one may mark time—hovering each morning and evening over the buried seed, wondering if and how life can come from this apparent death. Suddenly one day, apparently too fast for scrutiny, there appear shoots above the ground, now seeming almost to grow before one's eyes. While the farmer may work to help, what next happens seems beyond calculation. Before long there is a field of waving plants. How could so much have come from so little? Biologists are properly awe-struck. Farmers speak of miracle, and it is probably best to call upon poets if there are to be any words at all. Indeed, the several New Testament parables about seeds and planting are in their way poetry, using aspects of the wonder and mystery of seed growth to allude to the still more profound mystery inherent in the trust that God creates all life and will fulfill its intention.

There are four presentations of the story of the mustard seed in the several Gospels, behind which can be glimpsed two and possibly three older traditions. Matthew has evidently combined Mark's version of the story with one

from a source he shared with Luke.[1] As is to be expected, the evangelist has
fitted the parable into his teaching context and used it to speak to the concerns and hopes of the church of his locale and generation. By mingling the
two versions Matthew has fashioned an interesting mixture of narrative and
explanation—a kind· of combined fable and similitude, allowing him to use
the basic figure for several purposes at once.

His presentation begins with a statement rather than a question (as in
Mark and Luke), indicating that the major function is to teach more directly
rather than to involve hearers in a process of discovery. In narrative fashion,
and with words very similar to Luke's, the story then opens in the past tense
but quickly shifts to present, direct speech and the more expository form of a
similitude. The present tense is then retained and (differently from Luke's
the birds "made nests" and Mark's potential "can make nests") the birds
"make nests" in the tree. The picture that Matthew thus presents is of a tree
that is grown from the smallest of seeds and is even now a gathering place for
birds.

Perhaps one should not read too much into Matthew's use of this relatively
brief parable, but, given the context of the evangelist's concerns about the
life of the church and, more particularly, the teachings of the other parables
in his chapter 13, it is difficult not to imagine his audience hearing a series of
allusions in the story and understanding it in a quasi-allegorical manner. As
in the preceding parable of the wheat and weeds and its subsequent interpretation, the sower of this seed would be the Son of man, Jesus. As is
stated, the kingdom of heaven is like the mustard seed. It was planted in a
"field." Commentators point out that this description is probably horticultur-
ally more correct than Luke's "garden" or Mark's more general "ground"
(i.e., the mustard bush was usually cultivated in a field rather than known as
a wild bush or grown in a garden), but here it may well also refer to Israel or
at least the general setting of Jesus' ministry.[2]

This seed or kingdom began as something very small, but now has grown
to be not only the greatest of shrubs but a veritable tree. The kingdom and
the church should probably not be simply identified, but the church is presumably what Matthew has in mind as like the tree, in the branches of which
the birds make their nests. Jewish Christian hearers would almost surely recall the image of the tree used in the Scriptures as a figure for the nation that
would grow and become a haven for other peoples. "The beasts of the field
found shade under it, and the birds of the air dwelt in its branches" (Dan.
4:12). "In the shade of its branches birds of every sort will nest" (Ezek.
17:23). This awareness would lead naturally to the understanding that this
tree of the kingdom/church has now become a gathering place for the Gentiles.

While there are end-of-the-ages overtones in this use of the figure of the
great tree and in the verb used to describe the nesting of the birds,[3] the
evangelist's focus seems more on what the church as the kingdom now has

become than on what it will be. One of his purposes is thus to chide and argue with the continuing people of Israel of his time who had not recognized Jesus as the Messiah or the coming of the kingdom. The kingdom, not yet here in its fullness, is already the promised new home for the Gentiles. And, yes, it began as something very small and insignificant. But this, too, was in the plan of God, and see what it now is!

What can result from what is small and seemingly insignificant to begin with is still more obviously the point illustrated by the companion parable of the "woman who took and hid leaven in three measures of meal, till it was all leavened" (Matt. 13:33). The use of the word "hid" seems to emphasize how unimportant this crucial element can seem to normal vision. It may also allude to the insight that the hearing of parables and the good news of the gospel more generally have a secret character that is not realized by those who are unable truly to see and hear.[4] In keeping with other Gospel parables the amounts involved are not paltry. Three measures of meal would be a good deal to bake at one time and should make enough bread to feed at least a hundred people.

Luke evidently also found these two parables joined together, but he does not link them with other seed parables or have them in a context concerned with the hearing of parables.[5] Both are quickly told—the leaven in form virtually identical with Matthew's simile and the mustard seed without being combined with Markan language (Luke 13:18–21). His preceding story tells of a Sabbath healing, coupled with Jesus' response to an objection to healing on the Sabbath. The passage concludes, "All his adversaries were put to shame; and all the people rejoiced at all the glorious things that were done by him" (13:17). The two parables then seem to reflect on the wonderful ways in which the kingdom of God is now manifesting itself. Probably Luke would have thought of the birds as a figure for the Gentiles come to nest in the tree of the kingdom. He does not develop this image, however, and his hearers may only have envisaged people like the woman Jesus had healed finding a home and protection in the branches of the kingdom.

The evangelist, of course, recognizes that the kingdom began with what was small by the world's standards, but he does not wish to suggest that it was in some way insignificant or obscure in the teaching and ministry of Jesus. In many ways Luke's Gospel is a success story from beginning to end, only temporarily impeded by the opposition of the religious officials and the crucifixion. The parables are then heard as assurances: See what the kingdom is becoming—what it has and will become. To make this success significant and dramatic, however, it is necessary to stress the opposition encountered, as Luke does in what follows the two parables. He also wants to remind his hearers of the hard truth that there are those who will try to enter the kingdom but will not be able. The question "Lord, will those who are saved be few?" (though it does not seem to fit very well with the thrust of the parables) may be influenced by the idea of small beginnings.

The *Gospel of Thomas* also makes use of both parables although they are not joined together.[6] The similitude of the mustard seed is presented simply without much adornment. "[The kingdom of heaven] is like a mustard seed, the smallest of all seeds. But when it falls on tilled soil, it produces a large plant and becomes shelter for the birds of the sky" (saying 20). The only evident Thomas-like addition is the stress on the largeness of the plant, which reminds one of the large fish in the net parable, the large loaves that result from the leaven, and the lost sheep that is the largest.[7] These are the specially prized ones. In this case, however, the emphasis on size follows the basic plan of the core parable, and Thomas is also otherwise consistent with the outline found in the other versions: from small mustard seed to a substantial shrub or tree in which birds find some form of shelter.

Into this basic pattern Mark seems to have introduced phrases emphasizing the smallness of the seed and the size of the grown plant, thus creating some repetitiveness and what appears like grammatical awkwardness, although the chiastic a-b-c-b-a patterning ("when it is sown on the earth, is the smallest of all the seeds on the earth, yet when it is sown . . .") nicely concentrates hearing on the tiny seed. Commentators are not agreed on the evangelist's primary way of understanding the parable, and it is quite possible that Mark was contemplating more than one idea. Probably of most importance in this regard is the context, having to do with Jesus' use of parables and the awareness that the seeds, representing the word of God, do not always produce good fruit. In some ways Mark appears to be of two minds about the parables. He wants to stress his understanding that their true value and meaning can only be known by those to whom the secret of the kingdom of God has been given; yet that secret is not meant to remain obscure forever. "For there is nothing hid, except to be manifest; nor is anything secret, except to come to light" (Mark 4:22). Already the hearers of the Gospel—who know what is to come—have perceived the great mystery that leads through death to the awaited glorious appearance of Jesus as the Son of man and his judgment. One day all the world will know of God's purpose, although in this present time the parables remain opaque to many. Into this somewhat ambiguous and perhaps even paradoxical setting the parable of the mustard seed fits very nicely, for it is possible to emphasize either the way the smallness of the seed may cause its potential to be unrecognized or what that potential in fact is. By means of parable it can also be said that both ways of perceiving the seed are correct.

The preceding parable of the seed that grows the planter "knows not how" influences the hearing of the mustard-seed story. Patience is required but also faith that the seed will produce. As is the case with the parable of the sower, revelation may need to be given to hearers if they are to recognize that the word/kingdom is in fact producing in abundance. Those who do hear and perceive, however, will realize that this promise is not just for the future. More realistically than Matthew and Luke, Mark keeps to the figure: the little seed becomes a surprisingly large "shrub" rather than a tree with lofty branches. It is, however, of sufficient size that birds can make nests under its protection, and the phraseology again recalls the scriptural figure of the tree that becomes the haven for other nations.

It may be that this final consideration was more in the mind of those who passed the tradition on before the Gospel was written than it was of Mark himself. They would have wished to include the understanding that the destiny of Israel was now being fulfilled through the Christian community as Gentiles came to found their home in it. Indeed, the evidence suggests that the little parable was frequently used in the early church and that its attractiveness was due in no small measure to its openness to interpretation, an openness that continues among preachers and commentators today.

It is, however, probably best in keeping with the parable as a whole to try to hold both the tiny seed and the ten-foot shrub in the mind's eye at once. The essential parable witnessed to by the several Gospels appears little concerned with the process of growth. What would have captured the imagination of the people of the first century was how rapidly so relatively much came from so little. In some ways a mustard shrub may not be all that impressive, but if one is standing next to this big bush (virtually twice a person's size) while contemplating a tiny black speck of a mustard seed, one has to be fairly blasé not to be surprised and even awe-struck.[8] It seems more than likely that early Christians told the story as a form of assurance—to say, See what the kingdom has become or is becoming (as Jesus foretold), or to hold out the promise of what was yet to be. One can also well imagine that some Christians meditated on the parable with the crucial events that were the root of their faith in mind. From a seemingly dead body buried in the earth had burst forth their great and growing faith. The fourth evangelist, although evidently not much interested in the kind of parables found in the other Gospels, does present Jesus reflecting in a similar way: "Unless a grain of wheat falls into the earth and dies, it remains alone; but if it dies, it bears much fruit" (John 12:24).

It is, of course, considerably more difficult to make an informed guess with regard to whether and how Jesus may have used this parable. What can be said is that it seems to be congruent with several other of the early parables and emphases of Jesus' ministry. Especially is this true with regard to the surprise of what happens and one's amazement at the results. Looking at themselves and others in the motley collection around Jesus, and seeing the growing opposition he was encountering, the disciples must have had questions. Perhaps like John the Baptist they at some point asked, "Are you he who is to come, or shall we look for another?" (Matt. 11:3; Luke 7:20).

Or they may have wondered how the kingdom really could manifest itself, struggling against such great odds. The parable might have been part of Jesus' response, and/or it may have been used to answer those of his opponents who challenged his teaching that the kingdom was even now manifesting itself in the world. Yes, these were only small beginnings looked at in one way—and perhaps improbable people: fishermen, tax collectors, and the like. But the eyes and ears of faith saw and heard differently. As was the case with the story of the seeds sown, many of which did not produce, the final result will yet surprise. Or again, invited guests may have turned down the invitation, but the house will be full. The party will take place.

Those who continue to try to follow in the ways of the kingdom also continue to find hope and encouragement in the story, for it is still true that love and efforts for justice and peace seem paltry against the forces of human greed, fear, and anger. Why keep on sowing them? What will they produce? Yet, the parable is heard to say that in the mystery of God's purposes and providence they do yield. The little acts of caring that humans have to offer can bring surprising results.

Those commentators who point out that the mustard bush is still far from the most magnificent plant in the world may, however, also be right to suggest that there could be a certain tongue-in-cheek aspect to this story. Its size may be surprising when compared with its tiny seed, but the bush that grows to a height between eight and twelve feet and is relatively short-lived can in no way be accounted a great tree. The use of the figure might tend to undercut those who had political or worldly ambitions for either Israel or God's kingdom. It is instead an "unpretentious venture of faith."[9] At least one ought to be careful before using the parable as the text for a sermon evocative of Christian triumphalism. There is and has always been a perspective from which the ways of the kingdom are a lowly bush when measured against what the world counts as high and mighty. Even after the kingdom has made its surprising appearance it may still look rather improbable in the eyes of those who govern and run the world's business.

With this awareness in mind, one might doubt that the earlier uses of the parable spoke of a tree rather than a bush. It is understandable why later Christians developed the idea of the wonderfully protective character of the kingdom along the lines of the scriptural image, but the previous picture may have more modestly suggested how, in the shade it provides, small birds can find shelter.

It is possible that the parable was once used to allude to still another insight: that humans do not have that much to do with the growth that takes place, that it is first and foremost the activity of God. This thought was probably in Mark's mind and is one reason why he joined it to the story of the seed that grows the planter "knows not how." It may well have been because they did not want to encourage disciples already prone to laxity that Matthew and Luke do not use this story.

Any farmer can attest to the truth of the insight. It is not that farmers do not have to work hard. They have critical roles to play in the sowing and harvesting, but there is also a time for letting Mother Nature or the process of growth do its work. This principle of growth comes from God. It cannot be rushed, and there often is not much that a lot of activity can do to improve upon it. Indeed, too much scratching at the root or walking out in the fields could be counterproductive. "The earth produces *of itself* [*automatē*]" and "when the grain *is ripe* [passive verb: *paradoi*]" suggest the natural operation. In this sense the parable of the seed that grows one knows not how also echoes the exhortation to patience heard in the story of the wheat and weeds and perhaps in all the Gospels' seed parables. Christians live in the difficult and in many ways perplexing time between sowing and harvest, but one can trust that what God has begun God will bring to conclusion.[10]

There is a message here for those in the church and world who believe nothing can happen without their endeavors. It is sometimes too much human activity, too much competition, overproduction, the overuse of resources, creating consumer demand and trying to fulfill it, which can, in fact, corrupt the environment and dehumanize rather than enhance life. Some people more than others need to be reminded that humans also have a more passive role to play in the creation—one of listening, admiring, sitting on the porch, and looking out over the fields.

Yet the parable seems to offer at least a double message, for also now "at once" or "suddenly" (when the grain is ripe) the man is to put in his sickle, "for the harvest has come." (The phraseology is drawn from Joel 3:13 and its vision of the day of judgment.) There is a critical time for the ingathering and an inevitability about the process. It may appear to be a long wait, but there will be a harvest. In Jesus' message, that time may well have seemed very near. Some commentators see the major thrust of the parable moving in this direction. The emphasis is on the time of reaping and action. Although Mark may have used the story with other purposes in mind, it was earlier meant as a parable about the urgency and consequent activity that is called for now that the harvest has drawn nigh. The central focus of the parable is not on the seed but on the human (*anthrōpos*).[11]

That interpretation may well serve as a corrective to those who would only hear this parable as an exhortation to patience and for waiting upon God. Probably, however, hearers must again yield to the deliberate ambiguity of the way of parable and recognize that wisdom may be found in multiple themes, even those that rub against one another.[12] There is a time of waiting and a time of action. Humans bear responsibility but they are not finally in charge. As one of Christianity's shorter prayers expresses it, "Teach us to care and not to care."[13] It is not that disciples are to care sometimes and not at others. Rather are they to be careless while caring. Both caring and a careless trust in God are signs of faith. Indeed, it is only the latter that may make it possible to care when all else indicates that there is no reason for caring —when the cause for hope seems minuscule at best. There is a mystery at work to which the secret of seeds alludes. Why there is life and what it finally will produce are still to be known. Be ready, for that time of harvest comes.

15
WASTE AND GRACE

The Sower

"Listen! A sower went out to sow. And as he sowed, some seed fell along the path, and the birds came and devoured it. Other seed fell on rocky ground, where it had not much soil, and immediately it sprang up, since it had no depth of soil; and when the sun rose it was scorched, and since it had no root it withered away. Other seed fell among thorns and the thorns grew up and choked it, and it yielded no grain. And other seeds fell into good soil and brought forth grain, growing up and increasing and yielding thirtyfold and sixtyfold and a hundredfold." And he said, "He who has ears to hear, let him hear."

Mark 4:3–9; see Matt. 13:3–9; Luke 8:5–8

Along the way so much is lost in life while yet also there is much gain. How is that loss and yield to be understood?[1]

What seems in some ways like the simplest of parables can also be heard as one of the more mysterious. Although some scholars maintain that the parable and its interpretation have always belonged together, it seems more likely that the versions of that explanation found in Mark's (4:13–20), Matthew's (13:18–23), and Luke's (8:11–15) Gospels were an attempt to apply the story to subsequent circumstances.[2] Some nineteen centuries later, with the development of critical historical and literary methods of reading, it has become possible to separate the parable from its interpretation. Yet although modern scholarship appears to have been successful in enabling an earlier form of the parable to stand forth, it has proved far more difficult to know how it then would have been heard or, for that matter, to know how it might best be understood today.[3]

The interpretation accompanying the parable in the three Gospels had probably already been added to the narrative before the time of the evangelists in the preaching and teaching life of the churches.[4] While it is, of course, difficult to be certain how the parable together with its interpretation was used in first-century Christian communities, it seems that it may have been heard with as many as three purposes in mind: as a warning about what could happen when the word was not well and rightly received, as an explanation of the lack of success the preaching of the word of God sometimes encountered, and finally as assurance with respect to the ultimate fruit of the word. Perhaps the interpreted parable was found to be especially valuable as a way of understanding the frustration and concern a number of Christians must have felt over the evident failure of the word to take root and produce as powerfully as they thought it ought to. How could it not always bear fruit when it was the word of God?

The interpretation explains that in some cases Satan (like the birds) snatches away the word before it can grow. Sometimes the word does begin to grow but on rocky ground, and, since it is without any root, tribulation and persecution do it in. Others who do hear are (like the seed among the thorns) choked off by the cares and riches of the world. Only those that are sown on good soil produce abundantly. So it is with the church's mission. Its sowing of the word of God does produce abundantly, but only when it falls upon the right kind of soil.

The interpretation rocks somewhat unsteadily back and forth between viewing the seeds as the words or as disciples, and the disciples as seeds or like the soil conditions, but it makes sufficient sense to have appealed in one way or another to generations of believers. Mark was clearly very glad to make use of it to offer encouragement and assurance to Christians of his time: despite difficulties and appearances to the contrary, the word of God was producing and would produce plentifully. But a special emphasis was then given to the story by setting it at the head of a collection of parables in this Gospel and using it and its interpretation as a guide for understanding the purpose of parables.[5] Between the story and its explanation Mark set words attributed to Jesus that have proved to be among the most difficult of Gospel sayings:

> And when Jesus was alone, those who were about him with the twelve asked him concerning the parables. And he said to them, "To you has been given the secret of the kingdom of God, but for those outside everything is in parables, so that they may indeed see but not perceive, and may indeed hear but not understand; lest they should turn again and be forgiven." (Mark 4:10–12)

Since this teaching seems to conflict with several sayings attributed to Jesus and appears to make illogical his extensive use of parables, many scholars see these words as largely a Markan creation or at least a distortion of earlier tradition.[6] But the difficulties they present to modern hearers should not inhibit the recognition that Mark meant them to accompany the parable and interpretation as words of comfort and encouragement for those hearing his Gospel. Others do not understand the meaning of the parables. There are reasons for this which this parable explains. *This can all be seen as part of the divine plan. But to you* (although the first disciples had difficulty in understanding, 4:13) *has been given their understanding*—the mystery (*to mystērion*) of the kingdom of God. "Privately, to his own disciples, Jesus explained everything" (4:34). *You are the ones who hear the word and can accept it and bear fruit abundantly.*

Matthew also uses the parable and presents Jesus then speaking about the meaning of parables, followed by the parable's interpretation (13:3–23), at the beginning of his lengthy collection of parables. A reading of this entire chapter with its additions and changes shows Matthew making it clear that Jesus' true disciples (both those who were first with Jesus and those of Matthew's time) do understand the parables (13:51: "Have you understood all this?" They said to him, "Yes," and the implied rebuke to the disciples of Mark 4:13 is eliminated), while he spells out the scriptural text (Isa. 6:9–10 in 13:14–15) indicating that Jesus fulfills God's will by teaching in parables in order that others do not "understand" (Matt. 13:13). The interpretation then further explains how and why this is so, and the evangelist twice emphasizes (in negative and then in positive terms) the importance of not only hearing the word but "understanding" it (13:19, 23).

In other more subtle ways Matthew continues the process of fitting the parable and its allegorical interpretation more closely together. The "rocky ground," for which Mark uses a singular word in his parable and its plural in the interpretation, becomes plural in both instances in Matthew, probably to agree with his understanding of the seed as plural throughout the parable and interpretation. With Mark, Matthew sees this teaching as encouragement and assurance for the contemporary church, but, more than Mark, Matthew also uses it as exhortation and advice: Do not be among those who only hear the word but do not understand it.

By disassociating this material from other parables and providing the context of a preaching tour of Jesus, Luke has shifted the emphasis of the parable and interpretation from a concern with the use of parables to the theme of Christian preaching and discipleship more generally (8:5–15). Although he retains the hard saying that for others the secrets of the kingdom are in parables so that they may not see and understand, he abbreviates it and also eliminates Mark 4:13 with its reference to the disciples' difficulty in understanding. The disciples are able to understand the parable without any serious difficulty, and probably, from Luke's perspective, many others do as well. With the addition of the words "that they may not believe and be saved" (8:12), he shifts the responsibility for the unbelief of some individuals much more to the work of the devil. In other ways, too, Luke typically smooths out the Markan material, especially the allegorical interpretation.

The overall result is much more the homiletic exhortation to a faithful Christian life (avoiding the dangers of shallowness of faith and of yielding to life's cares, riches, and pleasures) that has provided the themes for most subsequent preaching on this passage. Those who have no root are said to be ones "who have faith for a while and in time of temptation fall away" (8:13). Luke's wording alludes more to the disciples' life of daily temptations than to Mark's suggestion ("when tribulation or persecution arises on account of the word") of a great crisis of persecution before the day of judgment. The "hundredfold" final produce in Luke's parable is not taken up in the interpretation and, instead of Mark's praise for those "who hear the word and accept it" and Matthew's "hears the word and understands," there is Luke's recognition of those who, "hearing the word, hold it fast in an honest and good heart and bring forth fruit with patience" (8:15). Again the thought seems to be addressed to the circumstances of daily living and parallels the more Hellenistic descriptions of a person of honor and fortitude. "Faithful Endurance" could well be the title given to Luke's splendid little commentary.

It is debatable whether the absence of the interpretation in the *Gospel of Thomas*'s presentation of the parable (saying 9) means that Thomas had access to a source with a version of the narrative before the interpretation was added. What is of perhaps more importance is to see that Thomas attests to the way in which the basic features of the parable strongly asserted themselves and are unchanged in the presentations of all four of the Gospels: sowing, path, rocks, thorns, good soil, and yield.[7]

In then trying to see if it is possible to reach back to an earlier form of the parable on the basis of Mark's presentation (which is probably the oldest extant version), the opening word "listen" and verse 4:9 can likely be removed as the evangelist's way of framing the story. The largest addition to the parable seems to have occurred at 4:5–6. The description of what happens to the seed on rocky ground is repetitive and almost twice as long as the descriptions of what overcame the seed on the path and among the thorns. There is general agreement that something has been added to these verses (probably to correspond with the interpretation of 4:16–17) but not as to whether it has to do with the withering caused by the shallow soil over the rocky ground or the scorching effects of the sun.[8] These are different processes —the scorching taking place rather rapidly, the withering more slowly. There is no obvious basis for deciding which is more original (and it will not make that much difference for subsequent reflection), but it is probably best to remove the description of the withering. Like the birds and the thorns, the sun is an outside agent acting on the seed, and it is a little easier to see how the idea of withering was added to scorching. By also removing the description of the quick growth of the seeds (more germane to an interpretation of facile discipleship) and the redundant stress on little soil, a triadic statement like the scheme of the preceding and following verses emerges. In keeping with the pattern of the entire parable, it is likely that a simple coordination of phrase using *kai*, "and," was the earlier, oral construct of this statement.

The other possible additions to the parable consist of just a few words. "And it yielded no grain" in 4:7 was likely added in the light of the interpretation to emphasize the understanding that those who were choked off by cares and riches were unproductive. "Growing up and increasing" in 4:8 may also be an addition to stress the ongoing growth of the kingdom and Christian community. The phrase is absent in the *Gospel of Thomas*'s version.[9]

One notices that the sower quickly disappears from the parable and that the story could easily begin, "As a sower sowed." It is possible that the short sentence "Now a sower went out to sow" was added at some stage to try to give a greater role to the sower seen either as a disciple or Jesus, although the introduction as it stands does anticipate the triadic structure of the rest of the parable.[10] Otherwise the phrasing of the introduction has little effect on interpretation. It can here be recognized, however, that the story might better be called the parable "of the seeds" than "of the sower." This seems better than the alternative "of the soils," which is sometimes suggested, since, although it is the soil conditions that vary, the interest is on what happens to the seeds.

Finally, before setting out a reconstruction of an earlier version of the parable, we may concur with almost all commentators in the view that Mark's "thirty-," "sixty-," "one hundredfold" best preserves the sense of the earlier story. Matthew has reversed the order, perhaps to allude to what he regarded as the slowing zeal of Christians. Mark has retained the triadic structure, which Luke simplifies to one hundred and Thomas to a more mathematically neat sixty and one hundred twenty, probably on the principle of doubling.

Thus an earlier version of the parable might have been heard like this:

Now a sower went out to sow.
And it happened in the sowing that

some fell by the path/and the birds came/and ate it.
And other fell on rocky ground/and the sun rose/and scorched it.
And other fell among thorns/and the thorns grew up/and choked it.

And other fell on good soil/and brought forth grain/and yielded
thirtyfold/and sixtyfold/and a hundredfold.

The strong triadic structure that has guided this reconstruction is now evident. It is present internally within the individual lines or verses, and one notices the three instances of growth corresponding to three kinds of loss. Although the act of sowing itself is not stressed in the telling, it is still intrinsically essential, thus also giving an overall triadic structure of sowing, loss, and yield. In its brevity the story seems little concerned with the process of growth but presents, as it were, a series of snapshots of the field—a kind of triptych with the central panel most fully developed.

But what is being said? In what direction is the parable leading or luring its listeners? Toward what other stories in their lives may it be hinting? And is it to be regarded as a parable of Jesus, congruent with other of his parables and other aspects of his teaching? Here there are no agreements. The relative ease with which the early church's interpretation can be lifted away contrasts with the difficulty in interpretation.

It is certainly possible that the parable had an at least semi-allegorical significance in its initial design. One recalls a number of allegories and similitudes regarding vines, trees, and seeds, and their growth, in the Jewish Scriptures and the intertestamental literature. Sometimes these are tied to particular historical circumstances, but their reference can also be more general. The poet-prophet who composed the second part of the Book of Isaiah speaks of the grass that withers and flower that fades when the breath of the Lord blows upon them, while the word of God stands forever (Isa. 40:7–8). In Isa. 55:10–11 the word of the Lord is likened to the falling rain and snow that do not fail to bring forth and give seed to the sower and bread to the eater. More directly comparable to the Gospel story is this short parable from 2 Esd. 8:41:

> For just as the farmer sows many seeds upon the ground and plants a multitude of seedlings, and yet not all that have been sown will come up in due season, and not all that are planted will take root; so also those who have been sown in the world will not all be saved.

Along similar lines, the Gospel parable about seeds falling into four different circumstances could be a kind of meditation on prospects for salvation—a story certainly susceptible to fuller allegorical development.

Some interpreters find that the parable speaks still more widely to the human condition. Life is a series of strivings, losses, and successes indigenous to many ventures: fishing, hunting, mining, investing.[11] Despite much frustration and loss, the human race (clearly the story would now speak inclusively and not just to individuals) can take comfort and even new hope in the awareness that life has its successes and victories. Buoyed by the natural processes that bring about new harvest amid natural disasters, people can know that there will be food, and also seed for next season's sowing.

Should the story be given so ordinary a hearing? The answer depends in part on one's understanding of the naturalness of what is pictured in the three panels of the triptych.

The loss involved in the sowing process may or may not be a surprise to modern people, but it was probably not to the story's first audience. Some commentators have in the past argued for a practice odd by the standards of western farming: sowing before plowing.[12] The sower (perhaps at the second or autumn planting, when the sun and drought have leveled earlier grass and weeds) throws his seed and then plows it in. There would be a natural expectation of a degree of loss and perhaps some surprise as to where seed does not and does flourish.

The more normal method of sowing seems, however, to have been prevalent at that time,[13] although anyone who has seen the rocky and often uneven fields throughout much of the Palestinian region would recognize that there would have to be an expectation of natural loss even after the most careful preparation of the ground. The frustration might then be greater, and there could be a greater degree of surprise about where and when the seed does and does not grow, but the farmer has to learn to live with both. In any event, what happens in the parable does not seem dependent on the method of sowing. Nor is the care or lack of care of the sower emphasized. The act of sowing was likely meant to be quite natural and not unusual.

Is the measure of the loss that unusual? One commentator has seen a special note of violence in the action of the birds, the sun, and the weeds.[14] Yet they are, after all, three natural enemies of the farmer. Without denying that the hearer is given a sense of nature's onslaught, and that the fact of loss is stressed, one need not understand there to be anything strange or surprising about the depletion. At least some years that is what happens.

The question about the naturalness of the final produce is the most difficult to decide and the most critical for the understanding of the force of the story. It is possible, to begin with, that the description is so unspecific that hearers now cannot be sure whether it is the fruit of the whole field or of individual seeds or ears that is being described.[15] If it is the product of the field, there may indeed be some generalized emphasis on the magnificence of the yield. In logical terms, however, it is hard to understand how such a measurement could be made in terms of thirty-, sixty-, and hundredfold. It seems to make more sense and probably fits better with the wording of the parable to understand that some seeds produced plants that bore thirty, sixty, or a hundred times what was sown—a satisfying though not necessarily surprising result.[16] Alternatively, it has been argued that some ears were understood to have had these numbers of grain. "In that country each ear bears thirty-five seeds on the average, but up to sixty are often counted and occasionally even a hundred in one ear."[17] While some would see the progression from thirty and sixty to one hundred as a way of stressing the surprising plenitude of the harvest, it might be just a way of rounding off numbers in poetic terms while describing a good harvest.

It does not seem possible on internal grounds to determine whether these numbers are meant to describe a natural or unusual harvest. The decision will most likely depend on the expectation of listeners and how the parable is heard in relation to other stories and sayings of the early traditions.

One may first try to hear the parable as a story of proverbial wisdom, presuming the naturalness of what is taking place. It then essentially confirms rather than disturbs or surprises the normal understanding of life. It may on this basis, as has been noted, offer in its conclusion a message of encouragement and hope. This need not mean, however, that there is nothing mysterious or surprising about the process, for nature can still be both. First-century people did not understand the how and why of nature's loss and growth any more fully than the people of today understand it. There is always something uncontrollable and even awesome about these results. As one commentator has expressed it, the human relationship "to the earth and its processes is primordial and full of mystery. Folklore, mythology, and the 'savage' mind see tilling and planting as transactions with powers, chthonic and divine, and harvest as having the character of miracle."[18] Every kind of harvest can be experienced as a gift—a delight and surprise that from so little and with so relatively little human effort, and despite all the natural losses, there should be grain for food and new planting. One needs only a few ounces of nature mysticism to hear that music in the parable and also to hear similar strains in the other seed parables.

In hearing the parable as a kind of proverb one should not, however, so stress the final good as to overlook the loss that the parable dwells on. The story is realistic. Much is wasted in nature and life. There is lack of growth and there is death, sometimes hundreds of seeds for one plant, thousands of seeds for one full-grown tree. Present-day listeners now recognize that millions of sperm are produced to create one human being, and that there are billions of stars for perhaps but one or a relatively few homes for conscious life. Somehow one supposed that God was an environmentalist! Yet nature's God seems utterly extravagant and profligate.

Yet, as the parable suggests, that is only one way of viewing the process. From a larger perspective the result is ongoing life, and maybe somehow that makes it all worthwhile. Possibly there is even a perspective from which what seems only waste and death all works together and fulfills the purpose of life. The parable does not, however, tell that, and it may be too much to assume. One comes back to the realism of the story with regard to death and life, while recognizing that the parable's final optimism seems to hint at something more beneficent than only the ongoing round of nature. Despite all life's problems there are grounds for hope.

Again one may hear the parable speaking to the whole of the human condition and the many kinds of loss and gain experienced in relation to the natural order and with respect to all human creativity. One might think of the risks involved in offering love and trying to make sacrifices that could lead to greater understanding and justice. Many times these offerings will surely appear to come to nothing, but sometimes in unexpected places and ways they can bear fruit of such gracefulness that it seems to make the caring more than worthwhile.

I have a little horticultural parable of my own that I use to remind myself about the unpredictable character of grace when, in spite of my efforts or those of others, nothing much good seems to be happening in the world or church. To begin with, however, I must admit that I am not much of a gardener. Occasionally, however, I do venture out, trying to make grass grow here or there. I dig, sprinkle seed, scratch a little more, add a bit of new soil, water, watch, and wait—a week, ten days. Finally scraggly bits of grass do appear, but it never seems to grow in these patches the way it should. Then

I look over to the sidewalk where lovely tufts of vibrant green grass are growing out from the cracks. Likely there is some good reason for this phenomenon, but I am made to think of other times and places where a lot of effort in some areas seems largely wasted while yet in unexpected situations goodness flourishes.

Along with such other stories of surprising gracefulness this parable of the seeds may whisper to the desire to understand whether life can be seen as good and worthwhile in spite of so much loss and death. One may listen for the possibility of God's presence and providence. For reasons that are very hard to understand there must be loss in order to have gain. The interpreter may even begin to realize that the evangelist Mark may not have been that far from the target when he located the parable as he has—in a section about telling and hearing parables. In that endeavor, too, there is inevitable loss and gain, and the parable of the seeds overarches the reiterated theme of having, losing, finding (being found and being given a new opportunity to choose) that sounds again and again through the Bible and in many of the other parables. It speaks to a people who have repeatedly lost their way, and lost much along the way, but for whom now there is cause for new faith, if they will have it. In this sense this is a kind of keystone parable:[19] "And Jesus said to them, 'Do you not understand this parable? How will you understand all the parables?'" (Mark 4:13)

If this be thought a legitimate way of hearing the parable, one also may realize that the Gospels' allegorical interpretation, though relating to later circumstances, may still have a certain coherence with the earlier parable. And just possibly those troublesome intervening verses (4:10–12) could even be Mark's version of an attempt by Jesus or an early disciple to indicate why parables must sometimes be so mysterious and difficult to hear. If they are to be faithful to experience, parables must allude to life's often problematic and ambiguous character and to the mystery of both God's visible absence and God's unseen presence in the world. Perhaps only those who are willing to live with faith in that presence—in the face of loss and death—can hear the parable as one of providence.

No doubt there are a number of hearers of Gospel parables who will expect still more from this parable—a greater sense of surprise more congruent with other parts of the tradition. Certainly one could hear a note of extraordinary plenitude in the last words of the parable[20]—an added inflection that points the parable just beyond the natural and historical order to the fullness of God's purpose. Although between sowing and harvest there will be much disappointment and tribulation, finally there is to be miraculous abundance. One is again reminded of the parable of the great supper. Three guests are "lost" and it does not seem as if there will be much of a party, but in the end the house is full.

Finally, in the hearing of this parable, the audience cannot forget who is said to be the teller. He is the one who not only spoke about losing life; that was his destiny. He, too, might well have looked back on his ministry and seen much loss and waste. Immediately after his death his disciples saw only failure and tragedy, until the day they found they could tell the parables again. Through the eyes of their faith God had mysteriously been present in the loss, accepting that as part of creation, to which God was now bringing surprise—new life—in yet another extravagant story of grace.

PARABLE AND GOSPEL

"There is nothing hid, except to be made manifest; nor is anything secret except to come to light" (Mark 4:22). Parables, this saying seems to suggest, are not meant to remain concealed; they help to make known what is otherwise secret. Mark tells his listeners that "with many such parables Jesus spoke the word to them, as they were able to hear it" (4:33). Yet Mark goes on to say (4:34) that only to his own disciples did Jesus explain the parables, and earlier Jesus is pictured as insisting that, although the secret of the kingdom of God can be given to the disciples, "for those outside everything is in parables; so that they may indeed see but not perceive, and may indeed hear but not understand, lest they should turn again and be forgiven" (4:11–12). The parable of the seeds that are sown is then interpreted as a means of understanding why and how the parables, in many cases, do not bring about the genuine acceptance of the word of God. Even to Jesus' close disciples parables appear to be opaque until given special interpretation.

If Mark was not of two minds about the purpose of parables, he at least has let stand in his Gospel a complex point of view. Jesus taught many things in parables (4:2). These parables will come to light and are full of revelation for those to whom the secret of the kingdom of God is given. But parables are obscure to others (Mark 12:1–12 is a significant exception) and are used to keep outsiders from perceiving and understanding. The usual response in terms of historical understanding to Mark's perspective on parables is to maintain that Jesus, in fact, used his parables to teach—to try to help as many people as possible understand how God's purposes were active in the world. The parables were, of course, used with disciples, and at times Jesus did teach them privately and offer them special understandings in a more intimate manner, but primarily the parables were used in open teaching and preaching. Some of them may even have been especially designed to argue with those who opposed him, seeking to reverse their perspectives.

Then, however, as the years went on and Jesus' parables were retold in different settings, a number of them became harder to interpret. The immediately impending kingdom to which they often alluded had not yet come, and the stories had now also to be viewed in the context of the powerful but itself mysterious story of Jesus' passion, the empty tomb, and resurrection appearances. Some Christian communities may have been influenced as well by strongly dualistic views that tended to divide humanity into the minority to be saved and the rest who were forever lost. Those called to salvation were given revelation that was to be guarded carefully and kept from others.[1] This ideology could have helped some early Christians understand why the parables seemed to have so little effect on those who did not join them. The tendency then grew to give the similes and stories further interpretation—especially, allegorical interpretation dealing with salvation history—that could only be understood by Christians.

To bring scriptural warrant to this perspective and so to see what was happening as part of the divine plan, reference was made to Isa. 6:9–10, which spoke of a people heavy of hearing, with hearts grown dull and eyes closed, who God had determined would not understand and be healed. Mark, or perhaps disciples before him, then formulated the "hard saying" that is now found in Mark 4:11–12 and fitted it into the context of the story of the sower and seeds, with its developing interpretation, to offer a kind of theory about how parables were and ought to be heard.[2] Mark may also have found that this understanding fitted with his belief that the first disciples often misunderstood Jesus (especially with regard to the necessity of suffering),[3] and that only from the perspective of later interpretation could his teaching (otherwise too open to interpretation) rightly be comprehended.[4] Still retained, however, in the Gospel were other sayings that reflected the earlier use of parables to reveal and teach much more plainly.

FAITH TO HEAR PARABLES

This historical outline has much to be said for it, but an important and complicating caveat should be kept in mind. The outline suggests that the parables were originally rather transparent and easy to understand and that only over the years did disciples come to have difficulty with them, sometimes giving them complex and more secretive interpretations. As has been seen throughout this study, that view is inadequate with respect to both the themes and the methods of a number of the parables. Some similitudes and parabolic stories were and are evidently fairly direct in their teaching, but inherent in many of them, and in the reasons for using the way of parables, are challenges to normal understanding. Parables are sometimes difficult because they are meant to make hearers think and see afresh, but they also can be mysterious because they point to beliefs that are otherwise not easy to put into words. Often one can glimpse the maturing churches moving in the other direction—seeking to explain and simplify for their members the significance of otherwise problematic parables. Thus, before concluding that the theory with regard to the secrecy and difficulty of parables in Mark 4 is entirely a creation by the later church and/or the evangelist, one must recognize that what is being said is not wholly out of keeping with the inherent character of a number of the parables. In this sense, although Mark 4:11–12 has been shaped by later experience and understandings in the church, it is possible that it is a development from insights that were more basic to the traditions[5] or at least not as fully in contradiction with those traditions as at first might appear.

The call to "repentance" and the opportunity to experience the kingdom do come to all who hear the gospel. The proclamation of the kingdom's near-ness and the accompanying acts of power in Jesus' ministry are in one sense an effort to create new hope and trust, although in another sense they re-quire hope and faith to be heard and seen. Where that hope and willingness to trust come from is itself a mystery. It is, of course, one of the paradoxes of Christian life that faith is both a human responsibility and a gift from God. But either way one has to have it in order to have it, and the more one hopes and trusts, the more trust and hope one can have. The sayings that Mark re-cords in the context of the teaching on the hearing of the parables are hard, but they reflect this insight.

> Take heed what you hear, the measure you give will be the measure you get, and still more will be given you. For to the one who has will more be given, and for the one who has not, even what that person has will be taken away. (Mark 4:24–25)

A number of the parables seem carefully designed to ask hearers whether they are willing to make the commitment to have faith in the coming king-dom. With that faith they can then "hear" the parables.

A PARTICIPATORY WORLD

No doubt it sounds unfair and illogical to say that people must commit themselves to believing in the kingdom in order to hear about it—that in or-der to see it one must first believe it. That approach runs counter to much that modern people have been taught with regard to honest learning. They have been educated to be objective—to get the facts, and to make commit-ments only on the basis of evidence. To commit oneself before doing this would be to run the distinct risk of distorting the evidence.

In almost all branches of learning, however, it is coming more and more to be understood that the basic conception of learning that this model portrays itself involves a major distortion. It suggests a picture of an observer sitting outside the materials being examined. Perhaps most clearly from the field of physics has come the realization that everyone lives in what might be called a participatory world. In the study of literature the comparable understand-ing is known as the hermeneutical circle. The interpreter of literature is already subtly involved with the text being studied and can never be com-pletely objective about it. Most works of criticism and interpretation tell their audiences as much about the interpreter as about what is being inter-preted. Often this only becomes fully clear a generation or two later, when the predilections of an earlier age can better be seen. Although it can be ar-gued that the problem is now lessened because contemporary critics are much more alert to this proclivity, the more aware they are, the less likely they are to think there is a way to escape it except partially.

For a number of contemporary thinkers the result is a radical relativity. Although degrees of objectivity are possible and may even be deemed valuable, still in the end human beings are only supposing about life rather than knowing with any certainty. One contemporary critic has seen in Mark's discussion of parables the seeds of this view. He links Mark 4:10–12 to the modern reader's experience of "arbitrary and total exclusion . . . from the secret sense" of life. In the end it might be said that even the close disciples do not really understand Jesus' life or teaching, and the reader is left as one of the outsiders trying to puzzle out the riddlelike parables that finally lead only to silence.[6] Indeed, the abrupt conclusion of this Gospel—without any full resurrection narrative—could be said to be that final silence. "And they said nothing to anyone, for they were afraid" (Mark 16:8). At the last there is only enigma.

A SURPRISING GOSPEL

Together with several other contemporary studies of Mark's Gospel, this reading of Mark 4:10–12 helps one see how odd a book it actually is. The understandable tendency to read Mark in the light of the other Gospels and to have a generalized view of the story of Jesus tends to obscure this strangeness, but Mark runs counter to expectations in at least several ways.

One can first notice its form. As likely the first of the Gospels, Mark had little by way of models to copy. He has composed a kind of hagiography that also collects a fair amount of teaching and is even more a proclamation of Jesus' actions and their significance. It begins abruptly, offering almost no information with respect to Jesus' background. More than a third of the book concentrates on the painful story of his last days, and then the Gospel also ends so precipitately that there are theories about the last page being lost or even that Mark died before he could complete it. The astonished and trembling women who found the tomb empty flee from the garden. Although the evangelist almost surely must have known a few of the traditions about Jesus' resurrection appearances, he records none of them.[7]

That last note of "fear" repeats a theme found at other crucial points in the Gospel (4:40–41; 5:15, 33, 36; 6:50; 9:6), especially with respect to the disciples' great difficulty in understanding Jesus' teaching about the necessity of his passion and crucifixion as the Son of man. Even after he has told them this three times (and will do so a fourth; 8:31; 9:12, 31; 10:33–34) the disciples "did not understand the saying, and they were afraid to ask him" (9:32; see also 10:32). In addition to having problems with understanding the predictions of his passion and resurrection, along with the parables and other teaching, several of those first followers of Jesus are portrayed as being weak and looking out rather much for themselves. Just before Jesus' trial and passion they three times fall asleep rather than keeping watch with him. When he is taken prisoner, "they all forsook him and fled" (14:50). The apparent first among peers three times denies he knows Jesus, and this Gospel does not tell of Peter's rehabilitation.

In many ways the most important parablelike story in Mark's Gospel is the story of Jesus' restoring sight to the beggar Bartimaeus (10:46–52). This immediately follows James's and John's request that they be given places of honor in the kingdom and Jesus' response about the necessity of service (10:35–45). Mark has very carefully prepared for this story. The leaders of Judaism, with their trained eyes, are unable to see who Jesus is. The disciples, though they have had glimpses of Jesus' true character and the purpose of his life, are, to say the least, myopic. But a blind beggar, whose faith seems to arise solely from his need, perceives well enough who Jesus can be for him, and then is given his sight so that he may follow Jesus "on the way" that leads, before glory, to the destined passion in Jerusalem.[8]

In these and other ways the evangelist portrays Jesus as a surprising and even cryptic figure, known but also unknown to his closest disciples. Mark seems deliberately to undercut any picture of Jesus as "lordly" in terms of worldly religion. Yes, he did miracles, but even these create greater opposition than understanding. His power to do miracles is more than balanced by the call to service, which he models, and the necessity of suffering. This is not a hero's story, at least not in the normal sense.

GOSPEL AS PARABLE

Mark was likely in a difficult situation when he wrote his Gospel. It was more than a generation since Jesus' death and resurrection. Jerusalem had recently been destroyed by the Romans. Surely, if the kingdom were to come—surely, if Jesus were to return—it should have been by now. Despite some days of growth and signs of power, many of the fledgling Christian communities were experiencing various forms of persecution, as well as frustration that their preaching did not bear more fruit and that their Lord did not return. Quite clearly not everything was explained or changed by the resurrection.

One of the most important sayings in Mark's Gospel (first spoken by Jesus to his disciples before his passion, and then repeated by the young man beside the empty tomb, 14:28; 16:7) is Jesus' promise that "after I am raised up, I will go before you to Galilee." The young man adds, "There you will see him." Mark was trying to make it clear that the fallen Jerusalem was never intended to be the place of Jesus' return or, for that matter, the central locale for the church's mission. It is instead Galilee, which may well represent for Mark the non-Jerusalem and largely gentile world more generally, where the church is to do mission and one day see the Son of man in glory.[9]

The evangelist was also trying to direct attention away from the resurrection itself and toward the hoped-for appearance of Jesus as the Son of man. If there were members of Mark's audience who wanted to stress the triumph of

Jesus' resurrection and the beginning of his reign, they must have been disappointed by this Gospel. To the extent that they wished to view themselves and other Christians sharing in that triumph, they would have been further troubled. What the resurrection does seem to mean to Mark is that the church has reason to hope that Jesus will be seen again, the "Son of man, seated at the right hand of Power, and coming with the clouds of heaven" (14:62).[10] The empty tomb and the young man's words telling that Jesus is risen and is going before his disciples to Galilee close the Gospel in a mood of awe, fear, and trembling hope.

Yet, despite the several unexpected and mysterious features of this book, and a mood that poses more than answers questions, Mark's Gospel is not finally an enigma. Though the disciples at best are struggling to understand, others are "outside," and all is far from clear, still the community of listeners to Mark's Gospel hear the demons who recognize who Jesus truly is. They also hear the heavenly voice at the baptism and are present at the mount of transfiguration—the scene that prefigures the glory to come. With the centurion who, as the precursor of all gentile believers, proclaims, "Truly this man was Son of God" (15:39), they know that the crucifixion is not meant to be the end of the story and share the hope that Jesus will again be seen coming in heavenly glory. What this Gospel might, in fact, best be called is a parable—an extended narrative in several of its configurations not unlike the parables that Jesus told.[11] It begins and ends abruptly and makes little effort to explain itself. In this way it too is open-ended and calls for its hearers' participation and interpretations. The narrative is told in concrete and particular terms. Jesus is a real man with real emotions of compassion (1:41), violent displeasure, anger, and indignation (1:43; 3:5; 10:14). He groans and sighs (1:41; 8:12), shows surprise at unbelief (6:6), demonstrates his ignorance in certain circumstances (5:31–32; 9:33; 13:32), and shows love (10:21). He dies a very real abandoned death. Yet frequently the Gospel also is alluding to a kind of parallel story just at the edge of or beyond human vision, in which Jesus is known to be the one from God, struggling with forces of supernatural evil. Although most of the world cannot see who he is, Mark's audience at least catches glimpses at the baptism (1:9–11) and transfiguration (9:2–8), and the narrative seems deliberately to conclude unsatisfactorily in order to point its hearers beyond itself to the sight of the Son of man coming in glory, for which Mark's church waits. Seemingly always undercutting any sense of Christian triumphalism, and weighted by the gloom of the drama of those last days, the story nevertheless ends with the audience's eyes lifted toward Galilee in hope.

THE PARABOLIC CHARACTER OF
OTHER GOSPELS AND PAUL

It is important to stress the distinctiveness of Mark's story, and other early Christian writers give the story of Jesus their own more positive emphases, but it is also important to recognize that they share with Mark's Gospel in a number of its parabolic features. For both Matthew and Luke, Jesus' life becomes much more a success story, with the disciples his more loyal and comprehending followers. Matthew's Jesus is the great teacher who, although he is fiercely opposed by the Jewish leaders and finally put to death because of their machinations, manages to found a church that, as its risen Lord, he sends on mission. Luke tells of the Spirit-filled man of prayer and compassion who taught and healed and, although martyred because of the wickedness of a few, quickly rose to become the ascended Lord of a rapidly spreading Christianity. Still, there are questions and mysteries: why the disciples yet had as much difficulty as they did in understanding and following Jesus; why there was so much opposition; why, though he was the hoped-for messiah of Israel, Israel for the most part rejected him; why there was still a problem with interpreting some of the parables; why the kingdom Jesus proclaimed had not more clearly manifested itself; and, perhaps most poignantly, why God allowed this Son to suffer so, and why Jesus, though risen, still had not come again in triumph.

The Gospel of John presents some of these questions and paradoxes in terms of irony, compressed images, and words with double meanings. A number of figures who are in dialogue with Jesus in this Gospel have trouble understanding the meaning of his words, but the hearers of the Gospel are meant to hear more carefully and to become "insiders" and understand. There is, in this sense, a kind of parabolic character to all that takes place.[12] It is always happening on at least two levels of meaning. From the opening passage of the Gospel the earthly Jesus is also known as the one who came from and returned to God. He is seen and he speaks in a stereoscopic and stereophonic manner, as both the one who once walked the earth and the risen, exalted Lord. The hearers' perspective on time is altered as what has been and is and, in a sense, what is yet to be for Christians are blended into one voice.

Jesus is the light of the world, but only a few in the darkened world know him. "He came to his own home, and his own people received him not" (1:11). The words "lifting up" and "glory" refer both to Jesus' being lifted up on the cross (the passion and death, which are to be seen as glorious because they bring glory) and the lifting-up to resurrection and to the glory of God (3:14; 12:32, 34; 13:31). So even on the gruesome cross may Jesus be seen in glory, the bearer of salvation. In the central incident in the Gospel, Jesus raises Lazarus from the dead, but this act of giving new life becomes the cause of his being put to death by those who do not understand the life he brings (11:1–53). Yet it is that death which will lead to Jesus' resurrection and life for many others.

It is Paul, however, who states the central Christian mystery most bluntly. He feels compelled to do so by his Corinthian converts who, during the absence enforced by his illness, had been receptive to teachings that stressed the glorious and triumphant aspects of Christian living. These teachers (whom Paul archly refers to as "these superlative apostles," 2 Cor. 11:5; 12:11) were apparently able to do many miracles, while Paul could not even cure himself. At least some Corinthians had evidently begun to think of themselves as already risen to a life of the Spirit and as therefore above many others in the world. Already they reigned as kings. Although Paul believed in the power of the Spirit and in miracles, he felt that his recent converts were now indulging in a kind of worldly religion. In so doing they were misinterpreting the heart of Christian faith, which, as Paul was daily discovering, meant to share also in Jesus' humility and suffering. Jesus had not been known in the world as a superhero, and those who followed in his way were never going to convince others by demonstrations of worldly power—for the power that God had shown in Christ was not the kind of power or wisdom that the world understood. For those brought up in Judaism who would demand signs of power before believing, the crucified Christ was a "stumbling block," and for those Greeks who sought a rational and universal wisdom, this Christ was "folly" (1 Cor. 1:20–25). But "God has chosen what is low and despised in the world" (1 Cor. 1:28).[13]

A PARABOLIC TRADITION

In their different ways the several New Testament writers use forms of irony or paradox or a kind of parabolic approach because the story they are dealing with already had this character, and probably also because a number of the sayings and stories said to come from Jesus were imbued with these features. Despite all the evident vagaries and different emphases in the passing-along of the essential teachings, the basic tradition had a grip on the imagination and hope of early Christian communities that was tenacious. Clearly much of the tradition's capacity to generate awe and wonder came from that part of the story which told of crucifixion and resurrection. They were inseparable. The passion and crucifixion without the resurrection were at best tragedy—perhaps only meaningless suffering and death. But the resurrection told by itself would have been but one of the great sensations of history, to be marveled over, though not a cause to change one's life. Taken together with the passion and crucifixion, however, the resurrection meant that the one who had suffered and his suffering were of God. It was not just that the resurrection confirmed who Jesus was and that suffering could be overcome; it also signified that God was in the suffering and did not stand apart from human agony. It was in some sense a fulfillment of the prophet's words "I have made and I will bear" (Isa. 46:4). The Creator was not aloof from the often grim and terrifying realities of mortal existence. In Christ God had mysteriously been present in the day of torture, of blood and dirt and searing pain. As Paul would put it, "In Christ God was reconciling the world to himself" (2 Cor. 5:19).

The resurrection did not end this human suffering, but it was now possible to encounter it, as Paul among others would do, as being essential to the creation and never apart from God's own experience. The resurrection was the evidence for Christians that through the presence of God the suffering could be transformed. One needs to be clear: the resurrection did not cause the mysterious aspects of the story of the crucified Savior to disappear or answer all the disciples' questions. In some ways it added to them. An empty tomb at first creates only fear and astonishment. The appearances, of course, helped interpret what the empty tomb meant, but these, too, were in their way mysterious. Even Matthew tells us that some of those who saw Jesus doubted (28:17). In other of the appearances the disciples only slowly came to realize who Jesus was. At first he was mistaken for a gardener, a wayfarer, or a beachcomber (John 20:11–18; Luke 24:13–35; John 21:4–14).[14] These disguises are perhaps to be understood as a clue to the interpretation of the teaching that by feeding and giving drink to the hungry and thirsty, welcoming strangers and offering clothes to those without them, and visiting persons sick and in prison, "you did it to me" (Matt. 25:35–40) in the ongoing life of human suffering and need.

RETELLING STORIES OF JESUS

Although suffering continued and even mounted in their lives, and although the resurrection did not take away all questions and doubts, the disciples were now filled with a vibrant hope and orientation toward the future. It was from this perspective that they began to look back on Jesus' life and to retell his stories and stories about him. As they did this they came to believe that this hope was in fact pointing them in the same direction in which Jesus had sought to orient them with his teaching about the kingdom of God. Between what was now their master story of his ministry, death, and new life and what he had said and done they discovered analogues and parallels. He had spoken of giving and risking in his parables, of losing, of humbling and service and even death, before finding and being found in God's exaltation. He was an unexpected Expected One—as John the Baptist was among the first to recognize (Luke 7:18–23; Matt. 11:2–6). But his parables had often alluded to the surprising and unexpected, along with the need to look beneath appearances into the heart of what was happening, in order to begin to perceive God's ways.

Even in his telling of the parables there is a sense in which Jesus was and is participant in them,[15] but now the disciples heard Jesus not only telling but being told of in these stories. He stood both behind and in them as the Samaritan who extended care to a stranger and to Mary Magdalene, Zacchaeus, and Bartimaeus. He was the one who forgave and sought the lost and outcast. Around him was forming the new community of relationships to which a number of the parables allude. He was himself that which was seemingly lost and found. There were many stories about him that seemed to have a parabolic character, and there was a congruence between his actions and his words that gave confirmation and example to his stories, and interpretation to the things he did. He not only spoke of forgiveness and healing, of reaching out to the tax collectors, sinners, and those whose disabilities could have made them seem subjects of divine disfavor, of the coming of the kingdom, and living *as if* it were already breaking into the world; so he had lived and died. In acts of power, the very telling of which still left hearers in awe, he had cast out demonic forces and spoken of what seemed a personal struggle between himself and the power of evil. A number of the healing stories are reminiscent of the symbolic actions of the earlier prophets. Jesus evidently understood the healings that took place through his ministry as essential ways of manifesting the character of the kingdom coming.[16] How the kingdom comes is in many ways at least as important as the final goal, for it is in its ways of coming—in the healing and responses to calls demanding righteousness and God's kind of love—that the kingdom does come. That is why the only means to the kingdom's peace and fairness are those of peace and justice.

More and more the disciples came to see Jesus not only as the one who told of the kingdom but as the one who enacted it. More and more, to tell of the kingdom was to tell of him, and to proclaim him was to disclose in personal terms the kingdom's nature and purpose. He, his followers now believed, not only had spoken the word of God but had expressed it in his life. In his acts of forgiveness and healing, in his opening of the kingdom and reaching out to the outcast as the one who would seek out the lost, Jesus was perceived to have been acting for God. Still more wondrous stories were told about the stilling of a storm, the feeding of crowds, and transforming water into wine. The abundance of the food provided and the making of more than seven hundred gallons of wine were further signs of the extravagance of the reign of God. Through these stories the Christian communities were already coming to believe that the power manifested in Jesus' ministry was of the Creator God.

PARABLE OF GOD

The experience of the resurrection was both an expression and a confirmation of that faith. Despite all that human misunderstanding, indifference, pride, and cruelty had done to show what happens to hopes like those of Jesus, and despite their own desertions, the disciples found his trust in God now healing their distrust. He had told them that service and suffering need not be the end but that, though lowly and seemingly with little power in the world, they could and would be raised up by God. When now they looked to God to try to understand, it was as though the spirit of Jesus was still speaking to them, still telling the stories and calling them to faith. So profound was this experience in their efforts to follow in his way and in their worship that the disciples came to think and speak of this presence of Jesus and the Spirit of God interchangeably.

They were, of course, just adding mystery to mystery. The disciples believed that Jesus pointed them to God, but now they were also coming to believe that through his humanity—in his ministry, death, and resurrection—God had revealed something of God's own character. In this personal life God was to be glimpsed not only in the power of the resurrection but in the power of the service and suffering as well.

One way of trying to put this experience into words is to recognize that "Jesus, who proclaimed God in paradoxes, became himself the Paradox of God."[17] Jesus had tried to tell of the surprising ways that God's activity was in the world, and the churches came to the faith that in him that presence could best be perceived. For them his story was the master story to be used for interpreting all the others. It was the chief parable, the parable of God. In parabolic ways the story draws its hearers in and then surprises them with misdirection. It starts going one way and then turns another, while offering other stories and sayings that sometimes seem like riddles, with their talk of losing what seemed to have been important and finding what one was not looking for, of the blind seeing and deaf hearing, of service and lowliness being the life that God exalts through suffering. Jesus himself is never fully understood. He is both known and unknown in his own story. In this and other ways the chief parable keeps gesturing beyond itself as hearers can never really be sure how or whether God is present. It can be heard as telling of a human life as limited and circumscribed as any other, and yet it is of God. As the one who acts for God and in whose life God is acting, Jesus both is and is not God. He is fully human and yet divine.[18]

The story was also heard to allude to what God intended for human life and its destiny. In his humanity Jesus was seen as an exemplar and a kind of pioneer in exploring and leading toward this purpose. It was again, of course, both possible and impossible to follow him, because he was also of God in a way that no other human could be. Yet his way of service was to provide the pattern for his disciples. To follow him meant to believe that, despite all the evidence to the contrary, God's compassion and justice were already active in the world. It meant living by faith that this was so—*as if* this caring and justice were most important and would finally win out over the powers of evil.

This was and is the way of parable, for it calls for the willingness to live with paradox and mystery. It is the experience of God's reign already becoming yet still unknown, full of God's power yet powerless, totally dependent on God although requiring human responsiveness, gracious and welcoming while demanding all. It means living within the gospel story—participating in it while trying to interpret it—living without answers though with the direction of answers that the way of parable seeks to offer.

This ambiguity allows for human freedom, but it also means living before God without God as a metaphysical known who is present as a director of the world's events and a guarantor of the victory of God's ways. The only way of seeing and hearing God's kingdom is to be willing to image or imagine a world in which God's loving justice is beginning to rule, and individuals and communities of faith can do this only if they are willing to live *as if* this were so, that is, by being willing to try to begin to make the sacrifices and commitments required by trusting that the only ways to love's justice and peace are by acts of love, justice, and peace.

The Gospel parables lure hearers toward that commitment, and they provide a way of hearing and seeing such a world. They can be the catalysts for perceiving one's own life stories and those of the community as parables and discovering in them the surprise of God's presence.[19] In their turn these stories may then reflect on those in the Gospels and all be joined to and interpreted by the parable that is the story of Jesus.

ABBREVIATIONS

ATR	*Anglican Theological Review*
BTB	*Biblical Theology Bulletin*
CBQ	*Catholic Biblical Quarterly*
ExpTim	*Expository Times*
Int	*Interpretation*
JAAR	*Journal of the American Academy of Religion*
JBL	*Journal of Biblical Literature*
JTS	*Journal of Theological Studies*
NovT	*Novum Testamentum*
NTS	*New Testament Studies*
SNTU	Studien zum Neuen Testament und seiner Umwelt
WUNT	Wissenschaftliche Untersuchungen zum Neuen Testament

NOTES

PROLOGUE: TELLING IT SLANT

1. Wilder, *Jesus' Parables*, 74.
2. This terminology is drawn from Murray Krieger's conceptualization in *A Window to Criticism: Shakespeare's Sonnets and Modern Poetics* (Princeton: Princeton Univ. Press, 1964), esp. 33–36; it is used by Via in *Parables* (see p. 84).
3. Emily Dickinson, "Tell All the Truth."
4. From Wallace Stevens's poem "Man Carrying Thing," quoted by Philip Wheelwright in *Metaphor and Reality* (Bloomington: Univ. of Indiana Press, 1962), 96.
5. Paul Klee, *The Thinking Eye: Paul Klee Notebooks*, ed. J. Spiller (New York: George Wittenborn, 1961), 1:76.
6. See Drury, *Parables*. See also M. D. Goulder, who stresses the creativity of Matthew and Luke, in "Characteristics of the Parables in the Several Gospels," *JTS* n.s. 19 (1968): 51–69. On the significance of hearing the parables in their canonical form and setting, while using their history at earlier levels to enlighten them, see B. S. Childs, *The New Testament as Canon: An Introduction* (Philadelphia: Fortress Press, 1985), 531–40.
7. The impetus for much of Paul Ricoeur's *Time and Narrative* (Chicago: Univ. of Chicago Press, 1984–) is a leaning against a deconstructionist view that the references, telling, and hearing of stories only constitute a "vicious" hermeneutical circle. Ricoeur's study, translated by Kathleen McLaughlin and David Pellauer, is now in 2 vols. of a projected 3. See esp. 1:72.
8. The problems involved in determining earlier settings and forms for parables are emphasized in J. W. Sider in "Rediscovering the Parables: The Logic of the Jeremias Tradition," *JBL* 102 (1983): 61–83. Drury (*Parables*) is also highly critical of Jeremias's finding new versions of parables and new settings for them on the basis of unstable criteria.
9. For a critique of the limitations of the "severely historical approach," see Via, *Parables*, 21–24.
10. John D. Crossan, "Parable as History and Literature," *Listening: Journal of Religion and Culture* 19 (1984): 17.
11. So, e.g., Paul Ricoeur ("Biblical Hermeneutics," *Semeia* 4 [1975]: 134), who then goes on to insist, however, that no interpretation can exhaust the meaning of parables.
12. Via, *Parables*, 11.
13. This point is emphasized by Boucher (*Mysterious Parable*, 17–25), who criticizes those who view allegory as in itself a literary form or genre.
14. See below, chap. 15.
15. A shorter version of this parable is found in the *Gospel of Thomas*, saying 65. Klyne Snodgrass (*The Parable of the Wicked Tenants*, WUNT 27 [Tübingen: Mohr

(Siebeck), 1983]) views it as a story more about the rejected son than the wicked tenants. See also John D. Crossan, *Four Other Gospels: Shadows on the Contours of Canon* (Minneapolis: Winston Press, 1985), 53–62.

16. On the reasons for and uses of allegorical interpretation in the early church, see R. P. C. Hanson, *Allegory and Event: A Study of Sources and Significance of Origen's Interpretation of Scripture* (Richmond: John Knox Press, 1959), esp. 97–129.

17. See particularly Drury, *Parables*, for arguments in favor of the essentially allegorical character of many of the parables. His thesis depends in part on maintaining that Luke knew Matthew's Gospel and that, therefore, there need not be a pre-Matthean source for a number of the parables they hold in common. Also Drury evidently does not believe that the *Gospel of Thomas* gives information regarding pre-Synoptic forms of the parables.

18. The phrase "surplus of meaning" is Paul Ricoeur's. See his *Interpretation Theory: Discourse and the Surplus of Meaning* (Fort Worth: Texas Christian Univ. Press, 1976).

19. See Ricoeur, "Biblical Hermeneutics," 100.

20. Although *models* are of different types and uses in scientific thought and may link or combine a number of features, "the general idea is that metaphor is to poetic language as a model is to scientific language" (Ricoeur, "Biblical Hermeneutics," 85). For a fuller discussion, see McFague, *Metaphorical Theology*, 67–102.

21. On paradigm shifts and transformations in scientific imagination as transformations of the world, see T. S. Kuhn, *The Structure of Scientific Revolutions*, 2d ed. (Chicago: Univ. of Chicago Press, 1970).

22. Ricoeur, "Biblical Hermeneutics," 114.

23. Ibid., 115–28.

24. Ibid., 115–18.

25. Important distinctions should be made between understanding that an author intended a story to be polyvalent and understanding how it is so heard or read, and between understanding that one can ascertain what a story itself means (its coherence with itself and comprehensibility) and understanding what else it may be referring to. See the discussions by Bernard C. Lategan and Willem S. Vorster in *Text and Reality: Aspects of Reference in Biblical Texts* (Philadelphia: Fortress Press, 1985). It is my position that a number of the parables indicate that they were once told so as to require interpretation and were therefore deliberately left "open" to at least a degree, and that these stories use measures of "unreality" (extravagance and so forth) in order to cause hearers to wonder and try to think of other, somehow related, circumstances.

26. Wilder, *Jesus' Parables*, 76.

1. THE RESILIENT RASCAL:
THE UNJUST STEWARD

1. Dodd, *Parables*, 17.

2. See D. P. Seccombe, *Possessions and the Poor in Luke-Acts*, SNTU B/6 (Linz, 1982).

3. John D. Crossan, "The Servant Parables of Jesus," *Semeia* 1 (1974): 31–33.

4. See J. A. Fitzmyer, "The Story of the Dishonest Manager: Luke 16:1–13," in *Essays on the Semitic Background of the New Testament* (London: Geoffrey Chapman, 1971), 161–84. For a current bibliography, see idem, *The Gospel according*

to Luke X—XXIV, Anchor Bible (Garden City, N.Y.: Doubleday & Co., 1985), 1095–1164.

5. So Breech, *Silence of Jesus*, 101–13.

6. See Stein, *Parables*, 106–11. So also B. B. Scott, "A Master's Praise: Luke 16, 1–8a," *Biblica* 64 (1983): 173–88; and Via, *Parables*, 156–57.

7. See Derrett, "Fresh Light on Luke xvi.I: The Parable of the Unjust Steward," in *Law*, 48–77. For a review of the possibilities and some support for Derrett's position based on a close examination of the Greek text, see I. H. Marshall, *Commentary on Luke* (Grand Rapids: Eerdmans, 1978), 614–22.

8. On the steward as a type of the picaro or rogue figure, see Via, *Parables*, 160–61.

9. So Bailey, *Poet and Peasant*, 86–118.

10. It is, however, rightly pointed out that what was charged in this era in the lending of consumer goods was quite a bit higher than effective interest on money. The charge could then have been considered part of the original loan or what the individuals otherwise owed. See Derrett, "'Take Thy Bond . . . and Write Fifty' (Luke xiv.6): The Nature of the Bond," in *Glimpses*, 1–3.

11. Jeremias, *Parables*, 182. Similarly, see Dodd, *Parables*, 17.

12. Noted by P. R. Jones, *Parables*, 56.

13. See the reading of the parable by Scott ("A Master's Praise," esp. 179–85), who argues that it is more than a trickster tale in which the trickster wins out in the end. See the discussion in *Semeia* 1 (1974) between John D. Crossan and Dan O. Via, Jr.

14. L. J. Topel ("On the Injustice of the Unjust Steward: Lk. 16:1–13," *CBQ* 37 [1975]: 216–27) suggests that an attitude of forgiveness toward even such a rogue as the steward was one of Luke's primary interests in presenting the parable.

15. On these and other insights into Buechner's and Greene's heroes, see Horton Davies, *Catching the Conscience: Essays in Religion and Literature* (Cambridge, Mass.: Cowley Pubs., 1984), 81–107, 151–61.

2. THE JUST AND THE UNJUST:
THE PHARISEE AND THE TAX COLLECTOR

1. See Mark 2:15–16; Matt. 11:19; 21:32; and the derogatory implications of Matt. 5:46; 18:17. Cf. Joachim Jeremias, *Jerusalem in the Time of Jesus: An Investigation into Economic and Social Conditions during the New Testament Period* (Philadelphia: Fortress Press, 1967), 310–12. Sometimes one finds the phrase "tax gatherers and robbers."

2. So E. P. Sanders (*Jesus and Judaism* [Philadelphia: Fortress Press, 1985], 174–211) in the context of an argument that is otherwise highly critical of the way much New Testament scholarship has discussed Jesus' association with the outcast. Sanders is right to stress the understanding that the offense in Jesus' ministry was not that he associated with people who were ritually impure or the common people of the land but that he included in his company people who clearly had broken the torah, i.e., sinners for whom the regular Jewish term was "the wicked."

3. Cf. Bailey, *Through Peasant Eyes*, 154.

4. See ibid., 147–48.

5. In the Mishnah, *Pirke Aboth* 2.5.

6. It is not clear whether one should translate v. 11 so that the tax collector becomes an example of those who are extortionists, unjust, etc. (so Bailey, *Through Peasant Eyes*, 150–52; "like this tax collector") or whether the tax collector is re-

garded as another category of sinner, but, either way, the effect of the Pharisee's words is really to lump them pretty much together.

7. Jürgen Moltmann, *The Power of the Powerless: The Word of Liberation for Today*, trans. M. Kohl (San Francisco: Harper & Row, 1983), 96.

8. An insight stressed by Michael Walzer in *Spheres of Justice: A Defense of Pluralism and Equality* (New York: Basic Books, 1983).

9. Jon Sobrino, *Christology at the Crossroads: A Latin American Approach*, trans. J. Drury (Maryknoll, N.Y.: Orbis Books, 1978), 92.

10. There is increasing reason to believe that Jesus saw his major mission as working toward the restoration of Israel to its fullness as the kingdom neared. On this restoration eschatology, see Sanders, *Jesus and Judaism*, 91–119. Sanders views this as evident more in Jesus' actions than sayings, but creation of new community would appear to be a central concern of a striking number of the parables as well as of many healing activities.

11. Sobrino, *Christology*, 360.

12. See Matt. 5:21–22.

13. Cf. Gerd Theissen, *The Sociology of Early Palestinian Christianity*, trans. J. Bowden (Philadelphia: Fortress Press, 1978), 105: "The most important precondition for this [introjected aggressiveness turned into self-acceptance on the basis of the divine love] was the anxiety-free atmosphere which emerges from the parables." In Romans 2—3 Paul also shows how all have sinned and are equally in need of God's grace.

3. EQUAL PAY:
THE LABORERS IN THE VINEYARD

1. Irenaeus *Against Heresies* IV.xxxvi.7.

2. 2 Esd. 5:42. Cf. also 2 Bar. 30:2.

3. See Perkins, *Parables*, 144.

4. In Matt. 22:12 the address is used challengingly to the man who has no wedding garment. In Matt. 26:50 Jesus so addresses Judas at the time of the betrayal.

5. So Crossan, *In Parables*, 112. He argues that v. 15 is an addition imparting a moral consideration. In my interpretation, however, I suggest that the question "Is your eye evil because I am good?" is focused not so much on the master's generosity as on the workers' jealousy—so continuing the major direction of the parable.

6. For one explanation, see Derrett, "Workers in the Vineyard: A Parable of Jesus," in *Glimpses*, 48–75 (see esp. 73–74).

7. On the possibility that workers of the time who had sought employment were entitled to a minimum wage, see ibid., 60–63, although the receipt of an amount equivalent to that received by the twelve-hour workers would still be excessive and quite a surprise.

8. On this insight and the complexities of questions of justice and fairness in society more generally, see Michael Walzer, *Spheres of Justice: A Defense of Pluralism and Equality* (New York: Basic Books, 1983).

9. On this point, see also Breech, *Silence of Jesus*, 151.

10. On Matthew's use of the parable in this connection, see Luise Schottroff, "Human Solidarity and the Goodness of God: The Parable of the Workers in the Vineyard," in *God of the Lowly: Socio-Historical Interpretations of the Bible*, ed. W. Schottroff and W. Stegmann, trans. M. J. O'Connell (Maryknoll, N.Y.: Orbis Books, 1984), 129–47.

4. A MAN HAD TWO SONS:
THE PRODIGAL SON

1. There are other interesting parallels between the story of the prodigal and Joseph, who both suffer rejection by elder brother(s) and are restored from near death to life, indeed, to honor. Note, too, the ring and robe given to Joseph by Pharaoh, in Gen. 41:42.

2. R. D. Aus ("Luke 15:11–32 and R. Eliezer ben Hyrcanus's Rise to Fame," *JBL* 104 [1985]: 443–69) finds a number of intriguing parallels between the story (extant in several versions) of Eliezer's reconciliation with his father and the Gospel parable. He posits a common oral folktale that has influenced both stories. Yet what is also striking is the major difference. The discovery by Eliezer's father that his son is a success—that he has become a highly respected rabbi—is crucial to their reconciliation.

3. Derrett points out that it would be more expected for a father to make a division of the property when death was near. Such would avoid family disputes after his death. "For a son to ask for a share while his father was in good health was a confession that the son could not live in that home" ("The Parable of the Prodigal Son," in *Law*, 100–125; see esp. 105–6).

4. From the Talmud, *Baba Kamma* 82b; cf. Lev. 11:7.

5. According to a number of early manuscripts of Luke's Gospel, some scribes missed the point of the abbreviation of the second rendition of the younger son's words and completed the speech on the basis of the first. The description of the son's reception is remarkably like that of Jacob by his brother Esau, in Gen. 33:4.

6. A point made by Tolbert in *Perspectives*, 103–4.

7. See Drury, *Parables*, 143–45.

8. Luke uses the Greek words for repenting (*metanoeō*) and turning (*epistrephō*) in this sense eighteen times in comparison with eight times for Matthew and four for Mark. Note especially how in Luke 5:32 he adds to read, "I have come not to call the righteous but sinners *to repentance*." Apart from the prodigal son, the other six stories are the calling of the disciples (5:1–11), the paralytic (5:17–26), the anointing by the sinful woman (7:36–50), Zacchaeus (19:1–10), Peter's denial and repentance (22:55–62), and the penitent thief (23:39–41).

9. See Luke 19:10 and also, with respect to losing and saving one's life, Luke 9:24–25; 17:33.

10. See Crossan, *In Parables*, 74.

11. See above, p. 6, for a brief comment on a psychological hearing of the parable; for psychological and literary-structuralist perspectives, see Tolbert, "The Prodigal Son: An Essay in Literary Criticism from a Psychoanalytic Perspective," *Semeia* 9 (1977): 1–20; and Dan O. Via, Jr., "The Prodigal Son: A Jungian Reading," ibid., 21–43.

5. THE DINNER PARTY:
THE GREAT SUPPER

1. On the significance of hospitality in Jesus' ministry, in New Testament times generally and Luke's Gospel in particular, see John Koenig, *New Testament Hospitality: Partnership with Strangers as Promise and Mission* (Philadelphia: Fortress Press, 1985).

2. See Stein, *Parables*, 85–86. See Ps. 23:5 and esp. Isa. 25:6–9.

3. On Matt. 22:11–14, see chap. 9. Derrett ("The Parable of the Great Supper," in

Law, 126–55, esp. 126, 155), in holding that the parable is essentially a midrash (in this case a narrative commentary on Old Testament texts and their use contemporary with the time of Jesus), maintains that 22:11–14 was the concluding scene of the original parable.

4. Further on the source question regarding the parable, see Stein, *Parables*, 83–84; Perkins, *Parables*, 92–97; and Funk, *Language*, 163–87.

5. In the Palestinian Talmud, *Sanhedrin* 6.23c and *Hagigah* 2.77d. See Jeremias, *Parables*, 178–79.

6. "Compel" here implies not force but the issuing of the invitation in such a way that people who might otherwise believe that the man was only being polite would realize his sincerity. Cf. Bailey, *Through Peasant Eyes*, 108.

7. Generally on this matter, and with respect to this parable particularly, see John D. Crossan, *Four Other Gospels: Shadows on the Contours of Canon* (Minneapolis: Winston Press, 1985), 15–52.

8. On occasion the author-compiler of the *Gospel of Thomas* does offer interpretations of his own, though they are brief. With reference to literature on both sides of the question as to whether Thomas had a source or sources independent of the Synoptic Gospels, see John Horman, "The Source of the Version of the Parable of the Sower in the *Gospel of Thomas*," *NovT* 21 (1979): 326–43.

9. On earlier versions of the story, including one Jesus may have told, see Barbara Hall, *Joining the Conversation: Jesus, Matthew, Luke, and Us* (Cambridge, Mass.: Cowley Pubs., 1985), esp. 10–32, 59–60.

10. Linnemann (*Parables*, 89) contends that these are excuses to be late to the dinner rather than refusals to come at all. This is disputed by Jeremias (*Parables*, 178 n. 23) and others.

11. Cf. Stein, *Parables*, 159 n. 6.

12. See Derrett, *Law*, 138–39.

13. Three of the reasons listed in Deut. 20:5–8 for why a man need not fight in a war (built a new house, planted a vineyard, betrothed a wife) are mentioned or closely paralleled one or more times in the versions in Matthew, Luke, and Thomas. The teller of an early form of the parable could have been influenced by either Deuteronomy or a similar general tradition. See also 1 Macc. 3:56.

14. Funk (*Language*, 192) notes that this is a parable of both judgment and grace though neither is spoken of directly.

15. Similarly Funk, *Language*, 196.

16. Perhaps made most clear in the Qumran appendix to the *Manual of Discipline* when "every person smitten in his flesh, paralyzed in his feet, or hands, lame or blind or deaf, or dumb or smitten in his flesh with a blemish visible to the eye, or any aged person that totters" is excluded from the congregation of holiness (IQSa 2.5–10).

17. So Stein, *Parables*, 91.

18. So, e.g., R. H. Fuller, who includes the saying in "The Authentic Jesus Tradition: A Representative List of Passages," in *A Critical Introduction to the New Testament* (London: Duckworth, 1966), 101. Jesus' words are based on Isa. 29:18–19; 35:5–6; 61:1.

6. ONE OUT OF A HUNDRED:
THE LOST SHEEP

1. E. F. F. Bishop cites and discusses a number of these efforts in "The Parable of the Lost or Wandering Sheep: Matthew 18.10–14; Luke 15.3–7," *ATR* 44 (1962):

44–57. One of the more interesting arguments along these lines maintains that since the shepherd knew there were ninety-nine others, he must have counted them and put them in a pen. But ninety-nine is used in the story to indicate that all the rest of a large number were left when the shepherd went to search. It does not reflect a concern with accurate numbers. Bailey (*Poet and Peasant*, 149) maintains that such a large flock would have required more than one shepherd and that the hearers would have understood this.

2. Cf. Bailey, *Poet and Peasant*, 149.

3. Note also the large plant and the large loaves in sayings 20 and 96. W. L. Peterson ("The Parable of the Lost Sheep in the *Gospel of Thomas* and the Synoptics," *NovT* 23 [1981]: 128–47) has argued against the gnostic interpretation of the story and also sees the Thomist version as the more primitive. Against this latter view, see J. A. Fitzmyer, *The Gospel according to Luke X—XXIV*, Anchor Bible (Garden City, N.Y.: Doubleday & Co., 1985), 1078.

4. On the importance of "repentance" in Luke's Gospel, see above, p. 152 n. 8.

5. Matt. 18:4 says it is not the Father's will that "one of these little ones should perish [*apolētai*]." Luke's word and the Greek word in Ezek. 34:16 is *apolōlos*.

6. See Jeremias, *Parables*, 134.

7. But for the view that Luke's version of the parable is closer than Matthew's to the earlier presentation, see Bailey, *Poet and Peasant*, 151–53.

8. See below, chap. 8, on the parable of the wheat and weeds.

9. Rudolf Bultmann, *The History of the Synoptic Tradition*, trans. J. Marsh, rev. ed. (New York: Harper & Row, 1968), 199.

10. So, among others, Jeremias, *Parables*, 91; and Linnemann, *Parables*, 69.

11. Gunther Bornkamm, *Jesus of Nazareth*, trans. I. and F. McLuskey and J. M. Robinson (New York: Harper & Row, 1960), 183.

12. This insight is, of course, central to "liberation theology." See R. M. Brown, *Theology in a New Key: Responding to Liberation Themes* (Philadelphia: Westminster Press, 1978), esp. 75–100.

7. AS AN INJURED STRANGER:
THE GOOD SAMARITAN

1. This discussion follows Borsch, *Power in Weakness*, 85–98, 147–51.

2. This animosity is emphasized by Bailey, *Through Peasant Eyes*, 47–53. See also Oesterley, *Gospel Parables*, 162.

3. John D. Crossan in "Parable and Example in the Teaching of Jesus," *NTS* 18 (1971–72): 295 (= *Semeia* 1 [1974]: 78).

4. The question is closely paralleled in Luke 18:18; Mark 10:17; Matt. 19:16 in the story of the rich young man. Luke may have borrowed the question from that context, or there could be a more complex relationship with that story which continues on to present the commandments about regard for one's neighbor.

5. See Num. 21:1–3. Jeremias (*Parables*, 204) rightly points out, however, that this restriction would not technically have applied to the Levite. Bailey (*Through Peasant Eyes*, 44–45) details the importance of ritual purity for the priest. Further on the reasons why the priest and Levite might have found reason not to help and the "balancing of commandments [which] would be [their] normal mental response to such a situation," see Derrett, "The Parable of the Good Samaritan," in *Law*, 208–27, esp. 212–17.

6. The story probably presumes that the priest and the Levite as well were, like the Samaritan, riding. Cf. Bailey, *Through Peasant Eyes*, 43.

8. DO YOU WANT US TO GATHER THE WEEDS?
THE WHEAT AND WEEDS

1. See the analysis of the failures of liberal Christianity to sustain the integrity of Christian ethics as Christian, in Stanley Hauerwas, *Against the Nations: War and Survival in a Liberal Society* (Minneapolis: Winston Press, 1985).

2. Among other instances in Augustine's anti-Donatist writings, see *Answer to Petilian* III.3.

3. On the role of chap. 13 and this and the other parables therein in Matthew's Gospel see Kingsbury, *Parables*.

4. Kingsbury, *Parables*, 135. See also C. W. F. Smith, "The Mixed State of the Church in Matthew's Gospel," *JBL* 82 (1963): 149–68.

5. In addition to the parables of the net (13:47–50) and the separation of the sheep and goats (25:31–46), see esp. Matt. 7:13–14 (Luke 13:23–24); 7:22–23 (Luke 13: 26–27); 24:10.

6. The *Gospel of Thomas* (saying 8) has a parallel to Matthew's parable of the net with a different kind of sorting process. All the small fish are thrown back into the sea by the wise fisherman while the one large fish (probably representing the knowledge necessary for salvation) is retained. The Thomas version seems so heavily rewritten that it is difficult to learn much from it about an earlier version of this story.

7. Cf. John D. Crossan, "The Seed Parables of Jesus," *JBL* 92 (1973): 244–66, esp. 260.

8. See C. W. F. Smith, *Parables*, 59–60. On this parable see below, chap. 14.

9. The matter is complicated by the fact that Luke also omits the Markan story.

10. This aspect of Jesus' ministry is emphasized by J. Kallas in *The Significance of the Synoptic Miracles* (London: SPCK, 1961).

11. On the probable place of this saying in the authentic Jesus tradition, see R. H. Fuller, *A Critical Introduction to the New Testament* (London: Duckworth, 1966), 101.

12. See the discussion of these issues, including the recognition that the devil or Satan was at least sometimes seen to be God's agent in the complex and mysterious divine purpose, in Walter Wink, *Unmasking the Powers: The Invisible Forces That Determine Human Existence* (Philadelphia: Fortress Press, 1986), 9–40.

13. For a helpful discussion of the issues, see John Hick, *Evil and the God of Love* (London: Macmillan & Co., 1966); W. S. Towner, *How God Deals with Evil* (Philadelphia: Westminster Press, 1976); and John Bowker, *Problems of Suffering in Religions of the World* (Cambridge: At the Univ. Press, 1970).

14. See Crossan, *In Parables*, 85.

15. See Kingsbury, *Parables*, 71.

9. READY OR NOT!
THE WEDDING GARMENT. THE TEN MAIDENS

1. For the view that Matt. 22:11–14 was the concluding scene of an earlier parable about a marriage feast, see chap. 5, n. 3.

2. So, among many others, Jeremias, *Parables*, 65.

3. See Isa. 61:10. The image is naturally picked up in apocalyptic literature and is found at several points in Revelation: 3:4, 5, 18; 7:14; 19:8; 22:14. See also Derrett, *Law*, 142. In later years the white garment of purity was worn by new Christians immediately after baptism.

4. On this and other details of the story, see Jeremias, *Parables*, 187–89. There is a

parallel Jewish story in which a king invites servants to a feast. The astute ones dress themselves well and gather at the gate while the foolish go about their work thinking that the feast will require preparation. Suddenly the king calls them all in, and the foolish servants dressed in their dirty work clothes are made to stand and look on. In the Babylonian Talmud, *Shabbath* 153a.

5. On the way the parable focuses attention on the unwise maidens, see Perkins, *Parables*, 106–7.

6. C. W. F. Smith ("The Mixed State of the Church in Matthew's Gospel," *JBL* 82 [1963]: 149–68) points out how Matthew uses a number of parables to stress the double message that the church is now a community composed of various types but that a sorting-out will certainly take place at the end.

7. The "watching" theme is given special stress in Mark 13:33–37, where it is part of a story of a man who returns suddenly to his home. See also Luke 12:40, linked to one of his stories of the master who comes without warning, along with Matt. 24:44. The story of the master returning unexpectedly evidently has a complex history in the tradition, both in a more complete form and in bits and pieces. It is also at least related to the story of the talents or pounds (Matt. 25:14–30; Luke 19:12–27), where some version or parallel of it has strongly influenced the Lukan presentation. See also Luke 12:35–36 and the following n.

8. So, among others, Drury, *Parables*, 103; and Linnemann, *Parables*, 124–28. The other Gospel materials would be the similitude of the bridegroom who will be taken away (Mark 2:19–20; Matt. 9:15; Luke 5:34–35) and stories like that of the wedding garment (Matt. 22:11–14), Luke 13:25, and esp. Luke 12:35–36, which in turn leads to the suddenly returning master, the thief who breaks in unexpectedly, and the saying about the Son of man coming at an unexpected hour.

9. On these customs, see A. W. Argyle, "Wedding Customs at the Time of Jesus," *ExpTim* 86 (1974–75): 214–15. Argyle contends that the story as told is congruent with the practices of the time. Cf. Jeremias, *Parables*, 51–53, 171–75; and Lambrecht, *Once More Astonished*, 156–63.

10. See Mark 1:16–20; Matt. 14:18–22 (with Luke 5:1–11; Mark 2:14); Matt. 9:9; Luke 5:27.

11. On the character and purpose of the acts of power, see further Borsch, *Power in Weakness*, esp. 10–11.

12. On the imminence and immanence of the kingdom in the New Testament, and its now-then, here-there aspects, see Borsch, *God's Parable*, 27–44.

13. T. S. Eliot, "The Dry Salvages," in *The Four Quartets*.

14. On this point and the discussion more generally, see John D. Crossan, *Raid on the Articulate: Cosmic Eschatology in Jesus and Borges* (New York: Harper & Row, 1976), 133–63.

10. ON NOT BEING ABLE TO REPAY: THE UNMERCIFUL SERVANT

1. B. B. Scott, "The Kings' Accounting: Matthew 18:23–34," *JBL* 104 (1985): 442.

2. Jeremias (*Parables*, 213) holds that the parable was from the first told with reference to the last judgment. Linnemann (*Parables*, 179) maintains that even as it stands in Matthew "the text offers no support for this."

3. On the role of the torturers, see Derrett, "The Parable of the Unmerciful Servant," in *Law*, 32–47, esp. 46–47.

4. On the life setting of this chapter of the Gospel in Matthew's church and as a

context for this parable, see William Thompson, *Matthew's Advice to a Divided Community: Mt. 17, 22—18, 35*, Analecta Biblica 44 (Rome: Pontifical Biblical Inst., 1970).

5. The manner in which the story at least partially contradicts Matt. 18:22 is perhaps the chief reason for questioning the judgment that the narrative is a Matthean composition. The high number of Matthean words (see M. D. Goulder, *Midrash and Lection in Matthew* [London: SPCK, 1974], 404) is better accounted for by Matthew's rewriting and adaptation of the parable.

6. See Derrett, *Law*, 32–40. In the story of Joseph, son of Tobias (also written in the 1st cent.), one can gain some insight into the work and responsibilities of such a chief minister: Josephus *Antiquities* XII.iv.2–5. The sum of taxes collected from Coele-Syria, Phoenicia, and Judea with Samaria is said to be eight thousand talents, though the editor of the Loeb Classical Library edition (*Josephus* 7:92) comments that this is obviously too large a sum in the light of other estimates of revenue from the time.

7. So Jeremias (*Parables*, 210–11), though even he has to recognize that the amount is unrealistically large on almost any reckoning. In a number of contexts in Greek literature the word *daneion* seems to mean "loan" more than "debt."

8. For a discussion of Zacchaeus's "conversion," see Borsch, *Power in Weakness*, 27–34.

9. Some commentators are troubled by the manner in which the king goes back on his words of forgiveness, esp. so in the degree to which the king is seen as a figure for God. The story, however, seems little concerned with the king's or God's reputation, as it were. The interest lies in seeing what happens to someone who, having been forgiven, will not forgive.

10. If, as Derrett suggests, the first servant was responsible for collecting the king's revenues, he perhaps meant to show he was turning over a new leaf by vigorously prosecuting the first debtor he met (see *Law*, 41). The story, however, says that the second servant owed the hundred denarii to the first servant. Although it could be conjectured that it was owed to the king through him, this does not seem the intent of the story.

11. TREASURE:
THE HIDDEN TREASURE

1. On the parable and treasure stories more generally, see Crossan, *Finding*, esp. his bibliography of treasure stories (pp. 125–33).

2. R. M. Grant and D. N. Freedman, *The Secret Sayings of Jesus* (Garden City, N.Y.: Doubleday & Co., 1960), 183.

3. Cf. Matt. 6:19–20; Luke 12:33.

4. See C. W. F. Smith, *Parables*, 66. Linnemann (*Parables*, 97–105) is also among those who interpret the parables in this manner.

5. So Linnemann, *Parables*, 99, 170 n. 9.

6. See Kingsbury, *Parables*, 115–16.

7. Matthew clearly had an interest in sayings dealing with treasure. See also 13:52.

8. See Linnemann, *Parables*, 100.

9. It has been suggested, however, on the basis of the Thomas tradition that in earlier versions of the story the man was simply a merchant and not a merchant in search of fine pearls. See Jeremias, *Parables*, 199. Going even further, and more in keeping with the treasure parable, there may once have been just a man who found a pearl.

On the value and use of pearls in the Near East, see Kingsbury, *Parables*, 113 with nn.

10. See Derrett, "Law in the New Testament: The Treasure in the Field (Mt. XIII, 44)," in *Law*, 1–16.

11. There may also have been more technical questions involved such as whether and how the individual *lifted* the treasure up before he purchased the field. For a discussion of the legality of the man's actions, see Derrett ("Law in the New Testament: The Treasure in the Field," 31–42), who concludes that what the treasure-finder did could have been perfectly legal.

12. See Crossan, *Finding*, 103.

13. Dodd, *Parables*, 86 n. 1.

12. NO WAY OF SAVING:
THE TALENTS

1. Cf. Crossan, *Parables*, 101; and J. A. Fitzmyer, *The Gospel according to Luke X—XXIV*, Anchor Bible (Garden City, N.Y.: Doubleday & Co., 1985), 1230. Drury (*Parables*, 155–56), again holding that Luke made use of Matthew's Gospel, sees Luke's version as an adaptation of Matthew's.

2. See Lambrecht, *Once More Astonished*, 175, for the arguments both that the addition of the throne-claimant story is pre-Lukan and that it was added by Luke. It at least fits in with Luke's allegorizing tendency here.

3. See Josephus *Antiquities* XVII.xi.1.

4. With reference to the hearing of parables: Matt. 13:12; Mark 4:25; Luke 8:18; and similarly, *Gospel of Thomas* 41.

5. Cf. Crossan, *In Parables*, 102.

6. Derrett suggests that what the third servant was understood not to have was any profit, resulting in the principal being taken away as well. See "The Parable of the Talents and Two Logia," in *Law*, 17–31, esp. 30.

7. See Via, *Parables*, against Jeremias (*Parables*, 62), who thinks Matt. 25:28; Luke 19:24 is an addition.

8. Luke's smaller amount is sometimes also held to be more in keeping with the essential features of the parable, in that both Matthew ("faithful over a little," 25:21, 23) and Luke ("faithful in a very little," 19:17) contrast what the two investing servants are to receive with the relatively small amount they had originally been given charge over. But it is consistent with the character of a number of the parables to suggest that what could make the original stake look little is the greatness of the outcome.

9. On the other hand, the method of tying the money up in a cloth (Luke 19:20) would leave the individual liable for loss or theft. See Jeremias, *Parables*, 61 n. 51.

10. Derrett believes the servant is trying to make a wry little joke (*Law*, 25).

11. *The Gospel of the Nazaraeans* (fragment in Eusebius's *Theophania* on Matt. 25:14–15) evidently recast the story so that a servant who wasted his money with harlots and flute players is imprisoned while the servant who hid the talent is only rebuked.

12. See Dodd, *Parables*, 118–20; Jeremias, *Parables*, 61–62; and with a little different emphasis, Lambrecht, *Once More Astonished*, 186.

13. On Paul and the law, see Gunther Bornkamm, *Paul*, trans. D. Stalker (New York: Harper & Row, 1971), 120–29.

14. See Langdon Gilkey, *Shantung Compound: The Story of Men and Women under Pressure* (New York: Harper & Row, 1966), esp. 177–88.

15. See above, p. 73.

16. From "News From Lake Wobegon," as told by Garrison Keillor on the *Prairie Home Companion* of October 12, 1985.

17. So Jeremias, *Parables*, 61.

18. See also 1 Cor. 12:4–13; 14:27–31; Rom. 12:4–8.

19. The Gospels contain several versions of the basic saying: Luke 17:33; Matt. 10:39; Mark 8:35/Matt. 16:25/Luke 9:24; John 12:25. The chiastic pattern of save-lose/lose-save was clearly essential to the structure of the early form of the saying. See John D. Crossan, *In Fragments: The Aphorisms of Jesus* (San Francisco: Harper & Row, 1983), 89–94.

20. "Such security is death" (see the "existential-theological interpretation" of Via, *Parables*, 120–22).

21. See Mark 2:7; Matt. 9:3; Luke 5:21; Matt. 11:19; Luke 7:34; Mark 3:22; Matt. 12:24; Luke 11:15.

13. HELP?
A FRIEND AT MIDNIGHT. THE UNJUST JUDGE

1. Because the story is so briefly related, it is, however, difficult to be exact about the legal background circumstances. Often Jewish people (as was true with at least some early Christians; see 1 Cor. 6:1–8) would have tried to decide such matters among themselves using torah and their own community councils. It was not, however, considered wrong to use gentile courts in certain circumstances, and this seems to be what is presupposed here. Cf. Derrett, "Law in the New Testament: The Parable of the Unjust Judge," in *Glimpses*, 32–47.

2. See Jeremias, *Parables*, 153.

3. The Jewish Scriptures are replete with pleas in behalf of widows, warnings not to oppress them, and the promise of God's concern. See Exod. 22:22–23; Deut. 10:18; 24:17; 27:19; Job 22:9; 24:3, 21; Ps. 68:5; Isa. 1:17; 10:2; Jer. 22:3; Zech. 7:10.

4. On corrupt judges in this era, see Bailey, *Through Peasant Eyes*, 131.

5. Bailey (*Through Peasant Eyes*, 137–40) makes an interesting attempt to translate 18:7b as a statement (rather than a question) about God's patience with sinners: "Also he is slow to anger over them." This idea, however, seems to interrupt the flow of the thought.

6. Jeremias (*Parables*, 156) holds that all of vv. 6–8 are pre-Lukan and Palestinian, on linguistic grounds. J. A. Fitzmyer (*The Gospel according to Luke X—XXIV*, Anchor Bible [Garden City, N.Y.: Doubleday & Co., 1985], 1175–77) sees v. 6 as belonging to the parable proper and vv. 7–8a and 8b separately as pre-Lukan allegorizing additions that are at least closely related to the material in the preceding chapter. But on Lukan characteristics throughout the parable, see E. D. Freed, "The Parable of the Judge and the Widow (Luke 18:1–8)," *NTS* 33 (1987): 38–60.

7. There are striking parallels between the parable and Sir. 35:12–18, where the Lord is pictured as an incorruptible judge who will not ignore the "widow when she pours out her story." The parable clearly is related to this tradition but then makes a kind of joking play upon it by telling of a human judge who finally heeded the widow only because he was prevailed upon.

8. The translation is from Fitzmyer (*Luke X—XXIV*, 909), who defends it (pp. 910–12) as the best rendering of the text.

9. Jeremias (*Parables*, 157–59) emphasizes this function of the story. Other instances of "which of you" or a similar expression beginning rhetorical questions are

found in Luke 11:11 (par. Matt. 7:9); 12:25 (par. Matt. 6:27); 14:5 (par. Matt. 12:11); 14:28; 15:4; 17:7.

10. The majority of scholars see the ambiguous "his" possessing the caller's "lack of shame [*anaideia*]." C. W. F. Smith (*Parables*, 184–85) attributes it to the caller who so acts because he knows his friend must respond to him. Fitzmyer (*Luke X—XXIV*, 912) believes it must be a quality of the petitioner because the previous "his friend" refers to him, though, in fact, that reference is ambiguous too. For a full discussion, see Bailey, *Poet and Peasant*, 125–33.

11. See Bailey, *Poet and Peasant*, 123. As well as being a staple, the bread was used to eat the meal.

14. SURPRISE!
THE SEED GROWING SECRETLY. THE MUSTARD SEED

1. For an attempt to reconstruct what may have been the basic Q version of the parable, see H. K. McArthur, "The Parable of the Mustard Seed," *CBQ* 33 (1971): 198–210.

2. See Kingsbury, *Parables*, 78–80.

3. See Jeremias, *Parables*, 147.

4. See Matt. 13:10–15; Mark 4:10–12; Luke 8:9–10; as well as chap. 15 and the Epilogue below.

5. Carlston agrees with other commentators in holding that one reason that Luke has not used these parables in chap. 8 and in connection with the parable of the sower is that he there is stressing the importance of hearing and doing God's will, whereas these parables presuppose little human effort (*Parables of the Triple Tradition*, 157 n. 1).

6. The parable of the leaven is saying 96 in Thomas.

7. Sayings 8, 96, and 20, using the same Coptic word.

8. The mustard seed was not actually the smallest seed to be found in Israel at that time, but it was proverbially so—and that is the point for the purposes of the parable. See Oesterley, *Gospel Parables*, 253–59; and Matt. 17:20.

9. See Robert Funk, *Jesus as Precursor* (Philadelphia: Fortress Press, 1975), esp. 20–24.

10. So Norman Perrin (*Rediscovering the Teaching of Jesus* [New York: Harper & Row, 1967], 159), who regarded the story as an authentic parable of Jesus.

11. So Crossan, *Parables*, 85; and idem, "The Seed Parables of Jesus," *JBL* 92 (1973): 252. Partly on the basis of a comparison with the last part of saying 21 of Thomas, Crossan holds that Mark added 4:28 to the parable to shift the focus from the activity of the farmer to the fate of the seed. It is, however, far from clear that Thomas 21 is really a parallel to the Markan story, and the idea of the seed growing apart from human activity is also present in 4:27, 29.

12. Jones provides a helpful brief survey of different ways that the parable has been interpreted (*Parables*, 95–98).

13. T. S. Eliot in "Ash Wednesday."

15. WASTE AND GRACE:
THE SOWER

1. Parts of this chap. first appeared in F. H. Borsch, "Waste and Grace: The Parable of the Sower," *Historical Magazine of the Protestant Episcopal Church* 53 (1984): 199–208, with fuller nn.

2. Drury (*Parables*, 51–58) holds that the parable and its interpretation must have been created together, probably by Mark himself. Drury's effort to relate the soil conditions to particular incidents in the Gospel's story seems, however, somewhat artificial, and much of the Markan vocabulary in the parable proper is to be found in those verses we regard as Markan additions.

3. On the ancient and modern "hermeneutical eclipses" of the parable, see T. J. Weeden, Sr., "Recovering the Parabolic Intent of the Parable of the Sower," *JAAR* 47 (1979): 97–120.

4. On Mark's, Matthew's, and Luke's versions of the parable and their interpretations, see Carlston, *Parables of the Triple Tradition*, 21–25, 70–76, 137–49. For a defense of the possibility that the essence of the allegorical interpretation came from Jesus, see R. E. Brown, "Parable and Allegory Reconsidered," in *New Testament Essays* (Milwaukee: Bruce Pub. Co., 1965), 254–64; and, from different perspectives, J. W. Bowker, "Mystery and Parable: Mark IV. 1–20," *JTS* n.s. 25 (1974): 300–317; and Birgir Gerhardsson, "The Parable of the Sower and Its Interpretation," *NTS* 14 (1967–68): 165–93.

5. See Carlston, *Parables of the Triple Tradition*, 139–40. David Wenham ("The Interpretation of the Parable of the Sower," *NTS* 20 [1973–74]: 299–319) also argues that Matthew has the earlier version.

6. Further on Mark 4:10–12, see in the Epilogue, pp. 135–37.

7. John Horman ("The Source of the Version of the Parable of the Sower in the *Gospel of Thomas*," *NTS* 21 [1979]: 326–43) concludes that the *Gospel of Thomas* used a Greek-language source independent of the Synoptics for its version of the sower.

8. Weeden ("Recovering the Parabolic Intent," 99–100) argues for the primacy of the scorching sun, Crossan (*Cliffs of Fall*, 30–38) for withering, though he had previously held the description of the sun's scorching to be more primitive.

9. I am, however, somewhat less certain regarding the deletion of these words, since they are not taken up in the interpretation and since, together with the word usually translated as "yielding," they follow the triadic structure evidently so integral to the parable.

10. The Thomas version more closely matches the triadic structure of the rest of the parable by beginning, "Now the sower went out to sow, took a handful [of seeds], and scattered them."

11. See Amos Wilder, "Telling from Depth to Depth: The Parable of the Sower," *Semeia* 2 (1974): 134–51; and idem, *Jesus' Parables*, 89–100, esp. 94–95.

12. Cf. Jeremias's often-quoted argument in *Parables*, 11–12. But see the critique of his position by K. D. White ("The Parable of the Sower," *JTS* n.s. 15 [1964]: 300–307) and Jeremias's backtracking ("Palästinakundliches zum Gleichnis vom Säemann (Mark IV.3–8 PAR)," *NTS* 13 [1966–67]: 48–53). See also Drury, *Parables*, 55–58.

13. See previous n. and the discussion by P. B. Payne in "The Order of Sowing and Ploughing," *NTS* 25 (1978–79): 123–29.

14. Cf. Weeden, "Recovering the Parabolic Intent," 100.

15. Jeremias (*Parables*, 150) argues for the whole field. Evidently Thomas understood the parable to refer to the yield of the whole field, and Luke may have as well. Further on this issue, see Carlston, *Parables of the Triple Tradition*, 143–44.

16. So White, "The Parable of the Sower," 300–307.

17. Linnemann, *Parables*, 117.

18. Wilder, *Jesus' Parables*, 94.

19. Crossan (*Cliffs of Fall*, 49) speaks of the sower as a *metaparable*, a "parable about parables."

20. In particular, see Jeremias, *Parables*, 150.

EPILOGUE. PARABLE AND GOSPEL

1. See Joel Marcus, "Mark 4:10–12 and Marcan Epistemology," *JBL* 103 (1984): 557–74, on this influence, esp. as it may have come from Qumran.

2. There have, of course, been other efforts to understand how Mark 4:10–12 developed. In order to make it easier to attribute the saying to Jesus or otherwise to soften it, it has been suggested that one should translate "*so that* they may indeed see but not perceive . . ." as "*because* they see but do not perceive . . ." This, in fact, is what Matthew (13:13) understandably has done, and it can be maintained that this translation is also more in keeping with Isa. 6:9–10, and so more likely the intent of an earlier saying. The Greek of Mark 4:12 is, however, very clear and can best be translated "so that," with the force of "in order that."

3. On Mark's often negative portrayal of the disciples' understanding as a foil for his views of Jesus' teaching, see Werner H. Kelber, *Mark's Story of Jesus* (Philadelphia: Fortress Press, 1979), esp. chaps. 2 and 3. On the negative portrayal's purpose of establishing the credibility of a written gospel in lieu of an oral tradition, see Kelber, *The Oral and the Written Gospel: The Hermeneutics of Speaking and Writing in the Synoptic Tradition, Mark, Paul, and Q* (Philadelphia: Fortress Press, 1983).

4. James G. Williams (*Gospel against Parable*, 189–93) suggests that Mark viewed parables as both dangerous (because they allow too much freedom in interpretation) and necessary (because they keep the gospel narrative open to the beyond and transcendent). For this reason his Gospel includes only a limited number of parables.

5. Some scholars suggest that Mark mistranslated or reshaped an earlier Aramaic teaching to the effect of "To you is given the secret of the kingdom of God, but to those who are outside all things become riddles"; i.e., that the parables are more like the *mashalim* or dark sayings referred to in Ps. 78:2. See Lambrecht, *Once More Astonished*, 93.

6. See Frank Kermode, *The Genesis of Secrecy: On the Interpretation of Narrative* (Cambridge: Harvard Univ. Press, 1979), esp. 27–47. Kermode illustrates the relationship to Kafka with reference to the "Before the Law" parable from *The Trial*.

7. On the relationship between stories of the empty tomb and resurrection appearances, and with respect to the resurrection narratives in the Gospels more generally, see R. H. Fuller, *The Formation of the Resurrection Narratives* (Philadelphia: Fortress Press, 1980), and C. F. Evans, *Resurrection and the New Testament* (London: SCM Press, 1970).

8. On the significance of this story, including the use of the phrase "on the way," see "Bartimaeus," in Borsch, *Power in Weakness*, 99–109.

9. On the interpretation of the saying, and esp. the meaning of "go before" as "to lead," see C. F. Evans, "I Will Go before You into Galilee," *JTS* n.s. 5 (1954): 3–18.

10. See also Mark 13:26.

11. On Mark's Gospel as parable and its character more generally, see Kelber, *Oral and Written Gospel*, 117–29; John R. Donahue, "Jesus as Parable of God in the Gospel of Mark," *Int* 32 (1978): 369–86; and Robert Hamilton, "The Gospel of Mark: Parable of God Incarnate," *Theology* 86 (1983): 438–41.

12. A point emphasized in Raymond E. Brown, *The Community of the Beloved*

Disciple: The Life, Loves, and Hates of an Individual Church in New Testament Times (New York: Paulist Press, 1979), esp. 61–62.

13. For my description of Paul's correspondence with the Corinthians, see "Paul's Story," in *Power in Weakness*, 111–27.

14. On the biblical narratives of the resurrection and their interpretation, see Borsch, *God's Parable*, 1–26.

15. See Funk's way of saying this in *Language*, 196–97.

16. On the exorcisms and healing stories and their significance, see Borsch, *Power in Weakness*, esp. 10–11, 39–50.

17. Crossan, *Finding*, 107.

18. The more usual and intelligible way of trying to resolve this mystery, as Christianity developed, was to view Jesus as part human and part divine, although the orthodox attempt to give it definition (Act V of the Council of Chalcedon, 451 C.E.) insisted on the fuller paradox—"truly God and truly man."

19. On the value of parables and a parabolic way of teaching as well as living, see Mary C. Boys, "Parabolic Ways of Teaching," *BTB* 13 (1983): 82–89.

BIBLIOGRAPHY

Alter, Robert. *The Art of Biblical Narrative*. New York: Basic Books, 1981. A book dealing with the Jewish Scriptures and full of insights regarding the reading of all biblical stories.

Bailey, Kenneth E. *Poet and Peasant and Through Peasant Eyes: A Literary Cultural Approach to the Parables in Luke*. Grand Rapids: Eerdmans, 1983. *Poet and Peasant* originally published in 1976; *Through Peasant Eyes* in 1980. Bailey emphasizes the poetic character of the parables and offers considerable information on customs and mores of the Middle East which can help in the understanding of these stories. One should not assume, however, that the parables were always meant to make sense by being realistic in all their details.

Borsch, Frederick H. *God's Parable*. Philadelphia: Westminster Press, 1976. An earlier presentation of the story of Jesus as parable.

————. *Power in Weakness: New Hearing for Gospel Stories of Healing and Discipleship*. Philadelphia: Fortress Press, 1983. A study of healing and controversy stories in the New Testament, noting their parabolic features and concern with new community.

Boucher, Madeleine I. *The Mysterious Parable: A Literary Study*. Catholic Biblical Quarterly Monograph Series 6. Washington: Catholic Biblical Assn. of America, 1977. A criticism of the classes of parable and allegory as they have been used by many commentators and an attempt at clearer definition, together with a discussion of parables and mystery in Mark's Gospel.

————. *The Parables*. Rev. ed. New Testament Message 7. Wilmington, Del.: Michael Glazier, 1983. A more popular presentation of Boucher's insights regarding the structure and purpose of parables, with brief commentaries on individual parables.

Breech, James. *The Silence of Jesus: The Authentic Voice of the Historical Man*. Philadelphia: Fortress Press, 1983. A different perspective on the parables, which stresses the silence of Jesus about himself as their teller.

Capon, Robert F. *The Parables of the Kingdom*. Grand Rapids: Zondervan, 1985. An imaginative reflection on the seed parable and other parables, mainly those found in Matthew 13.

Carlston, Charles E. *The Parables of the Triple Tradition*. Philadelphia: Fortress Press, 1975. A redactional study of the parables that have versions in all three Synoptic Gospels.

Crossan, John D. *In Parables: The Challenge of the Historical Jesus*. New York: Harper & Row, 1973. *Finding Is the First Act: Trove Folktales and Jesus' Treasure Parable*. Society of Biblical Literature Semeia Supplements. Philadelphia: Fortress Press, 1979. *Cliffs of Fall: Paradox and Polyvalence in the Parables of Jesus*. New York: Seabury Press, 1980. *Sayings Parallels: A Workbook for the Jesus Tra-*

dition. Philadelphia: Fortress Press, 1986. Works by the dominant figure in parable research over the past fifteen years. Crossan has given particular emphasis to the parables as aesthetic objects in relation to parallel forms of literature, and to the parables' openness to interpretation, or polyvalence. The workbook is a valuable tool for the study of parables and other sayings. The parallels are from apocryphal gospels and other early writings.

Derrett, J. D. M. *Law in the New Testament*. London: Darton, Longman & Todd, 1970. *Studies in the New Testament*, vol. 1, *Glimpses of the Legal and Social Presuppositions of the Authors*. Leiden: Brill, 1977. Two volumes that collect sometimes revised versions of journal articles which present a number of illuminating parallels and background information for the parables and other Gospel materials. Some of these parallels, however, do more to show the widespread character of various themes found in the parables than dependence on particular texts. Nor are the parables always meant to be as true to normal life as Derrett assumes.

Dodd, C. H. *The Parables of the Kingdom*. Rev. ed. New York: Charles Scribner's Sons, 1961. A seminal study originally published in 1935 that views the parables as telling of the kingdom already come into the world.

Drury, John. *The Parables in the Gospels: History and Allegory*. London: SPCK, 1985. A study laying special stress on interpreting the parables in their settings in the Gospels and on recognizing the special interests and tendencies of the evangelists.

Fiebig, Paul. *Altjüdische Gleichnisreden und die Gleichnisse Jesu*. Tübingen: Mohr (Siebeck), 1912. A response by one of Jülicher's first major critics. Fiebig has pointed out that in the Jewish context parable and allegory were not readily distinguished, that there were no rigid forms, and that Jesus' stories were more variable than Jülicher had allowed for.

Funk, Robert W. *Language, Hermeneutic, and Word of God: The Problem of Language in the New Testament and Contemporary Theology*. New York: Harper & Row, 1966. A ground-breaking work in biblical hermeneutics, with valuable chapters on the parables of the great supper and the Good Samaritan.

Jeremias, Joachim. *The Parables of Jesus*. Trans. S. H. Hooke. 2d rev. ed. New York: Charles Scribner's Sons, 1972. Still a major reference for the study of the parables, with a wealth of detail regarding their settings. Jeremias views many of the parables in the context of Jesus' proclamation of the inbreaking but not yet realized kingdom.

Jones, Geraint V. *The Art and Truth of the Parables*. London: SPCK, 1974. Among the first modern interpretations to see the parables as aesthetic objects with significance beyond their historical context.

Jones, Peter R. *The Teaching of the Parables*. Nashville: Broadman Press, 1981. An informed, popular presentation by an experienced preacher and teacher. The book has extensive notes and provides a wide range of references.

Jülicher, Adolf. *Die Gleichnisreden Jesu*. 2 vols. Tübingen: Mohr (Siebeck), 1888–99 (2d ed., 1899–1910). By the author who began the modern study of the parables by showing that many of them could be interpreted in nonallegorical ways.

Kingsbury, Jack Dean. *The Parables of Jesus in Matthew 13: A Study in Redaction Criticism*. Richmond: John Knox Press, 1969. An analytical study of the evangelist's use and interpretation of parables in this chapter of Matthew.

Kissinger, Warren S. *The Parables of Jesus: A History of Interpretation and Bibliography*. ATLA Bibliographical Series 4. Metuchen, N.J.: Scarecrow Press, 1979. A valuable research tool, with sections on major interpreters of the parables from

Irenaeus through the present, and extensive bibliographies for all the major parables.

Lambrecht, Jan. *Once More Astonished: The Parables of Jesus*. New York: Crossroad, 1981. A critical introduction, with exegesis and reflection on major parables. Lambrecht offers insights into the surprising character of a number of the stories and into their theological significance. Valuable bibliographies are provided.

Linnemann, Eta. *Jesus of the Parables*. Trans. John Sturdy. New York: Harper & Row, 1966. An introduction and study of eleven major parables. The book helped to open the contemporary discussion of parables in that it went beyond historical-critical considerations to basic questions of interpretation.

McFague, Sallie. *Speaking in Parables*. Philadelphia: Fortress Press, 1975. *Metaphorical Theology: Models of God in Religious Language*. Philadelphia: Fortress Press, 1982. An informed theological reflection on the literary and metaphorical character of parabolic expression, begun in the earlier volume and carried forward in the later.

Oesterley, William O. E. *The Gospel Parables in the Light of Their Jewish Background*. New York: Macmillan Co., 1936. An older, classical study that offers numerous parallels and insights from the rabbinic literature.

Perrin, Norman. *Jesus and the Language of the Kingdom: Symbol and Metaphor in New Testament Interpretation*. Philadelphia: Fortress Press, 1976. A book the third and fourth chaps. of which include a valuable survey of interpretation of the parables. The chaps. also reflect Perrin's own efforts to advance the discussion. The author focuses particularly on the parable of the Good Samaritan.

Perkins, Pheme. *Hearing the Parables of Jesus*. New York: Paulist Press, 1981. A thoughtful study of a number of the parables from historical, psychological, and spiritual perspectives, with the ordinary reader in mind. The chaps. include study questions.

Ricoeur, Paul. *Semeia* 4 (see below). One among his many works that deal directly with or relate to parable interpretation. Ricoeur is a seminal figure in the field of hermeneutics.

Scott, Bernard Brandon. *Jesus, Symbol-Maker for the Kingdom*. Philadelphia: Fortress Press, 1981. A study of the form and function of parables and shorter figurative sayings in the Gospels, from a structuralist perspective, esp. in relation to the symbol of the kingdom of God.

Semeia. A journal of biblical criticism that has produced a number of issues important for contemporary interpretation of the parables, in particular 1 (1974), "A Structuralist Approach to the Parables," ed. Robert W. Funk (in this volume John D. Crossan provides a good bibliography, pp. 236–74); 2 (1974), "The Good Samaritan," ed. John D. Crossan; 4 (1975), "Paul Ricoeur and Biblical Hermeneutics," ed. John D. Crossan; 9 (1977), "Polyvalence Narration," ed. John D. Crossan.

Smith, Bertram T. D. *The Parables of the Synoptic Gospels*. Cambridge: At the Univ. Press, 1937. A still-valuable discussion of the nature of parabolic literature and a critical interpretation of some sixty parables or parablelike short sayings.

Smith, Charles W. F. *The Jesus of the Parables*. Rev. ed. Philadelphia: United Church Press, 1975. A comprehensive study that seeks to relate the parables to the ministry of Jesus, esp. to the theological significance of the cross and resurrection.

Stein, Robert H. *An Introduction to the Parables of Jesus*. Philadelphia: Westminster Press, 1981. A presentation that emphasizes the eschatological dimensions of the parables.

Tolbert, Mary Ann. *Perspectives on Parables: An Approach to Multiple Interpreta-

tions. Philadelphia: Fortress Press, 1979. A literary and hermeneutical reflection on the polyvalence of parables.

Via, Dan O., Jr. *The Parables: Their Literary and Existential Dimension*. Philadelphia: Fortress Press, 1967. One of the first interpretations of parables as stories that can also be viewed apart from their historical matrix.

Wilder, Amos N. *Jesus' Parables and the War of Myths: Essays on Imagination in the Scriptures*. Philadelphia: Fortress Press, 1982. A collection of studies written over a number of years by a pioneer in asking questions of the Jesus tradition from perspectives other than the strictly historical-critical.

Williams, James G. *Gospel against Parable: Mark's Language of Mystery*. Decatur, Ga.: Almond Press, 1985. A monograph that sees the parables, which reflect the transcendent and mysterious, as in tension with the gospel narrative. The Gospel provides a guide for the interpretation of parables.